Testing for Learning

HOW NEW APPROACHES TO EVALUATION CAN IMPROVE AMERICAN SCHOOLS

Ruth Mitchell

THE FREE PRESS
A Division of Macmillan, Inc.
NEW YORK

Maxwell Macmillan Canada
TORONTO

Maxwell Macmillan International
NEW YORK   OXFORD   SINGAPORE   SYDNEY

The Free Press
A Division of Macmillan, Inc.
866 Third Avenue, New York, N.Y. 10022

Maxwell Macmillan Canada, Inc.
1200 Eglinton Avenue East
Suite 200
Don Mills, Ontario M3C 3N1

Macmillan, Inc. is part of the Maxwell Communication Group of Companies.

Printed in the United States of America

printing number
1 2 3 4 5 6 7 8 9 10

Multiple-choice tests reprinted with the permission of the Psychological Corporation and The Riverside Publishing Company.

Enhanced multiple-choice illustration, writing prompt, standards for scoring writing and open-ended mathematics, and history examination reprinted with the permission of the California Assessment Program, California State Department of Education.

Humanities exhibition reprinted with permission from the Center for Collaborative Education, New York.

Purposes for portfolio assessment reprinted with permission from Portfolio Assessment Clearinghouse, San Dieguito Union High School District, Encinitas, California.

Questionnaires for students and parents reprinted with permission from Kathryn Howard, Pittsburgh Public Schools.

Criteria for mathematics portfolio contents reprinted with permission from the Vermont State Education Department.

The Primary Language Record reprinted with kind permission from the Centre for Language in Primary Education, Webber Row, London, England.

Library of Congress Cataloging-in-Publication Data

Mitchell, Ruth
    Testing for learning : how new approaches to evaluation can improve American schools / Ruth Mitchell.
        p.   cm.
    Includes bibliographical references (p.   ) and index.
    ISBN 0–02–921465–3
    1. Educational tests and measurements—United States.
    2. Education—United States—Evaluation.   I. Title.
LB3051.M634   1992
371.2'6—dc20   91-27896
                                                            CIP

To the teachers,
who know and love their students

Contents

Preface

Evaluation sends a message. It points to what is valued and ignores what is not perceived to be important. Educational evaluation—testing and assessment—has been telling students, teachers, administrators, and legislators that the system values rote memorization and passive recognition of single correct answers. This message has been powerfully conveyed by the ubiquitous multiple-choice tests which have dominated American educational evaluation for most of the past thirty years and have terrorized it in the 1980s.

Worse than the form of the tests themselves has been the message that a single test can determine what students know and can do. Multiple-choice tests would not be so bad if they were part of a spectrum of evaluations, including essays, cooperative productions, collections of work, and teachers' observations. But evaluation has narrowed to the "bubble" on a machine-scorable answer sheet.

At the same time as testing has been distorting what is taught and learned, turning it into pellets which are the intellectual equivalent of rabbit food, other forces have been pressuring schools to move in the opposite direction. Business executives and leaders of industry find that they want employees who can think for themselves and apply knowledge to new situations. Professional associations of teachers, such as the National Council of Teachers of Mathematics, the National Council of Teachers of English, the National Science Teachers' Association, and the National Council on the Social Studies (to name only a few), have rethought what they were teaching as part of their professional responsibility. These associations and others like them have all researched, written, and published curriculum frameworks within the past five years. The frameworks share a common emphasis on thinking, problem solving, conceptual understanding, solid academic knowledge, and the application of learning.

These components of a sound academic education have been advocated for thirty-five years by the Council for Basic Education, which enthusiastically endorsed the new curriculum frameworks, especially the National Council of Teachers of Mathematics' *Curriculum and Evaluation Standards for School Mathematics*. The Council's president, A. Graham Down, perceived a collision between what should be taught in schools and how it is tested. With his customary vision, he sought ways to promote evaluation compatible with the rich intellectual experience schools should provide. He asked me to look at the newly emerging kinds of evaluation which ask students to demonstrate directly, not through the proxy of a "bubble," what they know and can do and then to write a book about them.

As an advocacy organization, the Council operates largely through the written word, publishing studies of educational developments, a monthly journal of comment, and occasional papers examining specific educational topics. As befits the president of an organization that has lived on "soft" money for thirty-five years, Graham also sought financial support for the project, and received it from the National Science Foundation; The Lilly Endowment, Indianapolis; and the McKenna Foundation, whose generosity is gratefully acknowledged.

Assessment is as old as education itself. For most of its history, educational assessments consisted of recitations, oral demonstrations of mastery over a subject, or essays. In the United States assessment took these forms (and still does in some, mostly private, schools), until the middle of this century, when multiple-choice took over. By the 1980s, the bubble had eclipsed nearly all other forms of assessment in U.S. public schools. How students are assessed inevitably affects how they are taught. Assessment cannot be considered separately from teaching and learning, because assessments are the motivation for both teacher and student. Changing assessment therefore impacts on the classroom, the textbooks, the professional lives of teachers, the decisions of administrators. The topic here is a new system, not just modified tests.

I wrote the book for a general audience, not primarily for educational specialists in university departments of education, or in school or state education administrations, but for teachers, parents, school board members, taxpayers, legislators and their staffs, journalists, professional education-watchers, but above all the large number of general readers who care about what is happening in U.S. schools as a vital component of the economic, social, and political fabric of our civilization. The book largely consists of descriptions of programs, and weaves into them discussions of theoretical issues. Not all issues are treated in each case, but only where the circumstances presented an opportunity.

After a brief introduction to the players and the action on the evaluation scene, the book plunges straight into examples. It concludes with a brief historical description of how we got ensnared by a single form of testing, and some thoughts on how a broad-minded system can move our schools toward their goals.

I have consciously tried to use general language, not the technical jargon of education. The word "curriculum" appears only rarely in this book, when it absolutely cannot be avoided or appears in a quotation. "Teaching and learning" are used instead in order to gain both directness and accuracy. Philip Schlechty, president of the Center for Leadership in School Reform in Louisville, says in his 1989 book, *Schools for the Twenty-First Century*, that educational evaluation is "too important to turn over to the measurement specialist." I hope to persuade the general reader that educational assessment is not an arcane subject, but everyone's business.

Many people have contributed to this book, as I travelled around the United States talking to educators, attending conferences, watching students as they performed tasks. I want to thank everyone on the following list for their patience with my requests for information. The list is as complete as memory and records can make it; if anyone's contribution has gone unrecognized, please forgive me.

Walter Askin, California State University, Los Angeles

Joseph Flynn, Cleveland Education Foundation

Joan Lipsitz, The Lilly Endowment

David Florio, formerly of the National Science Foundation, and now of the Office of Educational Research and Improvement, U.S. Department of Education

Ramsay Selden, Council of Chief State School Officers

Maryellen Harmon, Center for the Study of Testing, Evaluation, and Educational Policy

George Madaus, Center for the Study of Testing, Evaluation, and Educational Policy

Ray Campeau, Bozeman, Montana

Alice Sims-Gunzenhauser, Educational Testing Service (ETS)

Walter MacDonald, Advanced Placement Program, ETS

Deborah Meier, Central Park East Schools

Patricia Bolanos, The Key School, Indianapolis

Grant Wiggins, CLASS, Rochester

Douglas Reynolds, New York State Education Department

Rodney Doran, University of Buffalo

Mary Ann Smith, University of California, Berkeley

Roberta Camp, ETS

Dennis Palmer Wolf, Project Zero, Harvard

Dale Carlson, California Assessment Program (CAP)

Susan Bennett, CAP

The staff of CAP

Richard Mills, Vermont Education Department

Ross Brewer, Vermont Education Department

Geoffrey Hewitt, Vermont Education Department

Robert Kenney, Vermont Education Department

Joan B. Baron, Connecticut Education Department

Stephen Leinwand, Connecticut Education Department

Michael Fischer, New York State Education Department

Joanne Lenke, Psychological Corporation

Fredrick L. Finch, The Riverside Publishing Company

Elaine Craig, Center for Civic Education

Sophie Sa, The Panasonic Foundation

Michael Holtzman, Consultant to the Panasonic Foundation

Gerald Kulm, American Association for the Advancement of Science

Eva Baker, Center for Research in Evaluation, Students, and School Testing (CRESST)

Jan Camplin, Lake Shore School District, New York

Sharon Partyka, Buffalo, New York

Marilyn Whirry, Manhattan Beach, California

Wynne Harlen, Edinburgh, Scotland

Anne Qualter, Liverpool, England

Myra Barrs, London, England

Anne Thomas, London, England

Betty Hagestadt, London, England

Heather Lewis, Center for Collaborative Education, Central Part East Schools, New York

Teachers and students of Central Park East Schools, New York

Michael Goldman, Coalition of Essential Schools

Kati Haycock, Children's Defense Fund

Steven Seidel, Project Zero, Harvard

Renika Zessoules, Project Zero, Harvard

Lois Easton, Arizona Education Department

Reuben Carriedo, San Diego City Schools

Grant Behnke, San Diego City Schools

Teachers in Cleveland, Ohio, Elementary schools

Kathryn Howard, Reizenstein Middle School, Pittsburgh PA

Willa Spicer, South Brunswick NJ Public Schools

David Sink, University of Birmingham, Alabama

Janica Loomis, Center for Law and Education, Birmingham, Alabama

Kathleen Fulton, Office of Technology Assessment, U.S. Congress

I owe a special debt to A. Graham Down for his encouragement and support, and for the same (and for indulgence when I was not in the office, but off enjoying myself watching real children in real schools) to my colleagues: Elsa Little, Barbara Manzon, Patte Barth, Amy Stempel, Catherine Meikle, Maryanne Annan, Stephanie Soper, Michelle Taunton, Karen Anderson, and Liza Benson. Amy Stempel acted as more than research assistant: she was an astute critic and framer of penetrating questions. Patte Barth, Graham Down, and Kati Haycock of the Children's Defense Fund read early versions of the manuscript, and thanks to their perceptive comments, would now find it unrecognizable.

For the first three months of research for this book, I was assistant director of Center for Academic Interinstitutional Programs (CAIP) at UCLA, and was therefore supported by the University of California. My colleagues at CAIP, Patricia S. Taylor, director; Rae Jeane Williams, UCLA Writing Project Director; Susie W. Hakansson,

UCLA Mathematics Project Director; and Janet M. Thornber, UCLA Science Project director, supported me from the beginning and have continued to encourage me since I moved to Washington. Thank you.

Another colleague at UCLA, Mike Rose, has encouraged me and argued with me for more than thirteen years as we shared a common dedication, first to improving writing instruction, and then, as our horizons opened out, to ensuring the best education for all students. Mike showed me how to interest the publishing world in this book, and therefore led to me the person whose patient editing has given it whatever quality it has.

Susan Milmoe, my editor at The Free Press, obviously understands how performance assessment works as a feedback mechanism, for she gave me the kind of response to my early drafts that I wish teachers could take for a model. Sharing my aims for the book, she showed me where and how to shape it toward them. I am grateful to her for faith in a project risky for both of us. Of course, the ultimate responsibility for the accuracy of facts and the quality of judgments is mine.

Introduction

The educational spotlight is on goals, standards, assessments. Since fall 1989, when President George Bush met with the governors of all fifty states to outline a strategy for improving the achievement of American students, energy at the state and national level has been invested in setting national goals and figuring out how to measure progress toward them.

This book is an important component of the national debate, because it describes for people both inside and outside the educational community the kinds of assessment frequently mentioned—"alternative," "authentic," "performance-based," or (my preferred term) "performance assessment." These terms mean little or nothing to those who quite naturally have taken educational testing for granted as a matter for psychometric specialists. The goal-setting process and the consequent need for valid measurement have thrust educational testing into the foreground, so that everyone concerned with the quality of education not only needs to know what is available, but has a legitimate right to an opinion on it. The President and the governors have made education everyone's business.

The history of the past two years reveals an interest in education as a national issue that has not been seen in Washington before. Following the "education summit" in Fall 1989, when the President closeted himself with the governors to discuss what they perceive as a national emergency, the National Governors Association announced the national goals for American education in spring 1990. As listed in *America 2000*, they challenged the nation to redirect its efforts so that by the year 2000:

1. All children will start school ready to learn
2. At least 90 percent of high school students will graduate
3. American students will achieve competency in English, mathematics, science, history, and geography at grades 4, 8, and 12; and will be prepared for responsible citizenship, further learning, and productive employment in a modern economy
4. U.S. students will be the first in the world in science and mathematics achievement
5. Every adult American will be literate and able to exercise the rights and responsibilities of citizenship
6. All American schools will be free of drugs and violence

But how do we know whether we're achieving these goals, especially goals 3 and 4, their academic core? Designing indicators of progress became the business of the National Education Goals Panel, which was set up by the National Governors' Association to monitor progress. The Goals Panel appointed advisory committees for each of the six goals, groups which include people whose work is described or words quoted in this book. The Goals Panel was charged with producing the annual Progress Report—the nation's "report card"—a summary of where we are on the way to the six national goals.

When the first Progress Report was published in September 1991, there wasn't much information available on the national level. The report was cobbled together from existing assessments. The framers of the report included the National Assessment of Educational Progress and the number of students taking the College Board's Advanced Placement examinations and their scores—but they did not include the Scholastic Aptitude Test (SAT) nor the American College Test (ACT), nor any norm-referenced achievement tests. The National Assessment of Educational Progress and the Advanced Placement examinations were cited as national information along with statistics on high school course enrollments, public satisfaction with education, and data from international student achievement comparisons, such as those conducted by the International Evaluation of Educational Achievement.

Neither the National Assessment of Educational Progress nor the Advanced Placement examinations are regarded as satisfactory measures of progress toward the goals. The National Assessment takes a sample of students at certain grades and in certain subjects. When it was established by Congress in 1969, the National Assessment was prohibited from gathering information below the national level—states could not be compared to states, districts to districts, or students to students. In 1990, a pilot comparison of states was permitted, with voluntary participation by states. This resulted in the May 1991 report on the mathematics achievement of eighth graders in thirty-seven states. Obviously it isn't a complete measure of mathematical knowledge and skill.

The Advanced Placement program is an individual student examination, but it is taken only by the most academically advanced students who are intending to apply to prestigious colleges. Clearly this too is an inadequate measure of nationwide educational attainment. But Advanced Placement examinations challenge students to high academic achievement—in fact they are geared to first-year college courses—so they are a measure of how many students are being challenged in which high schools.

Obviously, if the annual Progress Report is to provide meaningful information, it must be based on comprehensive, timely information of the sort that would result from a national examination taken by all students. Such an examination does not exist, but it is being discussed widely, especially by the National Education Goals Panel's advisory groups for goals 3 and 4, the National Council on Education Standards and Testing, and the New Standards Project.

We have already seen where the National Education Goals Panel fits in. The National Council on Education Standards and Testing had its origins in the political background of the education reform movement. The charge was led by the President and the governors—the Senate and the House of Representatives had almost no role. In the middle of 1991, it became obvious that some better measures of educational progress were needed and that they could not be designed without standards. You can't measure how close you've got if there is no clear mark to shoot at. A Senate bill setting up a National Council on Education Standards was discussed in 1990, but got nowhere. Now the idea was revived and both houses of Congress passed legislation to establish the National Council on Standards and Testing. The Council's charge from Congress was to study the "desirability and feasibility" of national standards for American education. It is widely believed that the Council is essentially setting up a national examination system, something that will complement—

perhaps even replace—the National Assessment of Educational Progress, which by its nature has little effect on teaching and learning.

As such bodies do, the Council represents interested parties: there are four members of Congress; U.S. Department of Education administrators; representatives of business, industry, higher education, and the psychometric community; and the whole is chaired by two governors. Their first two public hearings symbolized two opposing ways of setting standards: starting from the top or starting from concrete examples.

Starting from the top involves deciding what kinds of knowledge and skills we want the educational system to produce. At its first public meeting, the National Council therefore asked representatives of the five core academic disciplines—literacy, mathematics, science, history, and geography—to describe what content they expected students to master after twelve years of schooling. This procedure turned out unsatisfactorily. The professional organizations (with the exception of the National Council of Teachers of Mathematics which produced *Curriculum and Evaluation Standards for School Mathematics* in 1989), are fighting among themselves about the definition of their disciplines and what knowledge and skills should be expected from students. The most public dispute is between representatives of social studies teachers' organizations, who believe that history is only one of a number of social studies, and the professional historical associations, who believe students should understand the narrative sweep of history primarily, and social studies will be absorbed along the way. The teachers' professional organizations in science and literacy (reading and writing in English) are equally preoccupied with internal disputes.

A further cause for dissatisfaction with top-down standard-setting is the fragmentation resulting from looking at education within these traditional boundaries. The Council for Basic Education since its founding thirty-five years ago has advocated a vision of an educated person as a productive member of society—one who works, votes, and engages in lifelong learning. The exact amount and nature of mathematics or science or geography courses taken in school should be subordinate to that overall vision.

The second approach to setting standards was exemplified at a subsequent meeting of the National Council, when three people whose work is described in this book explained performance assessment to the members. Tej Pandey described open-ended mathematics questions used in California statewide assessments (he displayed the "James" question which appears on page 68); Joan Baron demonstrated the real-life problems which make mathematics and science accessible for high school students in Connecticut, and Ross Brewer explained the first statewide assessment by portfolio (collections of student work) in Vermont. Their presentations showed how standards can be described in terms of tasks that students should be able to perform. If students can solve a problem about water use in their own homes, then they have learned important mathematics and can also write to communicate their solutions.

Both approaches to standard-setting are clearly needed. We need a vision to inspire our efforts, but we also need concrete examples of what the vision entails. It is fine to say that all high school graduates should be prepared to vote intelligently, but does that mean knowing the names of candidates running for president, understanding editorials in *The New York Times,* or being able to quote statistics about the exact area of federally protected wetlands in any given state? Such questions translate easily into assessments, so that standards can be approached practically as assessment issues.

That approach is being taken by the New Standards Project, a non-governmental group funded by the MacArthur and Pew Foundations, which is designing a national examination system—an innovation in the United States, although common in many other countries. The New Standards Project has a vision of regions or clusters of states or school districts designing their own examinations, including in them "anchor" tasks. These tasks will be performed by all students taking the examinations, and will be scored nationally. This is the process known as "moderation" in Great Britain, Australia, and some other countries. Scores on the examinations will be equated ("calibrated") to the anchor tasks, providing comparisons to a national standard. Individual students and their schools will thus know where they stand.

During summer 1991, the New Standards Project established that calibration among different responses to different writing tasks is possible, although a great deal of psychometric sophistication will be needed to make it work for a national examination system. At a working conference attended by more than 350 writing and mathematics teachers and another 80 or so policymakers, the New Standards Project decided on two policies: (1) any state, cluster of states, or regional organization entering into the Project's national examination system must guarantee the resources to enable every student to reach the standards exemplified by the tasks; and (2) the tasks themselves must include the "three p's"—performance, project, and portfolio. You will find examples and explanations of the three p's in chapters 2 through 6.

This has been a severely reduced summary of the present ferment in American education. I have focussed on goals and standards to demonstrate how central performance assessment is to their attainment. I have not mentioned the President's America 2000 strategy, or the state versions ("Colorado 2000") springing up in response; or the New American Schools Development Corporation, or Educate America, or the American Achievement Tests; or the proposals to change the requirements for Chapter 1 compensatory education, so that norm-referenced multiple-choice tests can be replaced with performance assessments for reporting purposes; or the separate standard-setting efforts by the National Academy of Sciences, the U.S. Department of Energy, and the U.S. Department of Labor. It is easy to get confused by the multiplicity of publications, meetings, conferences, and task forces, not to mention their cross-connections.

A consensus is building, however, on the role of assessment as a lever to crank the system up to higher achievement. High standards demand assessments which teachers not only can, but should, teach to, and that students must study for. As you will see from the examples, these assessments are in the early stages of experimentation, but they should not be judged and rejected for lack of qualities which need time to develop. Performance assessment has a vital role in the present educational drama: it will not only chart progress toward the national goals, it will also help us reach them.

1

From Testing to Assessment

If learning is being able to bubble in answers on a test, then
. . . our kids are learning. But I don't think that's what
learning is. All it shows is that they have test-taking skills. If
we really want to have global thinkers, we'll stop spending
our time training them to take the Georgia criterion-referenced
test.

—Georgia teacher[1]

Americans expect school in the 1990s to be about the same as it was when they were children. But the world outside school isn't the same as it was even as short a time as five years ago. If school is supposed to be preparation for work, citizenship, and personal development, it ought to be different from what we went through.

An international economy—which is our future—depends on an educational system capable of producing workers who can think, solve problems, and adapt flexibly to changing circumstances. A society that will have to adapt to finite resources needs citizens who understand the complexity of issues facing them. By national and international measures, American schools are not producing graduates who come up to these standards. The educational system is not up to the job. A new model of schooling is a national imperative.

Retooling the system includes changing assessment—not so much because we need to know how we are doing (although we certainly do) but because assessment drives instruction. This is a bald statement of a truth that is unpalatable *if* the assessments or "tests" drive teaching and learning in the wrong direction. But if the assessments are models of what students should know and be able to do, then they provide a lever for lifting the system to a new plane of achievement.

I do not claim that a change in assessment is a panacea for the educational system. Assessment is an important motivator to engage students in the kind of learning we will need in the rest of the 1990s and the twenty-first century, but it alone will not bring about the needed changes in American schools. It is only one of a number of needed reforms: the professionalization of teachers, improved school financing, a vast infusion of technology into the schools, rethinking school schedules to get rid of the 50-minute period and the nine-month school year, and a serious increase in public understanding about the purpose of schools. I claim only that a change in assessment is a necessary but not sufficient condition for a functional system of education in the United States.

WHAT IS ASSESSMENT?

Educational evaluation is a huge topic, and it is difficult to approach because of terminology. To make it more manageable, I will look at it from the point of view of the actors in the educational system—students, teachers, administrators, and parents—and in doing so point out what is and is not the focus of this book.

Some form of judgment on students' performance is an essential part of any learning. You only have to think about learning anything—from swimming to calculus—to realize that no progress is possible without judging how your activities, mental or physical, bring you closer to your goal. Informal feedback to students— "Yes, that's right," or "You might want to change this or that element"—defines an important component of teaching. In fact, students experience most evaluation as classroom feedback on their performances.

Richard Stiggins points out that 90 percent of evaluation takes place in the classroom.[2] This evaluation takes many forms: teachers' observations, teachers' responses to written and oral work (the As, Bs, and Cs recorded in the little squares of grade books), informal discussions with students about their work, and quizzes or tests designed by the teacher or taken from a textbook. To both teachers and students, the word *test* usually means these periodic evaluations. Teachers tell their classes at the beginning of the semester what counts toward the final grade—so many points for routine work and so many for the tests. Stiggins's research shows that teacher-designed multiple-choice tests emphasize memorizing and recall of facts and that teachers' essay assessments suffer from their lack of training in evaluation techniques. Teacher preparation programs typically include no training in evaluation, so test making and grading are frequently learned on the job from other teachers and hard experience.[3]

Whatever their quality, the results of the tests are fed into letter grades, which appear on report cards and are aggregated as grade point averages.

"STANDARDIZED" TESTS

Teachers' grades, like all other forms of assessment, constitute information. The quality of the information is affected by the form in which it collected, the assessment expertise of the teacher (or other collector), and the purpose for which it is collected. The grades may be used with other pieces of information to make decisions about whether the student should go ahead or stay in grade another year (retention) or which track a student should be placed in—academic, general, or remedial, in most cases. In fact, however, teachers' judgments embodied in tests and grades usually do not stand on their own—a sore point that is an important focus of this book. School districts use results on tests they buy from publishers in order to check on students' progress as their primary basis for decisions about students' futures; they use teachers' grades and observations only to modify these decisions.

An example of this process is formalized by the University of California admissions office. It requires applicants to submit both the results of the Scholastic Aptitude Test (SAT) and their grade point average (GPA) gained in the subjects (English, mathematics, science, history, foreign language) required for university entrance. It uses a complicated statistical formula to combine the two numbers in order to rank applicants; a high SAT can compensate for a low GPA, for example, and a low SAT may cast doubt on a high GPA. The system arose to combat grade inflation, a serious problem that emerged in the late 1960s as grades began to creep upward at the same time that student performance in first-year classes seemed to be deteriorating. The SAT is not connected to curriculum and was therefore regarded as an objective correction to the GPA, computed from the grades assigned by teachers.

Teachers' grades and teachers' judgments seem to suffer from suspicion, perhaps justifiably. In the past, teachers' grades on the same pieces of work have been found to vary widely and therefore seem to need objective verification. Nevertheless, teachers are closest to the students and can most directly influence their learning, so an improved assessment system should aim to educate them by including them.

The huge test publishing industry sells its products to superintendents or district testing directors with the same techniques that characterize marketing any other product: service to the customer (the school district) for the lowest price. Examples of these tests are the Iowa Test of Basic Skills, published by Riverside Publishing Company; the California Achievement Test, published by CTB/ Macmillan/McGraw-Hill; the Stanford Achievement Test, published by the Psychological Corporation–Harcourt Brace Jovanovich; and the Metropolitan Achievement Test, also published by the Psychological Corporation–Harcourt Brace Jovanovich. These are the four used most heavily by American school systems and states, but there are many more. There are forms of these tests for different grades and for different purposes, according to what the school districts want to test.

The National Commission on Testing and Public Policy estimates in its 1990 report, *From Gatekeeper to Gateway: Transforming Testing in America,* that students take 127 million separate tests in a year. Since there are 41 million students in American public schools, that works out to an average of three tests each, but since it is an average, some students must take many more than three. Students in remedial programs, such as Chapter 1 and English as a Second Language, are especially subject to heavy test schedules. Each of these tests involves preparation time, which, many teachers say, is not of the same quality as time spent on learning.

These tests are commonly referred to as standardized tests, which means they are given under the same conditions and ask the same questions across different populations in order to permit comparisons. They are expected to provide answers to questions such as: Is my child reading at the national level for her age? Is our district doing better than theirs on grade 3 reading? Are this year's students reading at a higher level than last year's? Comparison tables frequently appear in local newspapers, and realtors use these tables to enhance the desirability (and price) of a house in the service area of one neighborhood school over another.

The standardization of these tests is not the issue here. Two other features are much more important for the purposes of this book: norm referencing and multiple choice. A norm-referenced test is designed to show where a given student lies in comparison to a group of peers, usually a national norm. The items are chosen not to establish how much students know of what they ought to know but whether they are above or below the norm for their age and by how much. The reverse of norm referencing is criterion referencing, which is testing against an expected standard (what the child ought to know at that stage of development). However desirable this may sound, in practice many criterion-referenced tests are simply multiple-choice tests scored to district or state standards. Students—and teachers—could not tell the difference between most norm-referenced and criterion-referenced tests.

Multiple-choice testing means choosing a single answer from among a small number of preprepared possible answers. It is sometimes called bubble testing because the answers are recorded by filling in ovoids with a pencil.

Teachers administer these tests by making sure that each child has the necessary number 2 pencil. Then they watch while the students read the question booklets and fill in the bubbles on separate sheets. These sheets are collected and mailed to the test publishers, who score them by running them through machines that recognize the filled-in bubbles and then mail a report to the school district.

Administrators—principals, superintendents, and central office staff—care about the results of these tests because they are concerned with how their district or school looks to the outside world. "Those reading and math scores are still the bottom line," wrote an assistant principal in a letter to the editor of the *New York Times* in September 1990. These are the tests referred to when schools are said to have "high test scores" or to "score consistently below the national average." This is "accountability." Almost all states now have statewide tests of this kind, in response to pressures from legislators and taxpayers' representatives to monitor the expenditure of their money.[4]

The high visibility of these tests causes pressure on the teachers, who are asked, directly or indirectly, to teach to the test so that scores will rise. In the mid-1980s when this pressure intensified, workshops for principals and teachers were organized, usually by county departments of education but also by private consulting companies, to teach school personnel how to "align" their teaching with the test. They compared lists of topics on the tests with the topics covered in the school's textbooks. In cases where the textbook and the test came from the same publisher, teachers were told to make sure that they covered the test areas before any other material.

In classrooms where teachers are under pressure to raise test scores, students labor through workbooks that isolate skills from context and are arranged to familiarize them with the multiple-choice form of the tests. Some teachers resign themselves to acting as a guide to the textbook and design their own end-of-unit or end-of-chapter tests to match what the students will face at testing time. others resent the interference with their teaching. A teacher in Arizona told me that testing means "one curriculum 'til March, then the district's tests, then the state's test, and only then back to the curriculum." A teacher in an early childhood school in Dalton, Georgia, told a researcher:

> I was petrified that my class would do so poorly that I wouldn't be back next year. So I taught what the other teachers recommended to get them ready for the test. After the test I started teaching, good teaching. The class enjoyed it and I think they learned more the last three weeks of school than they did the first six months, because I was more relaxed, the students were more relaxed, and I was able to hone in on those areas where they needed help.[5]

Teachers recognize that teaching to multiple-choice tests is not helping students to learn, but they feel powerless to resist political pressure to raise scores. Some have even resorted to cheating by looking at the tests before they are administered and then teaching the children precisely those items.[6]

The most serious development in the mid-1980s was the intense focus, probably exacerbated by the media attention to educational accountability, on test scores as the *only* indicators of progress. Norm-referenced, multiple-choice tests have been around a long time, but they used to be regarded as one piece of evidence among many describing a student's progress or the quality of a district's programs. In the accusatory atmosphere following the publication of *A Nation at Risk* in 1983, the public and legislators turned on the schools and demanded results they thought they could trust.[7] They felt that the educational establishment had taken public money and thrown it away. They wanted the whole system tightly screwed down so that it could be controlled. In the years between 1983 and 1989, states instituted statewide tests that, until the late 1980s, were all multiple choice. The tests, originally intended as monitoring devices, became clubs to beat teachers and schools over the head.

NATIONAL TESTS

The district tests, closer to home, usually have consequences—"high stakes"—for both students and teachers. The statewide tests, which in many states are also norm-referenced, multiple-choice tests purchased from publishers, have an impact on administrators at all levels. National tests have a different impact. It may seem surprising that there are national tests in a country where responsibility for education is divided among fifty state authorities, but two kinds of tests are authorized by the U.S. government: accountability tests for programs funded under Chapter 1/Title I and the National Assessment of Educational Progress (NAEP).

Chapter 1 tests are required so that the Congress knows whether money it has appropriated has caused improvement in the test scores of children eligible for the programs. Children are admitted into Chapter 1 programs if they score below a cutoff point (established by the state and local authority, not the government) and must take a multiple-choice test once a year to measure their progress. This accountability measure must be nationally aggregatable; that is, it must be possible to add the scores across the states and localities and look at the achievement of subsets of the whole—African-American children or Hispanics, for example. Because published tests have national norms and therefore permit aggregation, the U.S. Department of Education keeps a list of "standardized" norm-referenced, multiple-choice tests that are acceptable for Chapter 1 reporting purposes. Chapter 1 students are therefore drilled by the bubble, so that their programs (and the funds) remain in their districts and schools. Overwhelmingly, the students in Chapter 1 programs are minorities—African-Americans, Hispanics, native Americans, and immigrants. The time taken preparing for tests is stolen from the precious little time there is to help these children catch up to their peers.

The other national test, the NAEP, was designed in 1969 as a monitoring system to keep records of how well the education system is doing over time. It is a national program evaluation. The NAEP is administered to a sample of students that is statistically selected to represent the population. A student would experience it as one more multiple-choice examination, but not an interesting or significant one. No results are returned to the school or the student. Instead, reports are issued about the state of the national ability to write and to compute and the amount of knowledge students have about history, geography, and science. The book *What Do Our 17-Year-Olds Know?* was based by its authors, Diane Ravitch and Chester E. Finn, Jr., on an NAEP test of students' knowledge of history and literature in 1986.[8] The reports of hesitant progress in skills that hit the headlines ("Tests of U.S. Students Show Little Progress," "Tests Show Little Gain in Education") come from the NAEP reports.

The NAEP was designed to be curriculum free in the sense that it is tied to no single textbook or curriculum; it tests what students at age 9, 12, and 17 should know regardless of how they learned. Historically NAEP has had more influence in Washington than in the statehouse or the classroom because its messages cannot be translated easily into information useful at the local level. You may be aware that students write reasonably correct prose but cannot construct a good argument, but you may be convinced that these are someone else's students, not yours. There is pressure on Congress to revise the original legislation authorizing NAEP so that its results can be reported for each state, not just the nation. Some want to use it for district reporting too, basing their confidence on its reputation as a kind of national report card. They believe that use of the NAEP at the state and district level will result in imposing a national standard for all schools without disturbing state control.

When students reach high school, they face another kind of national test, but one that is unconnected with the federal government: the aptitude tests that colleges use to select their applicants. The market is divided between the College Board's SAT and the American College Testing Service's ACT. The SAT is not a curricular test; it does not test knowledge and skills as they are taught in the classroom. Rather, it tests the general skills in language and mathematics that are believed to predict success in postsecondary education. The ACT is a test of content knowledge, but it is unconnected to any specific curriculum. Students face the Preliminary Scholastic Aptitude Test (PSAT) early in high school and then the SAT; National Merit Scholarships are awarded on sustained high scores between the PSAT and the SAT, and a great many other scholarships and financial benefits are tied to the SAT.

These aptitude tests are national in the sense that they are marketed nationwide and almost all aspirants to selective colleges (not all colleges are selective) take them. But the SAT and the ACT are used illegitimately when the results are quoted as indicators of educational quality, for two reasons. First, only college-bound high school students take the SAT and the ACT, thus distorting the picture, since not all high school students are college bound. Second, the SAT is curriculum free in a much more radical sense than the NAEP tests: it does not test what a student may have learned in literature, science, or history/social studies, and it reflects mathematical learning only to the extent that the student can recall the algorithm which will result in filling the right bubble on the answer sheet. But the SAT is a high-stakes test. It seems ironical that a test that contributes so much to decisions about a student's educational future should have only a tangential relationship to the student's educational past.

The SAT and the ACT have been well criticized by organizations like the National Center for Fair and Open Testing (FairTest) and have been the objects of numerous lawsuits, which have fairly well established that SAT and ACT scores are correlated with socioeconomic status.[9] Because residence patterns frequently dictate the quality of schools (compare Westchester County and New York City public schools), it seems fruitless to try to distinguish between the home and the school as the ultimate source of high SAT scores. In any case, scholastic aptitude tests are not the subject of this book. This book is concerned with tests or assessments that directly affect teaching and learning.

I shall also leave aside the other tests that students face from their earliest days: the intelligence tests that get them into or exclude them from Gifted and Talented (GATE) programs, the career aptitude tests that counselors administer in middle or junior high school and senior high school, vocational education tests, and tests administered by military authorities in the course of recruiting. All of these have been thoroughly scrutinized—and in the main rejected for their unintended adverse effects on the lives of children—by able critics, among them Stephen Jay Gould, N. J. Block, Gerald Dworkin, R. C. Lewontin, Steven Rose, and Leon J. Kamin, and FairTest.[10]

HOW TESTS WORK

The focus here is on tests that affect the relationship of the student, the teacher, and the subject taught—those tests that have most potential for leveraging improvement in teaching and learning. This means the classroom assessments that teachers administer for grades, the achievement tests used for accountability by districts and states, and the nationally aggregatable tests used for Chapter 1 evaluation. I shall focus for the most part on publishers' norm-referenced, multiple-choice tests.

The form and content of nationally normed, multiple-choice tests have corrupted the three-way relationship of teacher, student, and material. (Teachers' own multiple-choice tests are obviously not nationally normed, but they have the same form.) I will justify my charge with some examples of multiple-choice tests and invite you to remember similar tests from your own school experiences. Your memories may provide sharper examples, because the ones I will quote were never actually used. (Because of secrecy, publishers do not release actual items but make public only examples of the kinds of questions that appear on tests.)

Here is a Primary 1 reading item from a Stanford Achievement Test:

A Friend for Mouse

Mouse wanted a friend to play with. First, Mouse saw a cat. It wanted to chase him. Next, Mouse saw a bird. It flew away. Along came something as small and gray as a Mouse. Mouse had a friend.

What happened to the bird ? It—

○ hopped away
○ chased Mouse
○ flew away

A higher-level reading comprehension test from the Gates-MacGinitie Reading Tests published by the Riverside Publishing Company:

Wild cats warn other cats to stay away by marking the place that is theirs. And so do house cats. A cat may rub the side of its head against a chair leg. Some oil from a *gland* on the cat's head comes off. The smell of the oil tells other cats, "This place is mine."

C–1. How does the cat get the oil on the chair?
○ It jumps on the chair
○ It licks the chair
○ It rubs against the chair

C–2. The *gland* is on the cat's
○ paw   ○ chair
○ head   ○ tongue

Mathematics Computation from a Stanford Intermediate test:

Written directions: Read each question and choose the best answer. Then mark the space for the answer you have chosen. If a correct answer is *not here*, mark the space for NH.

$$523 + 168$$

   a 791   b 781   c 691   d 681   e NH

The * stands for what number?
$$3 + (2 + 7) = (* + 2) + 7$$

   a 9   b 5   c 3   d 2   e NH

15 is what % of 75?
   a 250   b 60   c 20   d 5   e NH

Language mechanics from a Stanford Intermediate test:

Written directions: Read the sentence. Decide which group of words belongs in the blank. Mark the space for your answer.

○ Capitalization
   The medal was given by _____
   a   general richmond
   b   General richmond
   c   general Richmond
   d   General Richmond

○ Punctuation
   I heard her_____ meet me after class."
   a   say, "Please
   b   say "Please
   c   say, Please
   d   say", Please

A sample of an item in Part 1 of Test NS[11]: Analysis of Natural Science Materials, from the Iowa Tests of Educational Development (ITED) Administrator's Summary, © 1990, published by The Riverside Publishing Company:

Conservation workers released 98 pheasants in a wildlife preserve. Some weeks later they found the bones of 26 pheasants at the entrance to a fox den in the area. One worker said, "Foxes ate our pheasants." This statement should be regarded as a

   a   verified conclusion
   b   scientific observation
   c   hypothesis
   d   fact

ITED Test E: Correctness and Appropriateness of Expression (Teacher, Administrator, and Counselor Manual, © 1989):

(For each underlined situation the student chooses the best alternative or the "No change" responses and marks the corresponding oval on the answer sheet.)

Henry David Thoreau was probably a century ahead of his time, yet his own generation regarded him as *quaint old-fashioned and eccentric*

   a (No change)
   b quaint old-fashioned, and eccentric
   c quaint, old-fashioned, and eccentric
   d quaint, old-fashioned, and also eccentric

Today, though, America proudly acknowledges that much of *your* enlightened thinking about the individual and society comes fromThoreau's philosophy of life, which he meticulously recorded in his book *Walden, Or, Life in the Woods.*

   a (No change)
   b its
   c it's
   d their.

Political science item from the Stanford Achievement Test, Advanced:

Judge, Jury, Witness
Which of these belongs on the list above?

   a doctor
   b store clerk
   c lawyer
   d teacher

Psychology/sociology/anthropology item from the Stanford Achievement Test:

Betty Rogers has to learn a new language. She also has to follow different laws and get used to eating different foods. She probably has to do this because she has____

   a finished going to school
   b started a new job
   c begun to earn more money
   d moved to another country

In order to give a slightly more rounded picture, here are a couple of examples from a teacher-designed grade 7 social studies midterm examination in January 1991:

3. The Armada was a fleet sent by

    a. Spain against England
    b. England against Spain
    c. France against Portugal
    d. Spain against Portugal

6. Another name for a Conquistador is

    a. God
    b. conqueror
    c. builder
    d. Spain

In fairness, I should add that the grade 7 social studies examination also contained an essay question that asked students to give their opinions on the U.S. actions in response to Iraq's invasion of Kuwait (this was about a week before the war began on January 16, 1991) and the strike at the *New York Daily News*. The teacher tests knowledge of facts as a separate issue from using them—a significant distinction.

Not all multiple-choice tests are like the examples I have given (although most of them are). For example, the Michigan-Illinois reading tests, developed by the evaluation staff of the two states' departments of education, ask students to read extended passages from published prose, not made up for the examination, and they include questions about the students' expectations of the passage and prior knowledge of the topic. They also use a format that permits more than one correct answer: some questions can have one, two, or three correct answers. There is a complicated formula for scoring these by machine.

Another category of multiple choice is developing in response to charges that multiple-choice questions cannot measure thinking abilities; this has been called enhanced multiple choice. Figure 1.1 contains an example from California.

In part (a) of the old problem, the student simply needs to know the definitions of *equilateral triangle* and *perimeter* and how to multiply 6×3. In (b), what is required is the ability to recognize or calculate multiples of 18. Both are rote computations; neither required understanding of concepts.

The new problem requires the student to analyze the situation and use spatial reasoning to see what is required, then make the same calculations as those in both of the old problems. Thus, understand-

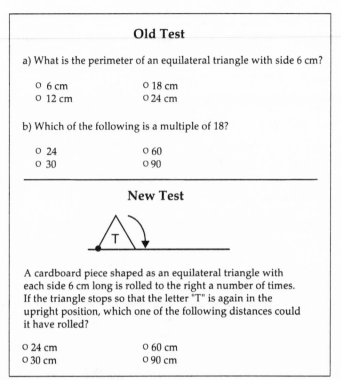

Old Test

a) What is the perimeter of an equilateral triangle with side 6 cm?

    ○ 6 cm   ○ 18 cm
    ○ 12 cm   ○ 24 cm

b) Which of the following is a multiple of 18?

    ○ 24   ○ 60
    ○ 30   ○ 90

New Test

A cardboard piece shaped as an equilateral triangle with each side 6 cm long is rolled to the right a number of times. If the triangle stops so that the letter "T" is again in the upright position, which one of the following distances could it have rolled?

    ○ 24 cm   ○ 60 cm
    ○ 30 cm   ○ 90 cm

FIGURE 1.1 An Enhanced Multiple-Choice Test Item

ing of concepts within several strands of mathematics is required to solve a situational problem.

No matter how sophisticated the techniques, however, multiple-choice tests corrupt the teaching and learning process, for the following reasons:

1. Even at their best, multiple-choice tests ask students to select a response. Selection is passive; it asks students to recognize, not to construct, an answer. The students do not contribute their own thinking to the answer.

2. Multiple-choice tests promote the false impression that a right or wrong answer is available for all questions and problems. As we know, few situations in life have a correct or incorrect answer.

3. The tests tend to rely on memorization and the recall of facts or algorithms. They do not allow students to demonstrate understanding of how algorithms work.

4. The form of multiple-choice tests means that test makers select what can easily be tested rather than what is important for students to learn.

5. Multiple-choice tests do not accurately record what students know and can do, either positively or negatively, as a personal example shows. In 1974, I passed by four points over the cut-score the German-language examination to qualify for the Ph.D., and I am on record somewhere as having a reading knowledge of German. But I cannot read any word of German that does not look like an English or Latin cognate. My answers were either guesses or choices based on probabilities. If the graduate examiners had really wanted to know if I could read German, I should have been required to translate a passage.

6. The tests trivialize teaching and learning. If all classroom activity—the books, the lectures, the discussions, the exercises, the homework—ends up in a few bubbles taking no more than a hour, then what is all the fuss about? The end is incommensurate with the means. Students know that much of passing multiple-choice tests is test wisdom—how to guess productively, what items to omit—and they invest only enough effort to get by.

The corrupting influence of multiple choice has produced a bad bargain between teachers and students: the teachers teach just enough—and in the appropriate form—for students to be able to select the right bubbles. Teachers routinely tell students preparing for the tests: "Don't think! Just mark what you know and move on." But thinking is what everyone needs, including the students.

A San Francisco businessman said at a conference on educational assessment in 1990, "We can only employ one out of five public school graduates now. We need employees with higher order thinking skills, flexibility, and the ability to learn throughout their lives. Businesses will move away from an area if indicators show that the educational institutions there are poor and will not produce employable graduates."[12] When the state of Vermont was holding a series of meetings in 1988 on its educational future, a student stood up and told the officials, "You have no idea how boring it all is."

Business and industry spends $25 billion a year on training programs within its own offices, factories, and plants to educate employees. Universities spend millions offering remedial courses in basic subjects to freshman who have passed multiple-choice examinations in order to be admitted. Certainly there is more wrong with schools than multiple-choice testing, but its influence has been pernicious.

THE CONSTRUCTION OF MULTIPLE-CHOICE TESTS

The way in which nationally normed tests are constructed reduces their educational value further because important content is deliberately omitted. (This is probably not true of teacher-made tests, since teachers do not have norm data.) The tests are developed and written by testing company experts, sometimes in cooperation with the school district's evaluation coordinator (not the staff concerned with teaching and learning) and sometimes not. They are tested on a student population, usually in schools close to the publishing company's headquarters, and items are rejected or accepted according to the students' responses.

Norm-referenced tests are designed not to give an unbiased picture of students' achievement in a particular subject but to spread the student out in a bell-curved distribution, so the test makers discard items that all or a large majority of the students know and keep only those that can be answered correctly by about half of the students. Thus, the core knowledge of a topic is likely not to be tested, since items probing the major facts were probably answered correctly by a majority of the test-taking population. The less central and more trivial facts are more likely to appear on the test. Although teachers do not know the exact material that will appear on any given published test, they know the kind of items likely to be tested, and they teach material relevant to those items.

Furthermore, as Bloom, Madaus, and Hastings point out in *Evaluation to Improve Learning*, there is an inherent bias in using the bell curve.[13] A bell curve is observed as a result of random factors, such as the distribution of height among adult males. But teaching is not a random activity, and therefore the bell curve is inappropriate.

An additional problem with norm-referenced tests is that they tend to misrepresent—upward—the level of achievement. The results are reported to the test publisher's customers, with information about the relative standing of the school, district, or state on a national norm. These norms have been computed by the test publishers from samples of populations who have taken similar tests. Thus, the school or district knows whether its students are at, above, or below the national average in reading, writing, and so on. Because of the bell-curved distribution intended by the tests, only half of the students tested can be above average; but apparently statistical miracles have been occurring: almost all children are above average.

Because the norms are frequently out of date, the tests produce what is frequently called "the Lake Wobegon effect," from Garrison Keillor's mythical Minnesota town where "all the women are strong, the men are good-looking, and all the children are above average." John Jacob Cannell, a doctor in Beaver, West Virginia, first drew attention to the problem when he found that children in the state were declared to be above the national average when they took a nationally normed test, despite the state's having one of the highest illiteracy rates in the nation.

He wrote a challenging book, *Nationally Normed Elementary Achievement Testing in America's Public Schools: How All Fifty States Are above the National Average,* which set the cat among the pigeons in the education community, already reeling from the charges made in *A Nation at Risk.*[14] Cannell's findings were substantially confirmed by a nationally funded research project conducted at the Center for Research on Evaluation, Standards, and Student Testing at the University of California, Los Angeles.[15] One researcher wrote, "In my opinion, there can be no doubt that current norm-referenced tests overstate achievement levels in many schools, districts, and states, often by a large margin."[16]

Norm-referenced, multiple-choice tests are apparently bankrupt as reliable indicators of achievement, as well as corrupters of teaching and learning. What can we do about it?

CHANGING FROM TESTS TO ASSESSMENTS

Evaluation provides important information needed to improve every aspect of the educational process. It is indispensable, not only for practical but also for sound pedagogical reasons.

There are four main purposes for assessment information, with many subsidiary reasons connected to them:

1. For decisions affecting the student's future, whether about appropriate placement or postsecondary paths
2. For accountability to political authorities
3. For information about the student's learning to both the teacher and the student

I will get to the fourth purpose which has emerged only recently, in a moment.

Norm-referenced, machine-scorable, multiple-choice tests are commonly used for the first three purposes: student selection and sorting (certification), accountability, and program monitoring. Anything that replaces these tests must ameliorate the problems caused by these tests and demonstrate that they can perform the functions as well as or better than these tests.

There should be no single replacement for these tests. An ideal evaluation system for American schools will include a variety of evidence about the progress of individual students and the quality of educational programs. I advocate a multi-indicator system that will make use of teachers' observations, collections of students' work (often called portfolios), group tasks, timed examinations, and even multiple choice where that is appropriate for a small area of specific knowledge. Reliance on a single measure, taken at a single point in time, no matter how sophisticated the measuring instrument is, cannot represent the complexity of what we want to know about students' intellectual, emotional, and social development or about how school programs affect these developments.

The ultimate aim of an educational evaluation system must be to train students to assess their own progress and their own products. That is why assessment methods should provide a model for students and why students should be able to learn self-assessment from the examples they encounter in school.

Seen in this light, multiple-choice tests fall short. They do not provide useful information or do they model life outside the classroom. When I was giving a workshop on performance assessment in New Mexico, I asked the teachers and administrators where they use multiple choice in real life. They were stymied for a moment. Finally someone answered, "the driver's license examination," and another came up with "at the racetrack." No one could think of any other situations.

This may be too flip a dismissal of a technique that worked when its purpose were circumscribed and before it was misused as a club to beat low-performing schools and teachers. Multiple-choice tests will have a place in a multi-indicator system, there is no doubt. In this book, however, I want to focus on the other techniques I have listed since they are not widely known.

These forms of assessment will be described using the general term performance assessment. The important distinction is between "assessment" and "test." A test is a single-occasion, unidimensional, timed exercise, usually in multiple-choice or short-answer form. Assessment is an activity that can take many forms, can extend over time, and aims to capture the quality of a student's work or of an educational program. There is a rapidly growing body of what are variously called "authentic," "alternative," "performance based," or "performance assessments." I prefer the term *performance assessment* because it accurately conveys the sense of a direct demonstration of achievement—a performance. The word *performance* is used to evaluate cars, stock markets, and materials. Why not apply it to education?

Performance assessments can fulfill the three functions I have listed at all levels. The examples in the following chapters include classroom assessments devised by teachers, especially portfolios of student work; districtwide assessments; state assessments; and even a national example (Advanced Placement Studio Art).

I define performance assessment as a collection of ways to provide accurate information about what students know and are able to do or about the quality of educational programs. The collective assessments reflect the complexity of what is to be learned and do not distort its nature in the information-gathering process.

I stress "a collection of ways" and "collective assessments" because I do not want to be misunderstood as advocating replacing norm-referenced, multiple-choice tests one for one with performance assessments. That is not my aim. There is no possibility of ejecting multiple-choice tests like the videotape from a recorder and sliding in a new tape. This tape is of a different shape and size and requires a new machine, and it is not one tape but a suite of them.

However, I do not want to lose the description "standardized," since standardization is essential to make an assessment system useful. Standardization permits comparisons among groups or individuals being assessed and also implies a comparison with a standard to be attained. The ideal would be standardized performance assessments that provide a rich array of statistically reliable information about students and programs.

A UNIQUE PURPOSE FOR ASSESSMENT

Performance assessment can be seen as a lever to promote the changes needed for the assessment to be maximally useful. Among these changes are a redefinition of learning and a different conception of the place of assessment in the educational process. Learning does not mean memorizing facts or algorithms; it means the ability to use them appropriately by weighing conflicting values, arguing with reasoned propositions, selecting facts, using evidence, and thinking clearly. If students are to increase their ability in these areas, both they and their teachers need constant feedback in a form both can understand immediately. Assessment thus becomes a part of instruction, even when the results of assessment are also used for accountability.

If students should be able to analyze, synthesize, interpret, and evaluate facts and ideas, then their progress should be charted by direct performances. If students should write well, they should be tested by reading their writing. If they should be able to solve problems using mathematical knowledge, the assessment must ask them to do it. The principle applies in all curricular areas. Knowledge of a foreign language should mean being able to communicate; knowledge of history and geography should mean understanding events in place and time. Ascertaining how well these skills have been learned means requiring their use in a meaningful context. Performance assessment includes conversations in a foreign language; observations of students conducting science experiments or of students' language development; open-ended questions, where students provide solutions for a problem that has no single right answer; exhibitions in which students choose their own ways to demonstrate what they have learned; interviews, giving students a chance to reflect on their achievement; and portfolios, selections of student work.

Multiple-choice testing assumes that a small number of items act as a proxy for knowledge of a larger set of things to be learned. This claim may be statistically true, but it begs the question about the nature of knowledge and gives no direct message about what is needed to raise its level.

This is where the fourth purpose of educational testing, unique to performance assessment, comes in. It can model desired teaching and learning, and it has been consciously designed to do so. In Fredericksen and Collins's terms, performance assessments have "systemic validity": "A systemically valid test is one that induces in the education system curricular and instructional changes that foster the development of the cognitive traits that the test is designed to measure."[17]

The forms of assessment—portfolios, open-ended questions, observations, exhibitions—can also be regarded as good teaching. Seizing the opportunity to change teaching and learning by making a test worth teaching to, two states, Arizona and Maryland, now have language arts assessments that require reading, writing, and revising over two or three days, intended as a direct inducement to teachers to follow the model of the assessment in their regular classroom work.

PSYCHOMETRICS

We need one more piece of background information before I can begin describing the performance assessments that are the heart of this book. Until recently, the evaluation of educational progress has been the business of the measurement community, the psychometricians. Psychometrics is the science of mental measurement, that is, assigning quantities to mental products. It depends on sophisticated mathematical and statistical techniques to extract maximum numerical information from minimum input.

The psychometric community is trained in graduate schools of psychology and education, and many of its members remain there. Those who move outside the academy become evaluation directors for state departments of education or large school districts that can afford the position or employees of the large test publishers. The most prestigious of these is the Educational Testing Service (ETS) in Princeton, New Jersey, which is the most renowned of testing companies. ETS designs and administers NAEP for the U.S. Department of Education and the SAT and the Advanced Placement program for the College Board. The psychometric community gets together annually at meetings such as those of the National Council on Measurement in Education (NCME), which are held in conjunction with the convention of the American Educational Research Association (AERA).

Introductions to psychometrics stress three virtues of good tests: objectivity, validity, and reliability. These mean, respectively, that a test must be free from the bias of subjectivity in both its design and scoring; must validly measure what it is supposed to measure, and not some peripheral features; and must be constructed so that the same answers would reliably produce the same score, no matter how and when the scoring is done. Objectivity led to the machine scoring of tests wherever possible (the famous SCANTRON machine is the most obvious example). Statistical sophistication has reached such heights that a layperson stranded at an NCME meeting would wonder what the talk about a "Cronback alpha of .87" or a "validity coefficient of .72" has to do with students' learning how to write.[18]

The psychometric community was at first hostile to and even contemptuous of the quality of performance assessments as they began to emerge, but they have begun to see in them a new challenge.[19] In their terms, performance assessments have high face validity (because they directly assess what students are supposed to know and be able to do) but low reliability (because they are scored not by machines but by people). This, of course, compromises the objectivity of performance assessments in psychometric terms. There is a trade-off between "authenticity," that is, importance in real-life terms, and reliability and objectivity. As validity goes up, reliability and objectivity go down.[20]

Psychometricians are beginning to use their immense statistical ingenuity to solve problems posed by the need for high authenticity and reliability at the same time. Test publishers such as the Riverside Publishing Company and CTB/Macmillan/McGraw-Hill are working with state departments of education (Riverside in Arizona and CTB/McGraw-Hill in Maryland) to produce startlingly innovative assessments, such as two- and three-day writing and reading assessments. The ETS itself is heavily involved with the development of portfolios and methods of scaling observational assessments.

The interest of the psychometric community is sorely needed if performance assessment is to reach its potential. As you will see from the program descriptions I provide, performance assessments today have all the courage of pioneers—and their foolhardiness. This is a movement that is just beginning. The first attempts are exciting but uneven, and they tend to go for big ideas and neglect the details. Performance assessments will play their vital role in improving America's schools if they can retain their freshness and challenge while increasing their focus and refinement.

INFLUENCING TEACHING AND LEARNING

I am interested in assessment programs that push teaching and learning in the direction of concepts, application, and student responsibility for learning. Some authorities make a distinction between the fairly relaxed degree of rigor needed for two of the three purposes of assessment (decisions about students and feedback to the teacher) and the higher degree of rigor needed for accountability. They believe that different kinds of testing are required for each purpose. Lorrie Shepard of the University of Colorado, who believes that "accountability testing . . . is having a pernicious effect on education," distinguishes between feedback and accountability:

> Large-scale assessments must be formal, objective, time-efficient, cost-efficient, widely applicable, and centrally processed. . . . In contrast, assessments designed to support instruction are informal, teacher-mandated, adapted to local context, locally scored, sensitive to short-term change in students' knowledge, and meaningful to students. They provide immediate, detailed, and complex feedback; and they incorporate tasks that have instructional value in themselves.[21]

When this passage was written in 1989, it was not as clear as it has become that a legitimate purpose for assessment is the modeling of instruction on a large scale. Shepard's distinction between accountability and support for instruction has been blurred, intentionally, by the design of accountability assessments that provide usable feedback about instructional policy and practice to teachers, largely because of their own participation in the process.

The first example I will provide is a group of state programs designed to change instruction by moving the classroom focus toward the kinds of outcomes needed for social and individual success in the next generation. I turn first to California, which has been in the business of performance assessment longer than other states, and to the subject of writing assessment (also with a long history of performance assessment), and then go on to examples from other states. These state programs show how an accountability assessment can change instruction through feedback to teachers and schools; this has already occurred in California.

There is hope for our schools if we quit trying to find in them the features we expect from our own experiences. What was good enough for our parents and for ourselves is not good enough for our children. Assessment is one area where schooling is going to be different—and, I believe, better.

2

Assessing Writing in California, Arizona, and Maryland

The teachers in Arizona can't serve two masters. If they want the teachers to do a good job of teaching, they can use the Essential Skills Document (ESD) . . . and throw out the Iowa Test of Basic Skills (ITBS) tests or teach the ITBS tests and throw out the ESD.

—Arizona teacher[1]

CALIFORNIA ASSESSMENT PROGRAM

In the late 1980s, the California Department of Education announced as a matter of policy that the California Assessment Program (CAP) would change its statewide assessments from multiple choice to performance assessments as soon as they could be developed by groups of California teachers. At the California Education Summit in December 1989, this policy was adopted, although it had been operating de facto for at least five years:

The current approach to assessment of student achievement which relies on multiple-choice student response must be abandoned because of its deleterious effect on the educational

27

process. An assessment system which measures student achievement on performance-based measures is essential for driving the needed reform toward a thinking curriculum in which students are actively engaged and successful in achieving goals in and beyond high school.[2]

The statement implies an intention to use performance assessment as a means of changing teaching and learning in California schools.

The CAP was, until it was cut from the budget by the Governor in August 1990, an accountability mechanism designed to report on the state of California schools. CAP scores were reported in newspapers throughout the state and influenced decisions of all sorts—from home buyers' location in one school district or another according to the CAP scores, to the allocation of special resources for low-performing schools. For a few years after the California school reform act of 1983, schools were offered "Cash for CAP," financial incentives for improvements of a certain magnitude. The funds ran out, and in any case, the motivation worked only once; a school that had made giant gains would be unlikely to make the same amount of improvement in subsequent years and so was not motivated to continue the same level of effort.

CAP used matrix sampling, a technique that economically elicits a great deal of information about programs from a single assessment. Students took different forms or parts of an assessment; in a single class of students, none may be answering the same question. There were no individual student scores from CAP but a score for each school.

CAP had a long history, going back to the early 1970s. By the time of its demise in 1990, most of its assessments were still multiple choice, but it had led the nation in implementing large-scale performance assessments in writing and mathematics. In 1991 a successor to CAP was going through the California legislature. A bold and innovative program, it will retain matrix sampling but add to it assessments that are embedded in normal instruction. Scores from both kinds of assessment will be combined to provide scores for each individual student. I will focus on California's writing and mathematics assessments to illustrate the assertions I made in chapter 1: that assessment is a lever for change in teaching and learning, that the form of the assessment should reflect directly what we want students to know and be able to do, and that accountability instruments can provide feedback to teachers and students.

At the time of its death in 1990, the CAP assessments were administered in grades 3, 6, 8, 10, and 12. (Its successor will move the assessment years to grades 5, 8, and 11, on the grounds that these are the years before transition to other levels—middle or junior high school, senior high school, and graduation—and therefore deficiencies revealed at these grades could be ameliorated in the final year before the students move on to the next level.) CAP measured progress in reading, writing, and mathematics at grade 3 and in reading, writing, mathematics, science, history–social science, and science at the other grades.

California went about its reform of teaching and learning in a progression that should please even the most traditional believer in curriculum first and then assessment. Beginning in 1984, the state department of education began a statewide process of revising subject matter in all the major academic areas. It was a consensus process, achieved through the appointment of statewide committees with representatives from all levels of the educational system, from elementary through graduate school. The results appeared almost annually: first the English/language arts framework, then literature, mathematics, history/social science, foreign languages, arts, and science. They are extensive descriptions of ideal teaching in these areas and have become national models. They advocate the understanding of concepts, not the memorization of facts and algorithms; writing and reading for meaning; application of knowledge to real-world situations; and cooperative learning as a delivery mode. The history/social science curriculum framework presents history as a narrative; it was partially authored by Diane Ravitch, who in *What Do Our 17-Year-Olds Know?* criticized the national state of learning in history.

These frameworks are called model curricula because they are recommended to California's 1,400 school districts. They cannot be mandated, but the state department of education expected them to be used as yardsticks against which school districts measure their own teaching and learning.

After the curriculum frameworks and guidelines were well along, the department of education in 1987 added the incentive of the CAP assessments in writing.

The teaching of writing in California was revolutionized when Charles Cooper of the University of California, San Diego began working in 1984 with groups of teachers to identify the kinds of writing students should be able to produce and thus to carry out the recommendations of the English/language arts framework. The genres of writing included narrative or story, report of information, evaluation or judgment, autobiographical incident, the solution to a problem, speculation about causes and effects, report of observations, interpretation, and discussion of a controversial issue. These and a few other types of writing were derived from observations of the kinds of writing or "rhetorical modes" required either in post-secondary education or the world of work. Cooper and the teachers' writing development team prepared teaching guides that contained descriptions of the features typical of each writing type, models from published writing, and classroom activities designed to develop mastery of the writing modes. Copies of these teaching guides were supplied to all schools with grade 8 classes throughout the state.

Teaching Writing for the Real World

It is worth underscoring the importance of Cooper's development of genre-specific writing instruction. Teaching writing according to purpose and audience, instead of assuming that "good" writing is good writing in all circumstances, was a breakthrough. Some states, such as Arizona and Maryland, have followed California and are assessing—and therefore teaching—writing according to a specified type. Other states and school districts try to evaluate writing from a single "prompt" or topic, not genre specific. The prompts frequently ask students to write about a favorite object, a turning point in their life, a gift that meant a great deal to them, and so on. (I call them "little locket" prompts, since the favored object often seems to be a locket with someone's picture or some hair inside. These answers raise considerable doubt about the student writer's interest in the topic. They look like something vaguely remembered from a sentimental story in a basal reader.) These topics are bland because they must be intelligible to a broad spectrum of students with different backgrounds who cannot be expected to have learned how to write specific genres. The prompts do not supply a context, a purpose, or an audience, possibly because they originate in a view of writing as a celebratory form.

Writing samples of this kind have their origins in the belles-lettres tradition of the occasional essay, highly regarded in the nineteenth and early twentieth centuries but now read (and sometimes written) only by a few English literature professors. It is significant that the lists of writing genres that Cooper and similar researchers worked out do not include an "essay," since it is basically an obsolete form.

The students who are asked to write on little locket topics have no context for them; if they want to communicate about favorite objects or celebrate great moments in their lives, they do so while hanging out with groups of friends or over the telephone.

Although still commonly assigned, the little locket essay prompt raises a great many problems. It assumes that all writing is essentially the same, and therefore an ability to write in one genre is equal to an ability in another; it makes the development of a common scoring scale difficult because of the wide variation in responses to a nongeneric prompt; and it does not offer an equal writing opportunity to all students. It tends to reward those who write with facility, since it is difficult to teach the features of a little locket essay. Students treat these prompts with contempt. They do not learn from them how writing can be a means to operate on and in the world. Instead, students need to learn what kind of writing is called for in what circumstances and how to apply a model of response.

Writing, of course, does not always fall into neat packages. Major attention-getting devices in effective writing include mixing genres and exceeding their boundaries, but students need to know the genres before they can appreciate what can be done above and beyond them.

Cooper and the teams of teachers also prepared prompts for the grade 8 and grade 12 writing assessments. Their prompts are starting ideas for writing, which usually include a scenario, an audience for the writing, and a purpose. Following is an example of a prompt (the example was never used in precisely this form; the exact wording of prompts is kept secret so that some can be used in more than one year to check reader reliability):

Writing Situation

Your English teacher has asked you and other students in your class to help select literature for next year's grade eight classes. Think about all the works of literature—stories, novels, poems, plays, essays—you've read this year in your English class. Choose the one you have enjoyed most.

Directions for Writing

Write an essay for your English teacher recommending your favorite literary work. Give reasons for your judgment that other grade eight students should read this work. Tell the teacher why this work is especially valuable.

Because the CAP used matrix sampling, as many as fifty prompts were developed, evenly distributed among the six or eight types of writing assigned for assessment in a given year. Prompts are distributed randomly; a student has an equal chance of being asked to write on any of the topics in any of the writing modes.

It is that feature—the impossibility of predicting the kind of writing any student will be asked to produce—that gives the writing assessment its power to change the teaching of writing. Because any student may have to write a persuasive or a narrative or describe an autobiographical incident, all students must learn to write all the genres expected for that level. From the teacher's point of view, both good writing instruction and preparation for the assessment— teaching to the test, if you like—require the teaching of all the kinds of writing; thus, preparation for the assessment is also good teaching. Since the CAP reports scores by schools, teachers have an on-site incentive to prepare the students well.

The Effect of CAP Assessments on Instruction in Writing

The CAP system has worked so well that it has had greater impact on instruction statewide than any other program. In an evaluation of the writing assessment, the Center for the Study of Writing found that 94 percent of California teachers questioned assigned a greater variety of writing tasks than they did before the CAP assessment, and 78 percent said they assigned more writing. In one year alone, the percentage of students who wrote eleven or more papers in a six-week period jumped from 22 to 33 percent.[3]

The papers are scored by group grading, which is accomplished by reading the students' writing. It now seems entirely natural that writing should be judged by reading it; however, in the first years of the Bay Area (now the National) Writing Project's dissemination during the late 1970s,[4] the participants were treated to psychometric explanations of the need for objectivity, reliability, and validity in the testing of writing. These explanations were provided as proof that reading actual samples was unnecessary as a measure of writing ability. Writing Project fellows were told that scores on multiple-choice tests correlated well with writing samples. Why go to the trouble and expense of having students write and teachers read if the same effect could be gained from a bubble test?[5]

At that time they did find the same effect, for the people reading the writing samples were looking for the same features as the test makers, which is why they agreed. These features were grammatical and usage errors, now recognized as essential but not central factors in the writing process. (In fact, the CAP tests that used multiple choice were called "editing tests" from the mid-1980s.) Dale Carson, CAP director, remembered those days in a speech he gave at an international conference on assessment in Germany in 1988:

> The most laughable example of this phenomenon (if it were not so tragic) is that there has actually been debate about the degree to which multiple-choice exercises focusing on grammar, punctuation, spelling, and/or recognizing the best way of stating a sentence can legitimately be used to assess writing proficiency. . . . For assessment programs that purport to measure the outcomes of education . . . it is unconscionable that we have even considered the use of such exercises.

The scorers of CAP writing assessments are teachers, working under the administrative guidance of an experienced agency such as the Educational Testing Service, which organizes reading sessions in several locations throughout California. The participation of teachers is the vital link between the standards embodied in the writing assessments and classroom practice.

Group Grading

Group grading is a technique for increasing the objectivity and reliability of assessments scored by people as opposed to machines. A group of graders (also referred as raters or scorers) assembles in teams around tables, each with a leader, who is usually experienced in the technique. The entire group—all the members of all the teams—first has to agree on standards, so sample papers, usually selected by experienced readers to illustrate all the possible scores, are distributed for the entire group to read.

This activity is called calibration in some cases and standard setting in others. It is the most important activity of the group grading process and may take as much as half the time allotted (usually measured in days) for scoring a large number of papers. The teachers (in the case of grading CAP writing assessments) first assign grades to the samples and then discuss what made them award a 6 or a 4 or a 1. The group must reach consensus so that these samples can be used as standards. It can be a strenuous process, but it is extremely valuable because it allows teachers to see clearly what they reward in writing and to reconcile their value systems with those of the larger group.

Different kinds of scales developed as group grading spread throughout the writing instruction community during the late 1970s and early 1980s. Holistic scoring awards a grade to a piece of writing based on its total impact on the reader; it does not analyze the writing into constituent parts. Analytic scoring does that; it awards separate scores for rhetorical effectiveness, use of arguments, tone, and so on, including correctness of grammar and usage. Primary trait scoring looks first for the expected features of a genre of writing, such as reporting, narration, a complaint letter, or a poem.

The CAP essays are graded according to a modified primary trait scoring system. Each essay has a rhetorical effectiveness score, which assesses its mastery of the type of writing attempted; a general feature score, rewarding ability to achieve coherence or an attractive style; and a conventions score, which assesses the ability to use the grammatical and idiomatic structure of the language. Figure 2.1 shows the six-point scale for essays of the evaluation type. The descriptions of achievement have been worked out from a combination of desirable features in an essay supporting a judgment and the evidence of what can be expected from grade 8 students. This scale is called the rubric and is used as a template to guide the scoring. (*Rubric* is an interesting word to use in this context; it describes the red or "rubric" letters that were used in Christian prayer books to give directions on the proper conduct of the religious service.)

The calibration sessions in group grading can be used to establish a rubric or to apply an already prepared one. There is considerable room for interpretation of key terms. What exactly constitutes evidence? What does "move along logically and coherently" mean in practice? Without thorough discussion, the standards can remain foggy, and the grading will lose reliability.

After the calibration session, with the standards fresh in their minds, the graders begin reading. Two people read each paper, without seeing the grade the other assigns it. If the scores agree within a specified tolerance, a final grade is assigned, usually the aggregate of

Achievement in Evaluation

Score Point	Description of Achievement
6 Exceptional Achievement	The student produces convincingly argued evaluation; identifies a subject, describes it appropriately, and asserts a judgment of it; gives reasons and specific evidence to support the argument; engages the reader immediately, moves along logically and coherently and provides closure; reflects awareness of reader's questions or alternative evaluations.
5 Commendable Achievement	The student produces well-argued evaluation; identifies, describes, and judges its subject; gives reasons and evidence to support the argument; is engaging, logical, attentive to reader's concerns; is more conventional or predictable than the writer of a 6.
4 Adequate Achievement	The student produces adequately argued evaluation; identifies and judges its subject; gives at least one moderately developed reason to support the argument; lacks the authority and polish of the writer of a 5 or 6; produces writing that, although focused and coherent, may be uneven; usually describes the subject more than necessary and argues a judgment less than necessary.
3 Some Evidence of Achievement	The student states a judgment and gives one or more reasons to support it; either lists reasons without providing evidence or fails to argue even one reason logically or coherently.
2 Limited Evidence of Achievement	The student states a judgment but may describe the subject without evaluating it or may list irrelevant reasons or develop a reason in a rambling, illogical way.
1 Minimal Evidence of Achievement	The student usually states a judgment but may describe the subject without stating a judgment; either gives no reasons or lists only one or two reasons without providing evidence; usually relies on weak and general personal evaluation.
No Response	
Off Topic	

FIGURE 2.1 Six-Point Scale for Essays

the two grades. But if the first grader gave the paper a 4 and the second a 2 or a 1, then a third person, usually the table leader, reads it, again without knowing the grades but understanding that there is a discrepancy.

Various techniques are employed to maintain standards. There are frequent pauses for calibration sessions, usually before beginning in the morning and after lunch for large-scale readings that spread over a few days. Papers already scored are circulated back into the piles to see if they get the same scores again. Table leaders randomly select scored papers and read them to see if they agree with the assigned evaluations. Most people who have been involved with group grading find the degree of agreement remarkable. There is, of course, the occasional reader who cannot accept the consensus standard; such a person has to be neutralized by rereading the papers—and by not being asked to return for further grading.

I have described the group grading process in detail because it is the basic means of scoring performance assessments. You will need to keep it in mind for the later examples in this book. Some assessments use the entire process, notably the free-response portions of the College Board's Advanced Placement examinations (described more fully in chapter 5 in the discussion of Advanced Placement Studio Art) and the open-ended mathematics questions of the CAP grade 12 assessment.

Others use reduced versions, with fewer people or following a tightly focused rubric. Among these are the New York State Elementary Science Program Evaluation Test (ESPET) (described in chapter 3), where teachers work in teams of whatever size is convenient at their schools to judge whether answers are worth a 0, 1, or 2. The scores are sometimes aggregated, as they are when six teams of judges score the entries in the "We the People . . ." competition in civics. Sometimes they are averaged.

The essence of group grading is approaching objectivity through a consensus of subjective judgments. When a variety of standards is represented in any group, which nevertheless has a common object and largely a common background, no single subjective judgment is likely to survive strenuous discussion. The technique is not unfamiliar, but we are not used to seeing it used in an educational setting. As Grant Wiggins has frequently pointed out, competitive sports such as diving and ice skating and artistic performances such as piano, voice, and violin competitions are judged by panels of experts who either discuss the performance until they agree or average their scores.[6] Art shows and science fairs are judged by juries who operate in the same way. To accept similar methods of scoring in education requires shifting expectations from numbers assigned by a machine to numbers assigned by direct human contact.

Feedback to the Classroom

The benefits of group grading vastly outweigh the disadvantages, as the CAP experience has demonstrated. Teachers who take part in scoring sessions experience standard setting and see in the essays they judge what material students need to be able to meet those standards. More than 400 teachers participated in CAP scoring sessions each year, for each grade (8 and 12). Their participation is perhaps the most powerful form of professional development (a better term than *staff development* or *in-service*) for teachers, as the CAP graders frequently exclaim. Assessment brings out the fundamental questions about teaching: What do we value? Are we teaching that or giving other messages? Is what we value in fact the most important aspects of the subject, or are we following tradition? Teachers who grade see firsthand what students are learning from writing instruction in the state, and they incorporate that into their own teaching and communicate the standards to their colleagues. They wrote in their evaluations of the experience:

> I am learning to analyze essays for distinctive qualities rather than rely on my general holistic impression. As a result, I see how important it is to teach my students the distinctive characteristics of each type of writing.

> I know good writing is damn difficult to do and damn rare. I know kids need to practice it more and see good models . . . in order to do better.

> More emphasis should be placed on critical thinking skills, supporting judgments, and tying thoughts and ideas together. Far too many papers digress, summarize, underdevelop, or state totally irrelevant facts.

> I will build cross-curricular writing lessons for my students because of my exposure to the student writing I saw grading these papers. Reading several hundred papers of varied quality gives me a sound sense of what is good and what is poor.

> As a social studies teacher, the CAP writing assessment had no real meaning for me. Now I understand the test and I will do more writing in my classes from now on.

Other teachers said they had "bought into the CAP system," would change their teaching methods, and would help their students make their writing "sparkle."

Fairness to Minorities

Great care is exercised to ensure that panels of teacher-readers include representatives of the ethnic groups in the California school population; however, the disproportion between the ethnic make-up of the teaching force as opposed to that of the student population makes this difficult to achieve to an acceptable degree. Although more than 50 percent of students in California schools are members of ethnic minorities, fewer than 11 percent of teachers are African-American, Hispanic, Asian-American, or native American.

This is a national problem, and it is getting worse rather than better because more teachers from these minority groups are leaving the schools than from the ranks of Anglo teachers.

Minority involvement in group grading is essential if minority parents are to be convinced that performance assessments are fair to their children. To a certain extent, the minority community sees machine-scorable, multiple-choice testing as a guarantee that their children are not victims of racist teachers. Bringing teachers back into the assessment process is not necessarily an advance in their eyes. A great deal of patient persuasion and demonstration of good faith will be necessary to show them at the objectivity they saw in multiple-choice tests was in fact shortchanging their children by not permitting them to develop creativity, conceptual understanding, and an ability to apply their knowledge.

The CAP writing scores are reported to the public in the same form as other CAP scores. It is a safe assumption that the public does not realize that the CAP scores represent different methods of scoring. The same service (once Educational Testing Service and then a New Hampshire testing service) that organizes and conducts the grading sessions also performs the statistical manipulations that translate the raw scores into scaled scores weighted for the relative difficulty of the writing assignments. It then transforms the resulting scores to the usual CAP scale, where the statewide mean is 250.

STATE WRITING ASSESSMENTS: A BROKEN CHAIN

Only a few states give their teachers the opportunity to develop professionally by scoring writing samples. In 1990, twenty-seven states used writing samples as part of their statewide assessments, but more than twenty of these states employed outside companies to grade the essays. These companies, most of them located in North Carolina, Minnesota, New Hampshire, and New Jersey, arrange for the essays to be read by groups of retired and moonlighting teachers they recruit in their own vicinity. The experience of grading is therefore wasted on teachers not in a position to plough back the knowledge they gain. Reasons given for what seems to be a perverse practice are usually fears of conflict of interest (that the state's own teachers will inflate the scores); the difficulty of conducting the sessions, especially gaining and maintaining consensus; and expense (teachers have to be paid for the time they spend grading their state's papers).

These objections are real and not to be dismissed lightly, but they are surmountable. Teachers do not grade papers from their own school, for example. As for the difficulties of maintaining reliable standards, they should be regarded as a learning process, providing opportunities to probe standards. The expense of writing assessments graded by teachers can be subsumed under the costs of professional development, since that is being accomplished at the same time. The costs of grading can also be posted as curriculum development, since this too is a result of teachers' involvement.

Probably the states that send their papers out of state for grading are following the old model of assessment as I described it in chapter 1: teachers administer the test by watching the students complete it, and then the papers are whisked away for "objective" grading before they can be tampered with. It is to be hoped that interstate exchange of ideas about assessment, now being formalized by national groups, will persuade these state education departments that they are missing out on a valuable tool for the improvement of teaching and learning.

ARIZONA: A STEP BEYOND

California's writing assessments suffered the fate of most other pioneers: they were used as models and then superseded by those who benefited from their experience—in this case, Arizona and Maryland. The assessments designed by these latter states reflect the writing process even more thoroughly than the genres developed by Cooper and the teachers in California.

A pedagogy of writing based on the practice of writers is the major contribution of the Bay Area (now National) Writing Project. Writing used to be assigned and then corrected; it was not taught as a process that anyone could learn. Writing teachers now take their students through a classroom process of brainstorming to develop ideas; writing a rough draft; sharing it with a group of peers or the teacher, or both; rewriting to incorporate suggestions; writing a final draft; and editing for grammar, spelling, and usage errors. In contrast, one-shot assessments ask students to compress the writing process into a single draft in a certain length of time: 45 minutes for the CAP writing assessment and only 16 minutes for the National Association of Educational Progress writing samples.

Arizona's writing test occurs over two days. On the first day, the students get as far as the rough draft stage, and on the second day, they reread their drafts and then revise and edit them according to a checklist of criteria.

The Arizona Student Assessment Program (ASAP) arose, like California's, from the state adoption of curricular frameworks, called, unfortunately, the Essential Skills Documents—unfortunately because in using the word *skills* they bring to mind basic skills, a concept that focused schools disastrously on lower-level skills acquired step by laborious step according to the behavioristic model of learning. (See chapter 7 where this is discussed in the context of a brief history of U.S. schooling.) The ESD nevertheless are solid descriptions of what children should know at grades 3, 8, and 12.

Taking the same road as California, Arizona wanted to reinforce the curricula with assessments. They looked first at the Iowa Test of Basic Skills (ITBS) and the Tests of Achievement Performance (TAP), norm-referenced, multiple-choice, machine-scorable tests they routinely bought from the Riverside Publishing Company for annual spring testing.

Researchers created a matrix and charted the items on the ITBS and the TAP that were covered by the ESD and the items in the ESD that were covered in the ITBS and the TAP tests. They discovered that while 100 percent of the items on the ITBS and TAP were covered in the ESD, only 26 to 30 percent of the ESD was assessed by the ITBS and the TAP. So in essence, from the usual tests, Arizona would receive only information about how well students were mastering 30 percent (at most) of their work; there was no information on the other 70 percent.[7]

Some psychometricians would argue that 30 percent is a reliable indicator of learning if the items were an acceptable proxy for the rest. But the Arizona state education department and the legislators who were backing the reform wanted to make sure that teachers understood what should be taught and how it should be taught by incorporating the message into assessments. They understood the feedback mechanism possible with assessment, while their psychometric advisers still saw testing as separate from teaching.

Using Assessment as Curriculum

The results of a bidding competition found Riverside Publishing Company working with the state department of education to produce exemplary performance assessments in writing, reading, and mathematics at grades 3, 8, and 11. The arrangement allows the company to retain the copyright while receiving royalties from the state department to permit copying of the assessments for school districts.

It also pioneered a different relationship between test publishers and their customers; the publishers do not sell an already designed product to the education department but work to its specifications and with teachers in the state. Arizona teachers will score the assessments when they are administered in spring 1992 and will probably design the state's history–social studies and science assessments in the next round of development.

Meanwhile, in an inspired move, the Arizona state department gave each school district a complete set of assessments to do with as it pleased for the school year 1990–1991. The assessments could be used as curriculum material, as district, school, or classroom assessments, or as material for professional development workshops—or they could be trashed if the school district could not face so much change. But the districts are fairly warned: like it or not, students will be assessed by similar instruments beginning in 1992.

Writing Assessment in Arizona

The reading and writing assessments in Arizona are matched so that the natural connection between the two is maintained. The interdisciplinary emphasis is a deliberate policy to move the curriculum in the direction of integrated learning. Each Essential Skills Document contains indications of links to other disciplines, on the grounds that "life is seldom parceled out the way school life is."[8] The five grade 3 reading assessments ask students to read and respond to a personal narrative, a story, an informative report, a communication, and a poem. The reading pieces are lively and interesting and do not shy from unfamiliar words such as *jesses* (in a narrative about retraining an injured owl to fly), *diplodocus dinosaur* (an affectionate name shared by two friends), and *captivity* (in an article on play in animals).

The grade 3 writing assignments are the converse of the reading assignments: the students are asked to produce a personal narrative, a story, a report, a communication, and a poem. At grade 8, summary and essay are added to both reading and writing. The communication for eighth graders is a letter to a public figure about a social problem. At grade 12, there are nine genres: the first four like those of the earlier grades (the letter is a job application), with the addition of a summary, a comparison/contrast essay, a persuasive piece, and an evaluation or critique.

The grade 12 reading assignments are particularly attractive. They include a witty and colloquial review of the movie *Star Trek V*, John Donne's sonnet, "Death, Be Not Proud," and Martin Luther King, Jr.'s "I Have a Dream" speech—the last an ironical choice for Arizona's twelfth graders, since the state is one of three in the nation that do not recognize King's birthday as a holiday. To make clear how the writing and reading assessments work, I will take one example of each to explain in detail.

For reading at grade 8 (reading personal narrative), the topic is Helen Keller and other disabled people. The teacher is instructed to ask the students first: "Have you ever worked with a disabled person, for example at the Special Olympics?" The class has a few minutes to talk about their experiences with the disabled. Then the teacher asks: "If you were asked to work with a disabled person and had never had any experience, you might want to find out what it would be like. What are some questions you might want answered?" Again, discussion ensues.

The first reading passage is a shortened and simplified version of the entry under "Keller, Helen," in the 1986 edition of the *Encyclopaedia Britannica*. Students are asked to answer on a lined sheet five questions "that you think a book about Helen Keller's life would answer." This portion is ungraded but must be completed. Then students read a three-page extract from Keller's *The Story of My Life*. In the test booklet, they write single-paragraph answers to two questions about the reading: one asks them to judge whether Keller's description helped them to understand disability and the other to suggest what more might be learned from a reading of Keller's complete autobiography. Although this is a reading assessment, students must pay attention to their writing; a "review checklist" at the bottom of the page requires them to check that they have answered the questions in paragraphs containing complete sentences and checked for spelling, capitalization, punctuation, and neat writing. Two additional exercises are uninspired comprehension questions asking the students to characterize actions from a list of words and match up events with the sequence of the narrative.

The final exercise is a one-page essay to be written in the test booklet in response to the question: "Why do you think Mr. Gibson gave the title *The Miracle Worker* to his play (about Anne Sullivan and Helen Keller)?" Again there is a checklist at the bottom of the page. The series of exercises is to be completed in 45 minutes on two succeeding days.

The scoring guide is in two parts: a table of guidelines and responses for the comprehension exercises and rubrics for the first two questions and the final essay. These are scored from 4 at the top to 1 at the bottom, with 0 for no attempt and n/s for illegible or unreadable papers, including those written in a language other than English. (A Spanish version of the ASAP performance assessments is being developed.) It is expected that answers receiving a 3 or 4 should be sufficiently free of mechanical errors (spelling, punctuation, capitalization, usage) that understanding is not impeded, but they are not expected to be perfect. "Content and creative thought are the focus of the evaluation," says the rubric for each question. The guide contains a comprehensive description of what should be expected of scores of 4, 3, 2, and 1, guided by the focus on what the student has to say.

The grade 8 writing assessment clearly builds on the reading experience expected in the reading assessment. The topic is:

Imagine that your community is putting together a time capsule to be opened in a hundred years. You have been chosen to write a description of an event in your life that will give eighth graders of the future an idea of what life is like for your generation. You are going to write a story about an event that made you feel happy.

Because of the scenario, the audience, and the purpose, this is not a little locket prompt.

Influence of Christian Fundamentalism

Arizona has problems that did not affect California and are probably a function of the size of the state's population. Christian fundamentalists exert a political power in Arizona beyond their numbers. To avoid conflicts with fundamentalists, who disapprove of topics in which children write about themselves, teachers are asked to explain that a personal experience narrative or autobiography must be written using the pronoun I but need not report the student's own feelings or experiences. These may be fictional or borrowed from some other source, and an astute teacher probably refers to the reading assessment to give children an idea of what to do. "Students who choose to write about themselves have considerable latitude about what to write. They can select what is not private and still do a good job writing."[9]

The Arizona Student Assessment Program is intended to give a complete picture of both the inputs and the outcomes of education by collecting information on school programs and the outside influences on performance, but it has had to modify its ambitions in the face of fundamentalist pressures. Because Christian fundamentalists object to even the mildest attempts to gather information about the home life of students, the Arizona department of education has been forced to abandon a large part of a survey of students' television-watching and other home activities.

How the Assessment Works

Responding to the grade 8 assessment about the time capsule, students spend 5 minutes randomly listing events that have made them happy. The time limit is deliberately intended to push the process. They are not asked to reflect but just to list as many events as they can remember. The reflection comes in the next section, lasting 15 minutes, when students choose one of the events and follow a guided process of developing it: they fill in a few lines about the experience, the setting, the people involved and what was said, the information the story conveys about life in the 1990s or life in general, and the opening and the closing. Then for 30 minutes they write the rough draft.

This is not the only possible process for developing writing, and some may object that it is mechanical and therefore unfaithful to what actually happens when a writer writes, but it is a serviceable and, above all, a teachable process. It gets writing out of the domain of inspiration and natural talent and into the sphere of effort; those who engage in this process will produce writing that communicates information needed in this context and will also have learned (and, I hope, internalized) a method of going about a similar writing task.

The rough draft is written on a separate sheet and then folded into the booklet for storage overnight. On the next day, the students spend 40 minutes rewriting and polishing their rough drafts. The final drafts are written into the test booklet. As in the case of the writing required in the reading assessment, a checklist helps the students revise. The story should be on the correct topic, should have good logic (that is, make sense), be complete; describe why the event was important and describe it fully, and focus on correct spelling, grammar, and usage.

Note that the items on mechanics are the last, not the first, to be checked—another feature of the writing process that downplays "correctness" in favor of meaning and communication of ideas. Students may use dictionaries and thesauri while working.

Directions to the teacher include the final suggestion that the students might want to read their narratives to each other in class. Contrast this with the emphasis on secrecy and security in administering norm-referenced, multiple-choice test.

Rubrics for scoring the writing give a score of 4 to a complete and logically ordered story that explains why the event made the student feel happy in the context of the modern world and shows evidence of careful proofreading. A 3 will be assigned to a story whose importance is not fully explained in prose slightly less well proofread than a 4 paper. A 2 outlines a story but does not flesh it out, and a 1 lacks coherence and probably includes so many errors that it is difficult to read.

The student submits the rough draft along with the general draft. Even though the rough draft and the final may look quite different (perhaps there is just doodling and scribble on the rough draft sheets), the reader scores only the final draft. After the examinations have been scored, they are returned to the teachers exactly as they were sent to the scoring center, with the rough draft folded inside the answer booklet. (This is unique to Arizona, as far as I know.) The teachers can then see the differences between the rough draft and the final copy and can adjust their teaching accordingly. The information provided by the rough draft is therefore used, but for instruction rather than assessment purposes.

The two-day assessment presents some problems, notably concerning standardization. How can what happens outside the test arena—the classroom—be controlled? If one student goes home and discusses the assignment with parents and siblings and then comes back and writes a superb essay, is it fair to compare that essay with the one by a child who never thinks about the essay after the class and watches television all evening? One control is the fact that both the rough draft and the finished product are given to scorers, so that a grader could detect a suspicious change of topic or viewpoint from the first to the second draft. The two drafts are intended to have a progressive relationship to each other, although this may rest on an ill-founded assumption. To have a complete change of mind overnight is not unusual for writers of all sorts—from professional novelists who change the direction of the book when they think more about the implications of the plot, to writers of reports who decide on a different approach and emphasis from one draft to the next.

I asked Fred Finch, vice-president of Riverside Publishing Company, about this problem, which surfaces whenever assessments include discussion, brainstorming, or work developed over more than one day. Finch replied that the loss of standardization is more than compensated for by the real-life conditions of the assessment. He pointed out that an employee given a report to write may or may not take it home and work on it there and may or may not discuss it with a spouse or fellow workers. Nevertheless, if the finished product is quite unlike the rough draft, can we assume that the student changed it because she suddenly realized her rough draft was going in the wrong direction, or did someone in her family write a story for her that she memorized and reproduced as a final draft? Problems of this nature remain to tease psychometricians and test developers.

Because of the classroom discussion that is an essential part of the reading and writing (and mathematics) assessments, it is not possible in Arizona to use matrix sampling as the CAP did. Instead, the ASAP will assign topics randomly to an entire class, thus ensuring that all the genres of writing are taught. A teacher will not know until the day of the examination which genre the students will be expected to write on. She or he will go through the process laid out for that kind of writing with the entire class. However, this process does allow the ASAP to assign individual student grades, although the grade will be based on the single kind of writing written on in the assessment. The grades will be reported as grades for that kind of writing only, not for writing ability in general.

These questions exemplify the problems arising from assessments that are situationally and systemically valid but psychometrically questionable. There are no satisfactory answers at the moment. When and if they come, the answers will probably arise, as did Fred Finch's answer to my question, from a different value system from that underlying norm-referenced, multiple-choice tests—a value system that prizes a close correlation with the real world rather than statistically defensible reliability.

MARYLAND'S READING-WRITING EXAMINATION

The Maryland School Performance Assessment Program (MSPAP), like CAP and ASAP, is using program assessment—accountability—as a lever to improve programs. In May 1990 the first assessments were tested statewide. They had been developed by the Maryland State Education Department's assessment team and Maryland teachers, with the technical assistance of CTB/McGraw-Hill. They were scored by groups of Maryland teachers, like the CAP and ASAP assessments.

Maryland, however, has taken the natural parallel between reading and writing to the point where they are integrated into one assessment. The students read two passages, one fiction and one nonfiction, and then go through a process of discussion and prewriting to produce written responses in more than one genre of writing (persuasive and informative, for example). The material is graded according to two rubrics: one for the answers to the questions designed to measure reading comprehension and the other for the persuasive or informative writing. The entire process models how to teach reading and writing together, directly in opposition to the skills approach, which breaks down reading (and then writing) into tiny steps, tests each through workbook drills, and uses basal readers with controlled vocabulary.[10] To show how it works, I will describe the sample grade 8 reading-writing/language use assessment.

Each student is given a reading book, which contains a map of North America on the first page, with Canada, Alaska, and Yukon Territory marked on it; a short story by Jack London entitled "To Build a Fire"; and an excerpt from *Hypothermia: Causes, Effects, Prevention*, by Robert S. Pozos and David O'Born, published by New Century Publishers in 1982. Each student also has a response book into which they will write their answers.

The assessment begins with a prereading activity, which focuses students on the topic—the deadly cold of the Yukon Territory and its dangers—by asking them to think about their own experiences of being cold. They are asked to spend 10 minutes writing a journal entry describing their experience on the appropriate page of their response books. Then they read London's "To Build a Fire" and respond to a series of questions probing their comprehension of the story. The first question can be answered with a drawing of the scene of the action if the student prefers to draw rather than write. A question later in the sequence asks the students to compare their own experience, described in the journal entry, with that of the man in the story who dies in the extreme cold. The final three questions probe the students' reading abilities by asking them to assess the difficulty of the story and explain why they rated it "very easy," "somewhat easy," "about average," "somewhat hard," or "very hard" and describe their reading strategies, that is, what they do to make sense of the story when they come to a word or a reference they do not understand.

On the second day of the assessment, the students begin by writing a 5-minute letter to the man in London's story giving him some advice that might have saved his life. Before they read the excerpt from *Hypothermia: Causes, Effects, Prevention*, there is class discussion about the topic, with the teacher writing on the board a cluster of the students' ideas as they respond to the words ("succumb," "insidious") that they will find in the excerpt. After they read the piece, they respond to a series of questions, again including the option to draw a picture or a diagram for at least one of them.

On the third day of the assessment, the students are expected to integrate the information from the two pieces into a written response to one of three situations: informing a group of friends of what they will need to do to stay safe on a winter weekend trip; writing a poem, story, or short play expressing their feelings about extreme states, not only cold but also heat, hunger, or fatigue; or writing a speech to persuade people to avoid travel in the Yukon. As in the case of

Arizona and California, teachers will cover these three kinds of writing because they know that one of them—but they do not know which one—will be used in the assessment.

In each case, the student is asked to go through a process of first brainstorming ideas and either listing them or making a web of words with lines connecting them to major ideas. (These graphic organizers are now a recognized part of teaching the writing process.) They write a rough draft, pause to consider whether it meets the needs of the situation, and then revise the piece. Finally, they use a proofreading guidesheet supplied in the response book to prepare a final copy.

The prereading and prewriting activities and the class discussion are recorded but not scored. The written responses to the questions and the essays are scored according to rubrics of substantially the same kind as the example from California.

The students have been introduced to this kind of teaching with similar examples, but they will be assessed on readings they have not seen before. For the students, being assessed is almost indistinguishable from regular classroom activities. For the teachers, this is a test worth teaching to.

3

■

Examples of Performance Assessments in Science and Mathematics

Students should be allowed to think more in classes, because if you don't think, you don't learn. A lot of times you sit there and watch and you don't think.

Texas student in a high school calculus class[1]

THE NEW YORK GRADE 4 ESPET

At first glance the classroom looks more like a kindergarten than the setting for a grade 4 science test. The balances catch the attention at once—five of them, apparently randomly distributed across the five rows and five columns of the desks. The balances are about 18 inches high and obviously homemade. The shaft is a dowel; the beam is fixed to it with a large nail across a notch, and the baskets, two ordinary plastic salad bowls, are suspended by paper clips bent over the ends of the beam. Lumps of modeling clay ensure the balance. At the foot of the balance shaft on the desk are a green plastic cup containing water, a clear plastic glass with a line around it halfway up, a plastic measuring jug, a ruler, a thermometer, and ten shiny new pennies.

On some other desks, an electrical battery is connected to a tiny light bulb, with two wires from the bulb terminating in alligator clips. A plastic bag containing what looks like a spoon and a paper clip, among other oddments, lies next to it. A single box sits on other desks. Another desk holds three pieces of paper marked A, B, and C, a paper encased in a plastic bag, a dropper, and a small plastic container of water. The last variation is a simple paper plate divided into three parts for a TV dinner, with labeled instructions, and a plastic bag containing a collection of beans, peas, and corn.

But if the materials make you think of a kindergarten, the almost silent concentration of the children sitting at the desks dispels the impression. They have the absorbed expressions of problem solvers happy at their work.

The boy with blond hair modishly short on top and long in back quietly exclaims, "Wow!" as he begins the electrical test. He has no trouble making the bulb light by bringing the two alligator clips together. The instructions tell him to test the objects in the plastic bag to see if they make the bulb light. He takes the wire from the plastic bag and places it on one of the alligator clips. No light. He puts a check in the "bulb does not light" column on his answer sheet. Then he tries the same thing with a toothpick, also in the bag. Same result, same answer. He repeats the pattern for all five objects.

Then he comes to the next question, which asks him to explain what happened, based on the results he noted in the columns. He looks again at the instructions and the questions, puzzled. Then he brings the clips together again—and the bulb lights. He lets out a soft "Ohhh" and then puts one end of the wire in one clip and the other in the second clip. Bingo. Rapidly he goes through the four other objects, connecting them to both the terminals, with the expected results. Then he furiously erases the checks for the wire and the other metal objects and checks the column marked "bulb lights." He spends the last few minutes of the allotted time emphatically scribbling his explanation.

Meanwhile, in the same row of desks, a girl has dumped out the beans and peas into the large division of the TV dinner plate as instructed and is classifying them by placing them into the two smaller divisions. She puts the lima beans and the kidney beans into one group and the pintos, peas, and corn into the other group. The first group, she writes, is "big and dull"; the second is "small and colorful."

You can see misconceptions in action. Back at the balances, a child spreads the pennies out in the basket, obviously believing that they do not balance the glass because they are clumped together. Instead of pouring from the large beaker into the glass, the students pour the water into the measuring cup first and *then* into the glass. They do not know what to do with the amount left in the measuring cup. When shaking the mystery box, their faces a study in absorbed concentration, they try to identify what is in it, ignoring the questions that ask them to describe what they hear.

At the end of 7 minutes, the teacher, at the front of the room, organizes a swift exchange of desks (called "stations"). The front-row children go to the back of the column, carrying their answer sheets with them, and all the others move up one desk. Thus, every child has a turn at all five stations, which, despite the initial impression of randomness, have been arranged so that adjacent stations do not have the same apparatus. Four classes of about twenty-five children each can be tested comfortably in a school day. The building mentor teacher is responsible for setting up and running the test, and classroom teachers bring in their classes at intervals of about an hour.

The situation just described is the manipulative skills test of the New York State Elementary Science Program Evaluation Test (ES-PET).[2] It is only one part of a seven-part assessment, but it is the one that interests both us and the children most. A number of the children expressed their feelings about it by asking if they could do it again tomorrow. More than one paper has the words "thank you" written at the end.

These students have the support of psychological research. Howard Gardner traces what he calls "logico-mathematical intelligence" to

> a confrontation with the world of objects. For it is in confronting objects, in ordering and reordering them, and in assessing their quantity, that the young child gains his or her initial and most fundamental knowledge about the logico-mathematical realm. . . . Over the course of development, one proceeds from objects to statements, from actions to the relations among actions, from the realm of the sensorimotor to the realm of pure abstraction—ultimately, to the heights of logic and science. The chain is long and complex, but it need not be mysterious: the roots of the highest regions of logical, mathematical, and scientific thought can be found in the simple actions of young children upon the physical objects in their worlds.[3]

Not every child will scale "the heights of logic and science." Many children will not want to climb them because their intelligence will be dominated by one or more of the other modes of Gardner's seven. But all children should be exposed to the physical objects that will allow them to discover the concepts of measurement and relationship.

The ESPET was instituted to give students in New York State's elementary schools the experiences Gardner thinks lead to scientific understanding. The intention to affect teaching and learning is the motivation for the assessment, as it is in California, Connecticut, and Arizona. In July 1958 science was mandated in the elementary course of study by the New York State legislature, but by the early 1980s, it was clear that nothing much had happened (as indeed was the case across the rest of the country). Despite the publication and dissemination of the *Elementary Science Syllabus* in 1985, not much science instruction of any kind, and especially not much hands-on teaching, was going on in grades K–3 in New York State elementary schools. The State Education Department and some state administrators saw a crisis approaching. As the number of African-Americans, Latinos, Native Americans, Asian-Americans, and immigrant children increases in the schools, they must receive early and motivating instruction in science to prepare them—and all the other students, especially girls—for a complex scientific and technological world. Of course this is a nationwide problem. Sue Berryman wrote in a RAND report for the Rockefeller Foundation in 1983 that students must be interested in science before grade 6; if they are not prepared to enter the science pipeline by grade 9, there is very little chance they can move into it later.[4]

The New York State science education leaders made the year 2000 a target date for excellent science teaching in the state schools. The center of their thrust at grade 4 is a program assessment that consists of a forty-five-item multiple-choice test, the five-station manipulative skills test, and five questionnaires on the perception of science education in the school—two to be completed by students and one each by administrators, teachers, and parents. Only the multiple-choice and manipulative skills test were required of school districts, although a number of districts administered all seven instruments. New York State was not without experience in hands-on science assessment; it has been assessing high school achievement in earth science for the Regents' Examination annually since 1970 using practical applications of knowledge. But to administer a performance assessment to all the fourth graders in the state was a different matter.

This was the first large-scale administration of a hands-on science test in the United States. In May 1989, 200,000 students in grade 4 classrooms throughout New York State were brought class by class into rooms set up like the one I described. The administration of a performance test in 4,000 public and nonpublic elementary school buildings in New York State presented problems of a different order of magnitude than finding enough number 2 pencils for the children to fill in the bubbles on an answer sheet. The performance test required preparation of kits of equipment in boxes small enough to be stored until test time. Each school district negotiated separately with a supplier, which explains minor variations in the physical appearance of some of the equipment. The number of schools with grade 4 classrooms in New York City—the largest school district in the United States—required eighteen-wheel trucks to deliver all the boxes from their New Hampshire supplier.

The ESPET has three important characteristics: it is a program, not an individual student, assessment; it is entirely designed by New York State educators at the state level, at the University of Buffalo, and at the local level; and the administrators of the test have solved the scoring problem to their own satisfaction.

ESPET, an Exemplary Program Assessment

The ESPET is designed to evaluate a school's elementary science program, but every grade 4 student took it, a requirement that raised eyebrows in technical evaluation circles; there is no need to test every student to estimate the success of a program, and if scores are recorded for every student, there is some danger of their being leaked as student achievement scores. The ESPET student scores remain in the schools and are not reported beyond that level, for reasons that will be clarified in the discussion of scoring. All students were tested not only to get a sufficiently large number to evaluate the program (a problem in some small rural schools) but also for social reasons.

The pilot and field testing in 1987 and 1988 proved that the manipulative skills test was a treat for the students who took it, and there were fears of widespread "Why can't I [or my child] do that?" complaints. In addition, if, say, every fifth student took the manipulative test, as originally planned, there might have been selection on the part of the school personnel in order to make the program look good, and certain students, perhaps minorities and disabled students, might have been routinely excluded. Instead, physically handicapped, as well as students from special education classes, took the manipulative test alongside others and were able to perform according to their familiarity with the apparatus, with allowances (usually additional time) for their difficulties with reading and writing.

Additionally, the fact that all grade 4 students in New York State took the test in May 1989 made an important statement: science education is intended for all students.

Assessment of Performance Unit (APU)

The manipulative test items were developed or modified from a large pool of hands-on science assessment tools developed internationally for the international assessments of science education (sponsored in the United States by the National Science Foundation) conducted by the International Association for the Evaluation of Educational Achievement. The pool draws on items developed in England and Wales for the Assessment of Performance Unit (APU), as well as for examinations in Israel, Germany, and Australia, among other countries. The items were developed by teachers and university researchers, not by testing professionals, a pattern also followed in California and Maryland.

The APU was developed in England and Wales for much the same reasons as those motivating the New York State science education leaders: to evaluate an instructional program that had been developed and instituted a few years earlier. The APU (now superseded by a new program of national assessment in England and Wales) was administered to 2 percent of the students. It consisted of paper-and-pencil tests where the students wrote their answers and manipulative tests, which were scored by observers, who were classroom teachers trained for the job. The observers completed a checklist and wrote comments as they watched students move through tasks in an organization that resembled that of the ESPET manipulative skills stations.

The APU has become the model for hands-on science testing in the

United States, in both the design of testing items (the APU is a bank of ideas on which U.S. test makers have freely drawn) and in the development of response mechanisms. With the APU tests, students write out answers, and they are observed. Each scoring method has advantages and drawbacks. The written answers are subject to each student's verbal ability and even small-muscle control in writing. It is possible that a student can perform the task and get justifiable results but be unable to express them adequately. On the other hand, there is no barrier of interpretation between the student's actions and reporting. That barrier can arise in the case of observation, where a student's actions could be evaluated quite differently from possible self-report. On the other hand, if observers are experienced and well trained, they can perceive how a misconception is driving a student's actions in the wrong direction and therefore pinpoint where program improvements are needed. With observers, training is crucial. New York's science education leadership avoided the issue by relying on students' written answers.

A Teacher-Owned and Operated Program

The ESPET is an in-house (or rather in-state) production. New York teachers and university researchers adapted and tested the items drawn from the APU. No outside vendors or contractors were used at any point in the design, administration, or scoring of the test (putting it in a class with Connecticut and Vermont, which also use no professional corporate assistance; the other states discussed so far use testing services for some component of their assessments). In New York, teachers work with university education professors to write items for a pool and have done so for a number of years. There is even a State Education Department publication on item writing, *Improving the Classroom Test*.

Despite this history of involvement in statewide testing, a number of principals and teachers were threatened by the prospects of the manipulative tests, offended by the implied criticism of their existing practices, and panicked by the sudden need for supplies and equipment they did not have.

A massive interlocking teachers-teaching-teachers system began to make inroads on these feelings. The state was divided into thirteen regions, each with a coordinator who had been trained by state department personnel and/or had worked on the development of the ESPET manipulative skills test. To use a religious metaphor, these were the disciples. Their signatures were among hundreds that accompanied the following letter to New York State commissioner of education Thomas Sobol in July 1988, ten months before the first administration of the test:

> We, the undersigned science educators, wish to express our pleasure and enthusiasm in the fact that there will be a hands-on manipulative component to the 1989 grade 4 ESPET (Elementary Science Program Evaluation Test).
>
> ESPET is the first test of its kind to measure both factual knowledge and the kinds of understanding that students acquire through hands-on activities.
>
> The manipulative component of this examination is essential in providing direction and support for first-hand problem solving experiences in elementary science in our schools.
>
> Further, it will provide school districts with the tool to best assess and evaluate local science education programs.

The regional coordinators trained ninety-three resource teachers, who trained the site coordinators who administered the test and informed their K–4 teachers about its purposes and procedures. A total of 6,543 people participated in the training between December 1988 and February 1989.

Teacher involvement in the administration of tests has been extolled as a particularly effective form of professional development; during the ESPET training, the learning curves of some teachers seem to take sharp upward turns. The training consisted mainly of having a group of teachers perform the tasks at the five stations set up exactly as they would be for the students. Resistance was occasionally stony. One regional trainer reported that more water was spilled on the floor during the first of the five stations than he ever saw when students took the test. But at about the third station, the noise level dropped, and the water stayed in the flasks and measuring cups. By the end of the hour, there was a buzz of conversation about the contents of the tests—not about the feelings that had caused the initial resistance.

One of those who was initially hostile was Susan Marciano, (not her actual name), and her case will stand proxy for similar ones throughout the state. Radiating energy Marciano proudly displayed the testing room from in her Buffalo elementary school.

I want you to know that I am a convert. I was skeptical. I have to tell you that I'm not a science teacher—I'm an elementary teacher. I had to have the science book in front of me. And I believed that you had to teach the kids—you had to tell them what to do. Now I know that isn't true—they can discover things for themselves and they learn them better.

What changed me was going to an in-service where they took us though the five-station process, set up just as you see it in this room now. I was scared at first. I thought, "Now they're going to find out I don't know any science." But just like the kids, I got interested. After the first station, I began to enjoy it.

Another School Takes the ESPET

Marciano is now science mentor for her building, one of the largest elementary schools in the state, with 1,340 students K–8. The ESPET apparatus in her room shows the minor variations from the first one described to be expected from different suppliers: the sealed box is a black box, the papers marked *A*, *B*, and *C* are different colors as well as textures, and the pans on the balances are opaque plastic bowls for cereal rather than salad. Marciano specified these alterations—for good reason, as it turned out.

Her school has a population markedly different from the one described at the beginning of the chapter. It is racially mixed and socioeconomically less prosperous. The children enjoy the test just as much, however, although the atmosphere is slightly changed by the dependence of these children on interaction with others. Their questions to the teacher indicate they either cannot read the instructions or do not know what they mean. They look around at each other and sometimes have to be reminded to keep their eyes on their task. The group did not include any special education students by school policy, but the teachers told me they were the "low" students. "Some of mine are borderline special education," one teacher said. It was clear that no one expected very much from these children, although several performed the five tasks as well as any others in the seven classes I observed. These students would have been happier mixed into heterogeneous collaborative groups and tested by group, but clearly they were trying to solve the problems, and the tasks absorbed them as they did the other children. Asked after the test how she had felt initially, a girl answered confidently, "I thought it would be boring until I started it. Then it was fun."

The balances, the water, the ruler, and the thermometer are intended to assess measurement skills. The child is asked the weight of the empty glass in pennies, recording the number needed to balance it; to measure the height of the glass; to find out how much water is needed to fill the glass to the line; and to take the water temperature. The children in Marciano's school could perform few of these measurement tasks, but they were not giving up. The question asked, "How many pennies heavy is the empty glass?" and one child solemnly counted the ten pennies, writing that as her answer. She obviously got no further reading the instructions than "How many pennies . . . ?"

The children did not know the purpose of the balance and the water but concluded there must be a connection; during the first 7-minute period, a boy poured water into one of the balance bowls (Marciano knew it would happen) and weighed it against the pennies. Because these children have a great deal of sensitivity to their surroundings and are easily distracted by what others are doing, the other four adopted the same approach, although with variations: some poured water into both pans, and others weighed the water against the glass with the pennies inside it. As the groups changed and other children came to the measurement station, a couple of them tried laying the ruler across the balance beam. At the conclusion of the 7 minutes, they neatly poured the water back into its container and cleaned up the inevitable drips.

These fourth graders had difficulties reading the instructions and carrying them out. They were told to sort the seeds into two groups but persistently put them in all three compartments of the TV dinner plate. A boy who enthusiastically tried everything with the electrical tester, including his shirt and his finger (which he cut slightly on the serrations of the alligator clip), made no attempt to write an explanation for his observations, although he obviously understood the principle of conductivity.

One teacher, watching her students pour water into balance bowls, count the seeds instead of sorting them, or drop water on the plastic container as well as the papers marked *A*, *B*, and *C*, turned away and said, "I could cry." It was a justified although painful reaction. The task now facing the lead teachers and school personnel is to make sure that such reactions are translated into energy that will change science instruction in the school, not into negative feelings about the unteachability of the students.

A Test Worth Teaching To

The State Department prepared a detailed scoring guide to assist school personnel in scoring the results and to help maintain reliability. Following the reporting of school scores, it is expected that a school committee will meet to survey the results and decide on changes in areas of weakness. The published *Guide to Program Evaluation K–4* includes grids to be filled out by this committee, first listing the weaknesses and strengths of the program, correlated to the relevant portions of the state elementary science syllabus, and then outlining an action plan, with time line, resources needed, and personnel responsible for each step. The State Education Department of Education, the Boards of Cooperative Educational Services (BOCES), and the large city school districts will provide the resources—both equipment and personnel—to help schools improve their programs.

Schools will vary in the depth of their changes. The motivation for making them is that the exact same test will be repeated using the same apparatus next year. Since the students who took the test this year will then be grade 5 students and not involved, the program and the teaching of it will be even more clearly on trial than they were this year.

Using the same test and the same apparatus again the next year raised fears of teaching to the test, apparently risking falling into the same trap this kind of testing was supposed to evade. The advantages of being able to monitor changes are perceived to outweigh the risk that teachers will reproduce in their classrooms what they saw as the manipulative skills test was being administered. In the administration of a test in 4,000 buildings, it is probable that more than one answer sheet was surreptitiously copied so that students could be trained to answer the questions.

One answer to the problem is trust—trusting the teachers to behave professionally and to care enough about the development of students' scientific knowledge not to cheat. A heartening feature of the ESPET scheme is the amount of trust institutionalized in it: teachers are trusted not to narrow their teaching and to score reliably; schools are trusted not to divulge individual student scores on the ESPET tests. In the case of teaching to the test, trust is backed up by the fact that the manipulative skills is worth teaching to—and this is precisely the point about performance assessments: they require activities that are not identified solely as test tasks but are also instructional tasks and even life tasks.

Suppose as the worst case (and it is unlikely to happen) that a grade 4 teacher in New York State decides that the students' scores on the manipulative skills test next year will be perfect. The teacher constructs the whole apparatus as it appeared in the test classroom—not hard since the total cost is about $100 for twenty-five stations and a complete set is unnecessary—and copies bootlegged answer sheets. And suppose that the students are drilled on the test items, time after time. By the time they take the test, these students will be able to read and understand the instructions. They will know what "property" means in the question, "What is another property of an object in the box?" (This word was the least known of the carefully chosen vocabulary in 1989.) The students will be able to write comprehensible answers on the answer sheets. Further, they will have acquired extremely important skills in using measuring instruments, predicting, inferring, observing, and classifying. In teaching as opposed to a testing situation, it will become clear that there is no right answer to a classification, only the development of a defensible criterion. In the case of the mystery box, it will be possible to teach the difference between reporting observations and guessing at reasons for them. In every case, the students' manipulative skills will be developed along with their conceptual understanding.

A class that did nothing beyond the five stations might have a monotonous experience, but the students would learn important science process skills. A year's work of this kind is a better introduction to science than reading a textbook and answering the questions at the end of each chapter. From observing children making discoveries while they were taking the test, it could be assumed that they would transfer their skills to other situations, an important instructional objective.

Of course, there is no question of advocating teaching to the manipulative skills test alone; the point is that such a course would not be reductive or fragmentary, as would teaching to a multiple-choice test, but constructive and likely to lead to further learning.

Scoring the ESPET

The five tests were assigned numbers for answers to each of the eighteen questions needing responses. In the station where weight, volume, height, and temperature were to be measured, students could earn 1 point for answers falling within a prescribed range, and 0 for all others. For the station that tested prediction, where students dropped water on paper of differing absorbency and then predicted what would happen on a paper they could only see, not experiment with, the answers received differential weighting. For describing what happened when the water was dropped, the students could earn 3 points for answers within a range; for predicting correctly, 1 point; and for giving an acceptable reason, 1 point.

These point assignments were made when the test was designed by university professors and teachers and refined during field tests in twenty schools in 1988. The results were scored in each school by the classroom teachers, led by the building mentor who administered the test, on a pupil-free rating day.

It was by no means a mechanical process. The instruction booklet urged that raters (the teachers scoring the test) thoroughly discuss the items and the criteria and practice with a few sample sheets before rating the students' answers. The role of teachers' judgment is acknowledged in this statement: "The samples of acceptable answers provided in this rating guide are not the only possible correct answers. Other answers which convey the same general meaning as those given in this guide should also receive credit." Raters recorded a considerable number of additional answers. One child found that "nothing worked" when he was using the electrical test, station 4. He wrote: "I conclude that something was wrong with the battery." He received full credit because his answer was based on his observations and deductions. "Good for soup," as opposed to "good for chili," was one unanticipated classification of the seeds. Raters also recorded answers that were not acceptable, thus refining the rating guide for next year's use.

Judgment was called upon continually. No partial credit was allowable in some cases where 2 points were assigned, making the decision particularly difficult. Where students' penmanship was poor or the expression cryptic, generosity had to season justice. There is, of course, no way of knowing what blanks in answer sheets meant: no attempt, no time, or no words.

Each school site rating team recorded individual scores item by item to produce a score for each student. School site personnel are asked to keep this score confidential, it is not intended to become part of a student's record. The students' individual scores are not reported to the state as such. What is reported is a frequency distribution of scores on three parts: the manipulative test and the two parts of the multiple-choice test. A difficulty score for each item is reported at the local level and not reported to the state. This is arrived at by a simple arithmetical formula, yielding a percentage, which is then compared to tables of state item difficulty percentages, supplied to each school.

The state item difficulties were arrived at in the field tests conducted in 1988 and are reported in terms of lower, overall (average), and upper groups. All the students who took the field test were ranked by their scores on the entire test and then divided into an upper and a lower group on these scores alone—that is, without reference to school population statistics. The state item difficulties were changed after the 1990 administration of ESPET, since the scores went up.

The local scores, tabulated for each item, are compared to the state item difficulties. Those that fall below the State Overall Group Item Difficulty are marked with a circle or with a square box for those below the State Lower Group Item Difficulty. These marks are intended to make areas for improvement easy to identify. On the basis of these analysis sheets, program evaluations and action plans are intended to be developed at the local level.

At the regional and state reporting level, the scores represent the achievement of students within a school program. Although ESPET is a K–4 assessment, not strictly a grade 4 assessment, and therefore technically assesses the entire science program in the early years, nevertheless the perception is that the responsibility rests with the grade 4 teacher, especially since the ESPET is administered in May, toward the end of the school year. At a school site, it is possible to compare achievement by classes and therefore potentially to compare teachers. The evaluation materials caution against this: "This program evaluation is not a vehicle for teacher evaluation." There is, however, the possibility of constructive evaluation of professional development. If a number of teachers attended professional development classes and in consequence increased the amount of hands-on instruction and some others did not, the emphasis would reveal itself in higher scores for students in the attendees' classes and not in the others. If this is so, it would represent a step toward evaluating the effects of changing teacher behavior on student achievement. Of course, such a sequence of events could only be recorded, not set up as an experimental situation.

Systems that depend on large numbers of scorers or raters must be monitored to protect the reliability of the numbers. In some countries, there is a system of moderation, which can take several forms. The principle is the rescoring of a representative sample of examinations by the staff of an outside institution. Sometimes it can involve a meeting of staffs from many institutions to score all their examinations in common. In the United States, there is no such process, but reliability is achieved by recalibration (described in chapter 2): grading groups periodically pause in their reading for group scoring of a few papers to make sure that their judgment is not drifting from a common standard.

New York State has a monitoring system for all of its statewide examinations. Between 7 and 10 percent of all examination papers are culled for rescoring at the State Education Department in Albany. A selected school must send a complete set of the required ESPET multiple-choice and manipulative skills tests. Teachers from school districts surrounding the state capital spend a few weeks in the summer checking the students' papers. Papers that show a high degree of rating error will be returned to the school's principal, who must arrange for them to be rerated at the school site before September 15. Serious problems with poorly rated ESPET scores would cause inaccurate item difficulty reports, and since they are the basis for action plans, they could have consequences for program improvement. The student papers were kept secure while in Albany, treated confidentially, and returned to their districts without disclosure of names or scores.

Recalibration keeps judgment on track. The 1989 reraters of the ESPET manipulative skills test found a high degree of reliability in following standards, but occasionally teachers made errors because of their own unfamiliarity with scientific concepts. In the measurement items, they confused centimeters and inches, centigrade and Fahrenheit. They were not always clear about what constituted an inference in response to the mystery box item. It is to be assumed that since these errors were found in a 10 percent sample, they indicate a fairly widespread need for professional development as part of district action plans.

Enthusiasm for the ESPET

Scoring the ESPET manipulative skills test has been accomplished by a chain of collective judgments that seem to reflect consensus. The participants appear satisfied with the kind and amount of information it is providing. Satisfaction with the rating process is, however, overshadowed at the moment by the general enthusiasm for the manipulative skills test itself. One of the rerating teachers said, "This preparation for the manipulative science test has brought a whole breath of fresh air and excitement—people just looking forward to doing it again. I can see it any place I go. In the past we've had the fifth grade writing and the sixth grade social studies tests which were new, but in no case have I seen the excitement that I've seen in the past three years in preparation for this test." Another teacher added: "If you believe that science is a curriculum area where it's more hands-on and doing things than maybe some other areas, then the test that evaluates how well the program is doing should be something that gets into hands-on, and it's exciting to see somebody finally realize this, and this state—no less—has realized it."

The success of the ESPET Manipulative Skills Test may have contributed to a major policy shift in New York State education. Chancellor Sobol has announced that assessment in New York will include portfolios and open-ended tasks as soon as they can be designed.[5]

More than New York State realized what the ESPET manipulative skills test had accomplished. Before the assessment was administered again in May 1990, Douglas Reynolds, New York Education Department Science Bureau chief who conceived the idea of the manipulative skills test and saw it through to its conclusion, and a team of teachers had traveled to conferences and workshops in a number of other states. They were in demand because they represented a large state with a diverse population that had successfully worked out the logistics of a hands-on science assessment. Their design was copied and modified on several levels; it became the prototype for the grade 6 performance assessment in science in California.

Even more important, the New York group showed that large-scale performance assessment in science need not be so expensive as to be unfeasible. The National Assessment of Educational Progress in the mid-1980s developed an excellent suite of performance assessment tasks (many adapted from the English APU) and pilot-tested them successfully; however, they were deemed too expensive to replace bubbles. These tasks are enshrined in a publication, *Learning by Doing: A Manual for Teaching and Assessing Higher-Order Thinking in Science and Mathematics*. As progress toward the national goals is assessed in the next few years, it will become necessary to emulate New York State's experience with a large-scale test. Clearly it can be done.

CALIFORNIA AGAIN—THIS TIME IN MATHEMATICS

What does performance assessment mean in mathematics? In what sense can we "perform" math?

The evaluation standards promulgated by the National Council of Teachers of Mathematics (NCTM) in its 1989 publication, *Curriculum and Evaluation Standards for School Mathematics* (known as "the NCTM Standards"), stress "using multiple assessment techniques, including written, oral, and demonstration formats."[6] They list the following characteristics as desirable and to be emphasized in mathematics assessment: assessing what students know, not what they do not know; making assessment an integral part of teaching, not just an activity to assign grades; taking a holistic view of mathematics, focusing on a broad range of tasks rather than isolated skills; using calculators, computers, and manipulatives in assessment, not only paper-and-pencil tests; and evaluating a school's program by systematically collecting information on teaching, learning, and achievement, not by simply looking at test scores.

Here is an example from the NCTM Standards for grades K–4: Students are given a large box of raisins and asked to estimate—*not* count—the number of raisins in it. To perform the task, they are given a balance, containers of different sizes, and a calculator. They must use a second method to check their first estimation and then record the results. This task is best accomplished in group, with the teacher observing the contributions made by each student to the group's success. It is intended to stretch the concept of mathematics beyond numbers and simple computations in order to develop estimation and problem-solving skills.

An example for a junior high class might pose this problem:

Five students have test scores of 62, 75, 80, 86, and 92. Find the average score. How much is the average score increased if each student's score is increased by 1, 5, 8, or X points? Write a statement about how much the average score is increased if each individual score is increased X points, and *write an argument to convince another student that the statement is true.*

This kind of assessment is designed to probe what students know about how a mathematical algorithm works—not just how to apply it—and to strengthen their abilities to explain it. Understanding why a procedure works is much less common among mathematicians than being able to plug it in and grind out a number. But calculators can do that. Instead of training students to behave like calculators, we need to develop their control over mathematics as a powerful tool through understanding why procedures work.

The following example is for grade 12:

James knows that half of the students from his school are accepted at the public university nearby. Also, half are accepted at the local private college. James thinks this adds up to 100 percent, so he will surely be accepted at one or the other institution. Explain why James may be wrong. If possible, use a diagram in your explanation.

These tasks all ask for writing, as well as formulas and diagrams. They are not answerable by a single number, in fact, none has a "correct" answer as such. In each case the results will have to be judged by the teacher or the reader. They all ask the student to use mathematical power, thought, and reasoning.

The "James" question comes from *A Question of Thinking,* a report on the first open-ended mathematics questions in the CAP.[7] It is an example of a growing class of mathematics assessments.

In 1987–1988 open-ended questions were added to the grade 12 level CAP assessment. Because of CAP's matrix sampling design, there were 360 multiple-choice questions and 5 open-ended questions; one was James and his faith in going to college. Each student answered 11 multiple-choice questions (only one with no calculator allowed) and a single open-ended question, which took about 12 minutes to complete. The scoring guides are drawn up by the scorers, who are mathematics teachers from throughout California, just like their colleagues who score CAP essays.

The CAP open-ended questions were scored in the same way as the writing samples, and the scores were reported separately and used in the scaled score for each school. The teachers who read the answers to the open-ended questions established two kinds of scoring guide: a general one for all open-ended questions and a specific one for the James question. The general one is reproduced in figure 3.1. Notice that mathematical competence alone will get the student only a 4. Mathematical understanding, reasoning, and communication are required to get a 5 or 6. The scoring guide for 6 includes the word mathematicians reserve for what they truly admire—*elegant.* All of the descriptions, however, are fully fleshed out, so that as guidelines they are as specific as the case allows.

The scoring guide for the James question (Figure 3.2) is a specific

<u>Demonstrated Competence</u>

<u>Exemplary Response</u> ... Rating = 6
Gives a complete response with a clear, coherent, unambiguous, and elegant explanation; includes a clear and simplified diagram; communicates effectively to the identified audience; shows understanding of the open-ended problem's mathematical ideas and processes; identifies all the important elements of the problem; may include examples and counterexamples; presents strong supporting arguments.

<u>Competent Response</u> ... Rating = 5
Gives a fairly complete response with reasonably clear explanations; may include an appropriate diagram; communicates effectively to the identified audience; shows understanding of the problem's mathematical ideas and processes; identifies the most important elements of the problems; presents solid supporting arguments.

<u>Satisfactory Response</u>

<u>Minor Flaws But Satisfactory</u> ... Rating = 4
Completes the problem satisfactorily, but the explanation may be muddled; argumentation may be incomplete; diagram may be inappropriate or unclear; understands the underlying mathematical ideas ; uses mathematical ideas effectively.

<u>Serious Flaws But Nearly Satisfactory</u> ... Rating = 3
Begins the problem appropriately but may fail to complete or may omit significant parts of the problem; may fail to show full understanding of mathematical ideas and processes; may make major computational errors; may misuse or fail to use mathematical terms; response may reflect an inappropriate strategy for solving the problem.

<u>Inadequate Response</u>

<u>Begins, But Fails to Complete Problem</u> ... Rating = 2
Explanation is not understandable; diagram may be unclear; shows no understanding of the problem situation; may make major computational errors.

<u>Unable to Begin Effectively</u> ... Rating = 1
Words do not reflect the problem; drawings misrepresent the problem situation; copies parts of the problem but without attempting a solution; fails to indicate which information is appropriate to problem.

<u>No Attempt</u> ... Rating = 0

FIGURE 3.1 Generalized Rubric for Open-Ended Mathematics Questions

application of the general rubric. The 4 is awarded for correctness, but it takes the ability to explain to get the higher score.

An important assumption lies behind this hierarchy: if students understand the concept rather than mechanically applying it, then they should be able to explain it in words and diagrams. In 1988, 20

Students are given an example of a logic problem that involves college acceptance. The student must give a clear and mathematically correct explanation of the faulty reasoning involving the assumption of nonoverlapping sets in the problem. For the highest score, responses must be complete, contain examples and/or counterexamples of overlapping sets, or have elegantly expressed mathematics. A diagram is expected.

Demonstrated Competence

For 6 points: The response is exemplary. It goes beyond the criteria for 5 points. For example, the response may include:

- Example(s) and/or counterexample(s)
- Mathematics expressed elegantly
- An explanation that is complete

For 5 points: The response is correct and the explanation is clear. It may be expressed in words, with a diagram, or both.

Satisfactory Response

For 4 points: The response is generally correct, but the explanation lacks clarity.

For 3 points: The response indicates a *partial* solution (e.g., the same 50 percent are accepted by both colleges); or the response indicates that the student *may* understand the solution but the explanation is incoherent.

Inadequate Response

For 2 points: The response is incorrect, but it shows evidence of mathematical reasoning. A mathematical explanation is developed. However, the explanation does not address the crux of the problem or the essence of the solution. The paper may include a mathematical misconception.

For 1 point: The response is incorrect. It is not a sensible mathematical solution of the problem. The justification may use irrelevant arguments, such as:

- Whether a student is qualified for college
- Where a student attends college
- Whether a student desires to attend college
- Whether a student has applied to college

Off Track: The student leaves a blank page or writes: "I don't know."

FIGURE 3.2 Scoring Rubric for James Problem

percent of the students of the students who answered the James question were given a 5 or 6, 12 percent a 3 or 4, and 65 percent a 1 or 2. Since the James question is not a particularly difficult piece of reasoning (although empirical evidence suggests that a number of adults, even teachers, do not grasp the principle of overlapping sets), the results indicate a need to reconsider how mathematical reasoning and communication are taught.

Open-ended questions requiring a written explanation rest on the assumption that those who understand a mathematical principle can explain it. These are fighting words to many mathematics teachers; their training and (in the case of high school mathematics teachers) their own expertise focus them on the accurate application of algorithms in mathematics teaching. They do not take kindly to incorporating writing into mathematics classes, no matter what the NCTM and the Mathematical Sciences Education Board may say. The publication of the scoring guides in *A Question of Thinking* is therefore important in helping them to understand how their students are to be judged. The students themselves can also understand what it means to communicate as well as calculate.

By the mid-1990s, California mathematics assessments will consist of three elements: open-ended questions, portfolios (similar to those that will be discussed in chapter 5), and enhanced multiple choice (an example is shown in figure 1.1).

One step beyond enhanced multiple choice is the 1990 revision to the SAT, scheduled to take effect in 1994. Students taking the SAT from 1994 will be able to use calculators and will not "recognize" an answer by bubbling in response a, b, c, or d. Instead, they will bubble in the appropriate numbers in columns and rows, just as they now do for their date of birth. The answer remains machine scorable, which is the point. To a certain extent, they will be constructing an answer, although it must be a number and there is no possibility of the students' explaining what it means or why their answer is correct.[8]

THE CONNECTICUT SCIENCE AND MATHEMATICS ASSESSMENTS

Connecticut's Common Core of Learning assessments in high school science and mathematics move assessment into another arena—cooperative groups. This seems at first to go against the grain, since little is more sacred in American classrooms than working alone and keeping one's eyes on one's own work. However, we are continually reminded by business and industry that real-world work is cooperative and collective. Ability to work as a part of a team is a prized asset and must be incorporated into school programs.

The Connecticut tasks are being developed by teachers to encourage conceptual understanding and application in the context of cooperative action.[9] The tasks seem so immediately appealing that readers begin to think about how they would go about them as soon as they see them. One task in mathematics asks students to find out what it really means to say one supermarket has lower prices than another: does it mean that some items are consistently lower priced or that all items are lower priced? If some, which ones? What kinds of mathematical knowledge are needed to make the comparison rigorous? A science task asks students to determine all of the energy costs involved in taking a shower, including all the energy transformations leading to it and then to design an alternative shower using less energy. Another asks students to find out what mixture of automobile antifreeze and water has the highest boiling point and would therefore work best at extreme temperatures. A topical task in 1989 was an investigation of the Exxon Valdez oil spill, in which students were asked to use vivid comparisons in order to make its magnitude easy to understand.

Here is an example in more detail. High school chemistry students are asked to work in a group to design an experiment that will analyze the lead content in the school's water. The task statement follows:

Your principal has recently become concerned over the issue of lead poisoning in your school. He has asked our class to study and report back to him on the safety of the school's drinking water. . . . You will design an experiment to determine that amount of lead present in your school's drinking water. You will also study factors which affect the amount of lead in the water . . . the source of the water (i.e. from various faucets or drinking fountains, the temperature of the water, the pH of the water, and the length of standing time of the water in the pipes).

The group took about two or three class periods to complete the task. They presented their findings orally in a briefing for the principal; all group members were required to speak. Because the developers of Connecticut's tasks are paying a great deal of attention to the skills of working in groups, they have developed checklists for both teacher and students to fill out, probing the students' perceptions of their contributions to the task and the teacher's observations. These checklists will be used in formative feedback to the students, and may play a role in a group grade.

Although grading a group performance may be an excellent way of assessing an instructional program it cannot provide the individual student with a grade or score that may be needed for career decisions, so the Connecticut group is developing transfer tasks, derived from the major group task, which will probe the student's understanding of the concepts involved. The transfer task in the polluted drinking water task was the preparation of a written report in the form of a letter to the principal, including:

a. A comparison of the allowable value of lead and the amount present in the school's water, based on your group's and the class's results.
b. An explanation of how your group determined the amount of lead in the water.
c. A discussion of how accurate you believe your results are.
d. Recommendations on how the school's water can be made safer for use.

This transfer task is like the report that members of an actual research team would be expected to produce. It is also obvious that students have to understand all the components of the group task, including those they did not take part in, in order to write the report satisfactorily. The transfer task increases the motivation to do well in the group; a student who slacks off on the group work is not likely to do well for his or her individual grade on the transfer task.

These tasks are developed according to a process that has emerged from the experience of involving large numbers of people in constructing them. The construction of a performance assessment task is almost always a group process among teachers, administrators, university education professors, test developers, and curriculum specialists. It is a messy, reiterative process, with the advantages of getting a lot of people involved and therefore personally invested in the assessment—and the disadvantages attendant on any quasi-democratic process.

The Connecticut State Department of Education has brought together a consortium of teachers from six other states—Vermont, Michigan, Minnesota, New York, Texas, and Wisconsin—and the Coalition of Essential Schools. The task will be tried out in many of these states before it is declared ready for use, so it must be robust enough to apply to a range of circumstances and populations.[10]

Development of a Performance Task

A task begins with an idea, which could come from the news (like the Exxon Valdez idea), from reading, or from conversations. The point is that it is an idea, not an objective or a fact. It must be tested for two important criteria: Does it center on an important concept or issue in its field? Does it tie the concept to a real-life issue and ask students to understand something of value to them in making sense of their lives and their environment?

The next stage, turning the idea into a prompt or task statement, asks the developer to define the objectives of the task. What kinds of knowledge, skills, abilities, and concepts will the student have to display in order to accomplish the task? If honest examination reveals that the idea does not elicit a reasonable number of these and/or they are not the ones appropriate to the student's expected stage of development, then the idea should be discarded.

If the idea gets through that hurdle, it should be expanded into a form where it could provide a task for a group of students. It should also be examined closely to see if computers, videotape, videodisc, or other technology would increase its challenge or its application. There is no point in enhancement for its own sake, but since these tasks are intended to approximate actual problems, additional dimensions of the task should be explored.

At this stage, the teacher's needs should be taken into account. Since ultimately these will become assessments for program accountability, they should be easy for a wide range of teachers (not just the teacher who developed the task) to administer. Notes to the teacher are written, with information on the appropriate place in the sequence of learning for this task, the materials and equipment needed, any anticipated problems or difficulties, the kind of assistance the teacher should expect to provide before and during the task, and any assistance the teacher should not provide.

After the notes to the teacher are written, the developer works out a scoring guide. This requires another close examination of the task's purposes and how easily they can be gauged from either processes or products. For example, in the supermarket comparison task, it is clear that process—how the students conceptualize the task and design their comparison—is as important as the product. Weight must be assigned accordingly. A rough rubric should be sketched out, delineating what is to be expected at each level of performance. The prompt statement for the students should be rewritten to communicate how their performance will be judged.

The prompt is shared with colleagues and then, after revisions, tried on the teacher's own class in a nonthreatening but serious situation. This field test reveals more about the qualities of the task than any amount of discussion and reexamination. The students are the sharpest critics of the task and of the fairness of the scoring system. They contribute extensively to the revisions that make up the final stage of preparation.

This, however, is still only the first of many tests. The prompts developed in this way are taken to meetings and workshops organized by Connecticut's state department of education, where they are subjected to further criticism by colleagues from the entire consortium and by the department's experts in evaluation. If they survive field tests by large numbers of colleagues, they will be added to a bank of prompts that will eventually be used for statewide program assessment in Connecticut at least and probably in most of the other states.

At the same time, the prompts are good teaching materials, like the writing and mathematics assessments in California. They do not have to be kept secure, since almost all of them have no correct answer and a wide range of acceptable ones; they can also be varied slightly from one administration of the assessment to the next.

Connecticut's History of Performance Assessments

Connecticut has a tradition of performance assessments. The Connecticut Assessment of Educational Progress, which began in 1980 and continued until 1987, when it was superseded by the Common Core of Learning (the assessments just discussed), included a few performance assessments in art, music ("Sing 'America' and complete a musical phrase"), science, and English/language arts. The foreign language assessments asked students to write letters and included interviews conducted in the target language. The most impressive achievement was the vocational education assessments. They were designed with the help of industry representatives, who not only advised on the development of the tests but also participated in the scoring and subsequent content revisions. The involvement of community groups in assessment design and scoring is a recurring theme in performance assessment and one of its most promising features.

In the case of the vocational education assessments, the Connect-icut Assessment of Educational Progress took a pioneering step to-ward linking school achievement with success in the workplace. The industry representatives set entry-level standards for drafting, graphic arts, business and office procedures, and ability to manipulate small engines. Since these assessments were designed primarily to assess the program rather than the individual students, only randomly selected subset of the students took the performance assessment. As in Cali-fornia, however, the randomness ensured that these assessments af-fected teaching and learning.

MARYLAND GRADE 8 MATHEMATICS

As in the case of their reading-writing assessments, the Maryland reformers have gone further than any other group in the direction of using mathematics assessments to model the kind of instruction they want to see. The Maryland School Performance Assessment Program (MSPAP) has designed mathematics assessments that take several days, include both group and individual activities, require students to use calculators, and simulate a real-world situation. Assessments such as these focus on what is valued in mathematics as scientists and mathematicians practice it, according to a Harvard professor: "The art of estimation should be emphasized: staying awake and using common sense instead of applying memorized rules mindlessly. That's how the scientist or mathematician does his or her arithmetic, and it is fun rather than drudgery."[11]

The following description of a grade 8 examination is a prototype of Maryland's assessments; the actual tasks may differ in the situa-tion presented to the students and the kinds of mathematics embed-ded in the task. There are corresponding kinds of tasks at grades 5 and 11, the other program assessment points for the MSPAP.

The students are asked to imagine themselves as developers pro-posing to build a restaurant. During a "preassessment activity," the teacher leads class discussion to make sure that the students know what is meant by the terms used in the assessment: "developer," "market research," "questionnaire," "survey plan," "zoning board," "ordinances," "building codes," and so on. This activity in itself should assist the process of connecting school with the outside world, showing that the mathematics studied in the classroom has real-world uses.

The first activity for the students is to develop a questionnaire and a survey plan, since the, as the developers, will be working with a market research firm to find out what kind of restaurant people want. They work in groups to list questions that should be asked and then as a whole class to design the questionnaire and survey. Then they change hats, and each student becomes a market researcher with questionnaire on clipboard, asking about twenty-five people they know to answer their questionnaires. The directions for the assessment give students "one or two days" to collect the data.

Displaying the data in appropriate charts and graphs is an individual student's task. "Remember," says the directions, "you conducted your own survey and your data and your displays should not look exactly like anyone else's."

Having decided what kind of restaurant they want to build, students now move back to being developers and consider the size and shape of the lots available in the community. They use their geometry skills to find the area and to figure out which of three lots will fit their needs (given the results of their individual surveys). They have to work within realistic restraints: the restaurant must be a rectangular, one-story building of 6,000 square feet; the parking lot must be at least 6,000 square feet, with parking for thirty cars, each of which must have a 10×20 foot space in which to park, with 20-foot-wide aisles between the rows and for the driveways; and there must be some landscaping to make the restaurant attractive.

The students do a scale drawing on graph paper and then a final drawing when they have adjusted their design the required dimensions. They choose one of the three lots available in their district and must show on a scale of ½ inch representing 10 feet where the restaurant and the parking lot are to be built. They calculate the costs of building the restaurant, given specific prices for building, parking lots, equipment, and so on, and are asked to defend their estimate of the costs.

The final summarizing activity consists of writing a paragraph explaining the decisions made, intended to accompany the scale drawing and the other display material in a presentation to the zoning board. The directions include: "Remember to support your decisions with information from your tables, charts, and graphs. Remember to include other information that you feel is important as they (the zoning board) consider your plan."

Scoring rubrics have been devised for each of the five aspects of mathematics assessed in this activity—communication, reasoning, problem solving, connections, and technology—and a rubric scoring the students' ability to understand the concepts involved and accurately apply the appropriate algorithms. The "technology" rubric asks whether the teacher observed the student using the calculator to solve the problem. In other words, calculators are not regarded here as enhancement but as essential to the completion of a mathematics task.

If mathematics and science assessments turn out to be as engaging as the examples outlined in this chapter, they will go a long way toward making these subjects accessible to the populations that have been largely excluded from quantitative studies. Lynn Arthur Steen has called mathematics "primarily part of white upper class male culture, readily available only to those who have the nourishment, solitude, and luxury to spend time in concentrated thought."[13] But there will be proportionately fewer white males in the U.S. population in the future, so female students and minorities constitute an essential pool of talent needed to keep the United States technologically competitive.

4

Getting Students, Parents, and the Community into the Act

In every class, in every subject, students will learn to ask and to answer these questions:

1. From whose viewpoint are we seeing or hearing or reading?
2. How do we know what we know?
3. How are things, events or people connected to each other?
4. What if . . . ? Could things be otherwise than they are?
5. Why does it matter? What does it mean? Who cares?[1]

Chapters 2 and 3 described statewide programs of performance assessment, showing that it can be used for accountability purposes on a large scale. The examples of performance assessment in this chapter bring us to the school level and into disciplines—art, history/social studies, integrated problem solving—that are not often assessed at the state level. Accountability sticks to the three Rs and science, although California, Arizona, Maryland, and New York are looking forward to assessing at least history/social studies within the next few years. This chapter also examines a couple of state experiments with history/social studies assessments and two assessments that are really competitions, although their quality should interest anyone looking for good ideas for motivating students towards thoughtful problem solving.

A COALITION OF ESSENTIAL SCHOOLS EXHIBITION

The individual student assessments at Central Park East Secondary School (CPESS) in District 4, Manhattan, are called "exhibitions," based on the concept developed by the Coalition of Essential Schools and the Rites of Passage Experience (ROPE) developed at Walden III school in Racine, Wisconsin.[2] The essence of exhibitions is a multimedia presentation of the results of learning in a particular area.

The details of exhibitions vary a good deal. In fact, the Coalition of Essential Schools has begun to codify them with a view to defining what is essential and what is contingent if an assessment procedure is to be called an exhibition. The example given here exemplifies the depth and breadth of experience that each student will go through in the process of completing the requirements for the exhibition. This is not only a test worth teaching to; it makes teaching, learning, and assessment into an inextricable whole.

This example is from a Central Park East Secondary School humanities classroom. At this school, the day is divided into two blocks of 2 hours each, one for humanities and the other for mathematics and science, with an additional hour of small group work called an "advisory," where students develop their individual interests. The school does not offer any other academic disciplines in its regular hours, 9:00 A.M. to 3:00 P.M., but the building is open from 8:00 to 5:00 P.M. so that students can attend classes in Spanish, the arts, computer programming, and physical education before and after regular school hours.

This humanities exhibition is intended to allow students to demonstrate command of major themes in history and culture. The instructions begin with this preamble:

During the first three years at Central Park East Secondary School, we explored the themes of power, authority, and immigration with a focus on the United States. This year we have expanded on these themes by applying them to three non-Western cultures: the Maya, the Chinese, and the South Africans. Our work is based on the following essential questions:

1. What is the relationship between culture and world view?
2. Who writes history, for whom and why?
3. What is "civilized" and what is "barbaric"?
4. How is political power achieved and maintained?
5. What happens when people of different cultures come in contact with each other?
6. How are cultures affected by imperialism?

The students wrestling with these questions are ninth and tenth graders, predominantly African-American, although some are Hispanic and a few are white. Some have traveled for 30 minutes or more on the subway to get to this school because admission is open to any student in the New York City public schools attendance area who has chosen the school and has demonstrated an eagerness to undertake rigorous intellectual work. Most of the students, however, come from District 4, the Upper East Side of Manhattan, because they attended Central Park East I and II or River East elementary schools. Some of these students might have dropped out by the tenth grade had they been assigned to a large, impersonal high school.

At CPESS the students work at their own pace in groups, as a whole class, or individually in rooms where there are apparently random arrangements of desks and tables, sometimes an old couch in the corner, and word processors along the counters around the room.

The high level of intellectual activity is indicated by the instructions for the unit on China. There are nine parts to the exhibition. The first part is the production of a paper on a Chinese dynasty, which will be the basis of an oral report to be delivered to the class in the week after the paper is completed. One of the instructions directs the student to make a contribution to a time line the class is developing by creating a picture or symbol for the dynasty chosen and a characterization of its achievements.

For the art portion of the exhibition, the student could choose among six options, including the following:

1. Go to the Metropolitan Art Museum or the Natural History Museum. Choose a poem from one of the scrolls. Illustrate it with your

own design. Materials: rice paper, Chinese brush and inks, or color inks.

6. In Chinese philosophy, the idea of opposites/balances is expressed in yin/yang with its own symbol. Create your own idea of balance and make up your own symbol. materials: water color, paint, wire, wood, print, etc.

Each student is required to keep a diary of progress toward completion of the project. The diary is used in evaluating the exhibition's quality.

Section 3 of the exhibition follows the reading of a book independently chosen and read by the student. Two essays on the book are required, one essentially a book report and the other an appraisal of its treatment of one of the six themes. Section 4 asks for a pen pal letter to a student in China (located through an international service). Two more sections ask for writing assignments on the role of women in Chinese literature. A creative writing section asks to write scenes for a novel they were assigned to read entitled *Gold Flower's Story*—for example:

b) Gold Flower's mother says: "it's not only you who hates society, but me too" (p. 12). Write a scene where Gold Flower's mother talks about her life and feelings.
c) Gold Flower is forced to have sex with her husband, Chang. Write a scene from Chang's point of view.

Section 8 is a group project that requires an oral presentation on an aspect of Chinese culture that has been researched in the library. Each group member is required to submit a checklist with the initials of the librarian certifying the learning of the research skills necessary for this project. (This should be contrasted with the detached "library research skills" taught as a unit of English in many conventional high schools.)

The final section asks the student to take a stand on a topic (Confucianism, filial piety, imperialism, or Mao Tse-tung, for example) and defend the position taken in a "thesis paper." Students earn a "competent" rating if they apply one of the "habits of mind" (the promise to the student in the epigraph to this chapter) and an "advanced" rating if they apply three more. Diary entries are required for all portions of the exhibition.

There is clearly more than a few days' work here, but the students know ahead of time on what they will be judged; there are no surprises. This is a compact between adults and apprentice adults, treated as they will be in the world outside the school. They are expected to pace their own work, although they are offered a great deal of help from the classroom teacher (the classes are small—no more than twenty students) and from their adviser. The exhibition will be judged acceptable, competent, or advanced by the student's teacher and at least one other teacher attending when the student presents before the class. Both teachers read all the written work before the presentation.

The fact that the students know what the exhibition consists of from the beginning of the course needs some emphasis. One of the least edifying aspects of multiple-choice, norm-referenced tests is the need for test security—making sure that no one sees the answers and can cheat on the test. A book has been written by a famous gadfly of American education, John Jacob Cannell, castigating teachers and administrators for their laxity in security.[3]

Keeping tests secret is demeaning; it is also unnecessary. If, however, students know what will be in the examination ahead of time and know the standards by which they will be judged, nothing is secret, and no one will trip over nonessentials. Students can also get involved in assessing their own work, which should be the ultimate aim of any educational assessment.

But understanding that surprise (and the accompanying anxiety and tension) is not an integral part of educational evaluation requires a considerable switch in attitudes by teachers, students, and parents, who often believe that school should be the same for their children as it was for them, despite the differences in the social and economic climate.

AN ELEMENTARY ART ASSESSMENT
CONDUCTED BY PARENTS

In Bozeman, Montana, a town of about 20,000 inhabitants 90 miles north of Yellowstone Park, the school community at Longfellow Elementary School has cracked a hard nut: the assessment of growth in learning about art.[4] The school adopted an art course of study, Art in Action, for grades 1 through 4 in which the children learn art history, art criticism, and aesthetics, as well as the production of art, and it wanted to know if the curriculum was successful.

The question—whether the instruction at Longfellow increases students' appreciation of art—arose from the traditional attitude of the school, its principal, and staff toward innovation: if we do something new, how do we know it's working? But there were no tests to buy—and this is a school that does so well on multiple-choice tests bought from publishers that there is no doubt it would have used one if it had been available.

The art teacher at Bozeman High School, Ray Campeau, took time off from his position and developed a test designed to show whether the children had learned the discourse of art. Campeau's name is synonymous with art in Bozeman. The students at Bozeman High School, through an art club organized but not controlled by Campeau, own an art collection that hangs in the school's corridors and boasts several famous names. Campeau is a reader for the College Board's Advanced Placement Studio Art examination and a member of the National Board for Professional Teaching Standards' Committee on Teaching in the Arts.

He wanted the Longfellow School art assessment to be cheap, sustainable, and a lever for good instruction. The design is simple. The same assessment is given twice a year: once in the fall as a preassessment and in May as a postassessment. Each child in grades 1 through 4 is interviewed about a work of art. The interviews take between 1 and 5 minutes (the oldest of these students is only 10), in the privacy of an office near the classroom. The atmosphere is friendly and relaxed, especially because the interviewer is a parent, and frequently one the child knows.

Campeau wants children to understand that what is on the canvas before them is a construction embodying ideas, feelings, and attitudes. An appropriate response is not a fantasy about the subject of the painting but an understanding of the ideas and how they make their effect through technique. When training the parents who took part in the assessment, Campeau impressed on them that a picture of a horse is not a horse but a manipulation of paint and space to suggest a horse to the viewer by taking a certain perspective and using light, shade, texture, and all the other resources of technique to communicate.

The process and the questions used in the interview were designed by a committee consisting of Campeau, the principal of Longfellow Elementary School, three teachers, and two parents, who were also aides in the classrooms. This may be the first performance assessment partially designed by parents.

The interviewer begins by saying to the child: "I want you to look very carefully at this work of art and tell me everything you can about it. Think of how you talk about art in your classes." The second sentence focuses the child's mind on art classes and the language used in them. The expression "work of art" was used so that the child might supply "painting," "drawing," or "watercolor," if possible. If the child has plenty to say, the interviewer does not need to say more. But if there is some reluctance and hesitation, the interviewer can say: "Are there any other things that you can tell me about this work of art?" and finally, if the stream seems to have run dry, "Is that everything you have to say about it?"

During the first year of the program, five parents, all volunteers, did the interviewing and the scoring, (there was no money for releasing teachers). The pictures chosen were representational. One of them selected for the second grade, a seascape, caused an unforeseen problem: 90 percent of the children had spent all their lives in Montana and had never seen the ocean, so they interpreted a curling wave as "snow coming over a mountain," when they could understand it at all.

The November tests were put away until May, and then both tests were scored at a sitting by a group of parents. The scoring consists of points given for accurate comments, thus:

- one point for a comment on technical properties such as line, shape, color, medium (watercolor or oil), or tools (brush or knife, e.g.);
- two points for a comment on formal properties such as unity, theme, variation, repetition, etc.;
- three points for a comment on the expression of the work, such as its feeling, mood, character.

The points were marked at the end of each line, tallied for each student, and then tallied for each teacher's class. The scores for the two tests were compared and a "growth" score computed.

Like the New York grade 4 science test, this scoring is a tightly controlled version of group grading. It begins with a standard-setting session so that all the parent-scorers agree on what constitutes a "comment on unity, theme, or variation." During the scoring, the parents discuss among themselves how to score problems posed by some reported comments. Since there are only 532 papers to be scored (two for each of 226 children), it is possible to conduct the scoring sessions informally.

During the first year of the Art in Action program, the pretest scores for all grades were low. The various grades, however, showed marked differences in understanding the works of art once instruction took place.

The first graders began the year by describing the picture literally and commenting on its reality. "It looks real." "It's pretty." "I see green over here." "Mountains like we have, and water on mountains like we have." "There is a reflection on the water." The more talkative students usually named every color they could see in the picture.

Growth over the year was strong, primarily due to many more children naming all the colors in the picture. "Little bit of purple and blue on the mountain . . . Black coming down stream. Maroon right there. Orange all over it. Little bit of yellow and green, dark pink and red in the pink." The literal descriptions became more detailed, although this is not what the Art in Action program emphasizes: "Two squirrels. Crack in mountain. Tall cliff. . . . Fish, bird, and Indian there." Of course, there were children who said nothing during the pretest and only one or two descriptive words during the posttest, but even that shows growth. One child in both tests became fixated on the ability of the artist: "Art is always beautiful. Artist always draw beautiful."

By the spring, second-grade, children began to talk about the artist's techniques. "Scratched in places." "Rock detailed because of bumpiness." "Mixes colors. Used fingers and a paintbrush." "The artist used a big brush, and fat brush, and a skinny brush." There was attempted discussion of shadow: "There is light and dark in the water." "It seems very dark." And some talked of perspective: "[They] sat on the shore and watched."

The main focus, however, was still on the reality of the piece and the colors used. The class on the whole seemed comfortable talking about the picture: what it was, what they thought it looked like, the colors represented. "Blue in water and white. Light blue in sky with orange. Purple. A little green. Some black." One student however, after an average response on the pretest, said nothing in response to the picture of the ocean.

By the spring, third-grade children were able to discuss technique. "It looks like they used thin and wide brush strokes." "To make the trees look like they go around—it's dark to make it look shaded." "Right here it pokes out." "One side of the mountain is lighter than the other because of the shadows." "The paint on the trees and mountains kind of gloppy, kind of sticks out." "It looks like things in the front are painted really dark greens or blacks and the things in the back are painted orange red or yellow." "It looks three-dimensional." They spoke in more complete sentences and began to articulate clearly what they saw. A few students still described what was represented, but the number diminished.

The pretests of the fourth graders showed responses similar to the pretests of the first graders. Because they had received no instruction in the third grade (this was the first year that the Art in Action program was introduced into the school), their age gave the fourth graders no advantage in the pretest: "It's a bunch of trees and fence. Bunch of different colors." "Just some flowers." "Looks like its fall." "Looks pretty." "Don't know."

But there was a wide difference in responses to the posttest; the fourth graders were able to express their thoughts in complete sentences and to move beyond the literal image of the picture. Some fourth graders noticed the blurring of background and figure in a portrait: "My focal point is the eyes," said one. "It's an original—you can tell by the texture," said another, making an observation not easily accessible to students who have studied from reproductions. "It looks like the painter used a knife and did a lot of spreading," was the response of another child. "The artist wanted it to look not real, impressionistic. It looks rushed." Several others mentioned the sense of haste: "looks like they painted it fast," and "He didn't paint all of the places." There are greater sophistication in the discussion of technique. "The hat looks 3-D because of texture." "Suggests glasses with little bits of circle." "Used rough strokes, not little ones." "Looks like a wide brush was used." "Lip has light highlights so it shows up from the dark around it." "Some of the painting looks like dry brush, some like sponge." "Looks like sun shining on it makes colors. One side of coat darker than other."

Throughout the grades, there was little talk about mood. "Lots of warm colors" and "It looks mysterious" were the only phrases that referred to the mood of the piece. Although the students knew that the artist was "painting to show how someone expresses his opinions," they ventured no guesses as to what exactly the artist might be trying to express. In the spring, while some need to define the image still lingered, students usually worked past that and focused on the style (watercolor, oil) and technique used in the work of art.

The scores showed that change ranged from 7 points of growth in one first-grade class to 157 in a fourth grade, with an average of 75 points per class. Growth seemed markedly higher in the second, third, and fourth grades. Although each child will accumulate knowledge over the years, only growth over a year is scored, so while the pretest score may go up (because of continuing instruction in Art in Action), the distance between it and the posttest score must be maintained if the instructional program is to be judged a success.

The physical setup for the interviews was usually the utility room where supplies are kept and materials prepared, often accessible only through the classroom. The interviewing parent prepared a comfortable corner. The picture was propped up on a chair, about eye level to a child. The parent sat beside the picture, with the response sheets on her lap. A child sat in a small chair opposite the picture, answered the questions, and then left with a message to send the next child in. The interviews did not take long; indeed, an entire class of twenty-five students could be covered in about 1½ hours.

Trying to avoid the mistakes of the first year, in fall 1990 Campeau chose impressionist landscapes painted in acrylic by a local Bozeman artist, Freeman Butts. They were characterized by broad, swift strokes of color; diagonal placements of linear features like rivers or fences; contrasting textures, from multiple layers of paint to bare, unpainted patches; and dramatic expressions of mood. Campeau chose them deliberately in order to force students to discuss the formal, technical, and expressive properties of the work, not tell stories about a horse, a man, or a house, as they had frequently done when faced with representational works.

These pictures are not easy for the children to understand. When I visited the school to watch the interviews, it was clear that the children were trying to relate the pictures to recognizable objects or scenes. One of the pictures was particularly hard for its first-grade viewers. Smaller than the others and in an ornate frame, it depicted autumn trees seen across a diagonal yellow river; it did not offer a figure or object for a young child to connect with. One little girl listened to the parent's request and then asked: "You mean what do I think it is?" She finally said she thought it was pretty. Others identified hills, bushes, trees, green fields, and snow. A number listed a few items of this kind and then said, "That's all."

The parent-interviewers were sensitive in their appreciation of what ought to constitute understanding of art. One said that children should be close enough to touch it in order to appreciate the texture. She used gestures to invite them to touch. (One child did tap the painting and then looked at his finger, as if he expected the paint to come off.) They criticized the original question as not specific enough and the language as a bit too formal. One parent noticed that the younger children seemed unsure of themselves during the pretest but relaxed in the posttest because they knew what was happening. "The older students liked the one-to-one attention," she added.

This parent was also eloquent about her reasons for enthusiasm: "In the past students were graded simply on their ability to draw. This new assessment centers around evaluating a student's knowledge of the properties of art: not everyone can draw—but *everyone* can enjoy art. I like it."

Longfellow School's assessment of learning about art suffers from the defects of pioneering programs put together on a shoestring budget. From a psychometric viewpoint, the Longfellow program is not exemplary. There is no attempt to standardize details of the interviews, such as the child's distance from the painting, whether the child is invited to touch it, or the amount of time given to each child. No account is taken of other variables than classroom instruction; children whose parents are artists or who spend a lot of time around artists may pick up the target vocabulary independent of the school curriculum. The scoring may lack reliability, despite frequent cross-checking among the scorers, the leadership team, and Campeau.

But its use of parents as interviewers is inspired and should give other districts ideas about how to implement performance assessments on low budgets. Using parents solves two potential problems at once: parents are involved and support the assessment, and the students are comfortable because parents (frequently friends and neighbors in this small town) are not threatening.

Insufficient experimentation with the kind of painting suitable for the assessment is a problem that perhaps needs the attention of researchers, who would have time to consider it fully. Campeau is probably correct in not wishing to use representational works, but the choice of the impressionistic landscapes did not meet the needs of the assessment. Research needs to be conducted to see which paintings (or drawings) permit children to see them as artifacts rather than as narratives.

Other interesting questions are raised by the Longfellow art assessment: Do children in the lower grades have the cognitive skills necessary to enter into and understand works of art? It will be interesting to see how the first graders from the first year discuss art when they reach the fourth grade. What happens when children are taught the language of art and are encouraged to use it? Does simply exposing children to the language of art when they are young enable them to grow into it when they are ready? These questions illustrate the point that assessment raises important questions about learning.

The Longfellow School art assessment exemplifies the creativity available at the local level in American schools. It is a cooperative endeavor; Campeau cannot operate without the full support of the school's staff, the parents, and the district administration. Presented with a challenge, they devised an assessment that is true to what is being assessed (psychometricians would say it has "face validity"), has enough reliability for the scale of the assessment, and has the built-in support of the community. It has potential as a model for assessment of programs in all curricular areas at the school or district level.

HISTORY/SOCIAL STUDIES ASSESSMENTS

Some creative history/social studies group performance assessments have been developed for grade 8 by New York State.[5] (They should become the basis for some of the performance assessments in New York's future.)[6] They are examined here because they are experimental and voluntary. Although New York State instituted performance assessment as part of its grade 4 science assessment, it did not mandate the performance assessments in history/social studies. The history/social studies assessments involve groups, which make for a more complicated grading challenge, and the science assessment worked only with individuals. But the New York State Education Department described the social studies assessments fully in several communications to schools, which may be construed as encouragement for the schools to use the assessment.

One of the group performance tasks asks eighth graders to develop a tourist guide for New York State as seen through the eyes of teenagers. The students divided the state into regions and researched the history and the culture of each region, putting the whole together in a final package. A second task was the evaluation of the changes brought about in New York State's economy by, on the one hand, the completion of the Erie Canal in 1825 and the opening of the New York State Thruway in the 1950s. They were to look at newspaper articles predicting the economic effects of these two developments and then find out whether the forecasts were accurate, given the different conditions in the nineteenth and twentieth centuries. This is a project that a group of students can accomplish, although for an individual eighth grader, the amount of data required might be overwhelming. A third project asks students to create a Hall of Fame for their locality or, if there already is one, to nominate someone for it. They were given as an example the Steuben County Hall of Fame, which includes baron von Steuben (for whom the county is named), who trained George Washington's troops, and Margaret Sanger, the advocate of birth control. These examples show that the project will take students far from their immediate locality in establishing the reasons for a person's claim to fame.

Like the Connecticut science and mathematics tasks, all of these projects provide observation and self-assessment forms, so that the process, as well as the product, can be evaluated. Like the Connecticut assessments, the social studies tasks will provide formative feedback as well as information about the quality of the program.

California is considering history/social studies assessments far beyond traditional modes: videotaped presentations of hypothetical trials or congressional testimony, for example, or computer simulations of decision making based on given variables. At the moment the California Assessment Program is experimenting with open-ended questions directed toward discovering students' ability to apply their historical knowledge. Grade 6 students were given a completely blank map of the United States, followed by these instructions:

Study the map above, then:
A. Shade the area where the 13 colonies were located.
B. Label the three groups of colonies: New England colonies, middle colonies, and southern colonies.
C. Write a short essay comparing and contrasting the three groups of colonies. In your short essay, be sure to tell:
  ○ what the geography and climate of each area was like.
  ○ how the people in each area made a living.
  ○ what ways of life resulted from the similarities and differences among the three areas.

These open-ended questions are scored by groups of teachers following the group-grading model explained in Chapter 2. They have found that students have some strange misconceptions about the origins of this country—some placed the New England colonies correctly, but then filled the rest of the map with the middle ones in the Midwest and the southern colonies in California and the Far West!

CREATIVITY OUTSIDE THE SCHOOLS

An important body of ideas for performance assessments arises from the auxiliary organizations that surround American schools. These organizations design competitions for students, such as the Odyssey of the Mind, organized by a group with the same name; "We the People . . ." organized by the Center for Civic Education in Calabasas, California, funded by grants from the Bicentennial Commission of the United States; the Physics Olympiad, organized by an international group of physics teachers; the Westinghouse Science Talent Search; and science fairs, which are frequently organized by local and state science museums.

These competitions are to be distinguished from the genre of competitions modeled on the spelling bee, such as the Citizen Bee, the Geography Bee, and the Academic Decathlon, which rely on low-level intellectual abilities and the recall of memorized facts—indeed, the competition equivalent of multiple choice.

In all of these competitions—"bees," "decathlons," Odyssey of the Mind, and "We the People . . ."—students participate in local competitions in school districts and then move up to county, statewide, national, and—in the case of the Odyssey of the Mind and the Physics Olympiad—international level. At each level, the students' presentations in the nonbee competitions are judged by a panel of experts, much as Olympic diving and skating competitions are decided.

"We the People . . ."

The national "We the People . . ." competition, run by the Center for Civic Education, has solved the problems of evaluating student performance in social studies with imagination, possibly because the designers are less daunted than are educators by the authority of evaluation experts. The burden of accountability forces educators to maintain traditional instructional programs. The "We the People . . ." contest can be imaginative and creative precisely because, like the other competitions, it is not part of the school's responsibility.

The Center for Civic Education is a nonprofit group that researches, develops, and implements programs of civic education in public and private schools, elementary and secondary, where these programs are incorporated into the sequence of social studies teaching.[7] In commemoration of the two hundredth anniversary of Congress, the Center for Civic Education designed "We the People . . . Congress and the Constitution," a companion program to the National Bicentennial Competition of the Constitution and the Bill of Rights. The "We the People . . ." curriculum and competition are funded by an act of Congress and administered by the Commission on the Bicentennial of the United States Constitution, which made a three-year grant to the Center for Civic Education. The program is administered nationwide in 435 congressional districts, four trust territories, and the District of Columbia.

The "We the People . . ." curriculum and competition were developed by the Center for Civic Education to increase understanding of and interest in the principles on which the United States is founded. Because these principles are embodied in the Constitution and the debates that surrounded its inception, the content of the curriculum and competition focuses on their application to both historical and contemporary issues.

The curriculum complements the regular school history/government curriculum in grades 11 and 12 and is designed for a wide range of achievement levels. The simulated congressional hearings are an elective and can be competitive or noncompetitive.

Competitive hearings require precise adherence to the format designed by the Center for Civic Education. The entire class must participate in the competition. There are six units in the curriculum, and the class divides into six teams to specialize in one of the topics: political philosophy, history and experience, the Constitution, establishment of the government, fundamental rights, and responsibilities of the citizen. At the competition, the presenting team faces the judges, and the rest of the class is the audience. There are three judges for each topic.

This program is another example, similar to the Longfellow Elementary School art assessment in Bozeman, of involving the local community in the assessment. The eighteen judges are professional people who volunteer their time to make themselves familiar with the "We the People . . ." textbook and spend a day judging the competition. The judges are provided with the textbook several weeks in advance of the competition and are expected to read at least the unit of the book they will be judging (and are encouraged to read the entire book) in order to understand what the students have learned and, on a basic level, how sophisticated their answers should be. When I watched a competition in a congressional district, the judges were five attorneys from local law firms, a university administrator, three graduate students in public administration, a university professor of political science, two professors of law from the law school where the competition was staged, a professor of education at a local university, the assistant to the vice-president for public affairs at the local electric company, an independent filmmaker producing and directing a documentary on the twenty-fifth anniversary of the Voting Rights Act, a police officer, a private consultant to local government, and an aide to the congressman of the district.

The judges' participation (like that of the parents in the Bozeman Montana art assessment) is an important link to the community. The students find themselves addressing adults for whom constitutional and political questions are professional bread and butter, a new experience for many of them. At the same time, the professionals, in many cases influential members of their communities, gain some idea of what is going on in the schools and the level of teaching and learning in history, social studies, and political science. One lawyer said, "There is something satisfying in seeing all these students getting a charge out of the Constitution. It makes me realize that all the gloom and doom I hear about education is not necessarily the whole truth."

Three weeks before the competition, the Center for Civic Education sends the participating schools and the judges the pool of possible competition questions so they can prepare responses. There are three questions for each of the six units. Students prepare answers to all eighteen but will be asked only one from each unit. Although the students receive the primary questions in advance, they have no idea what the follow-up questions will be. At the meeting in the morning before the competition begins at 10:00 A.M., the unit judges decide which of the three questions to ask. Each judging team asks the same question for each unit in order to maintain some standardization. The judges are assigned to a unit and remain a team throughout the competition. They physically move from room to room while the class stays in place (it is easier to move groups of three people than groups of twenty or twenty-five).

The judges introduce themselves to the team and take on the role of members of Congress who are hearing testimony. For the first 4 minutes of the 10-minute period, the students present a prepared statement in response to the judges' choice of one of the three questions. Students may use notes and are not required to memorize their response. In the other 6 minutes, the judges ask follow-up questions, which may be taken from questions provided by the Center for Civic Education but may also deal with current issues. Since I watched a competition in December 1990, one of the questions dealt with the constitutional right to declare war: does the president or the Congress have that right? Judges are to judge student teams on the content of their presentation only. No points are to be taken off for using notes during the 4-minute prepared presentation, and students are not to be penalized for an accent, dialect, or poor grammar. The students have been instructed that regular school clothes are appropriate for the competition, and judges may not mark teams down on the basis of appearance. Students may sit or stand, depending on what is most comfortable to them. Differing opinions within the teams are encouraged. Judges are asked to score on the basis of how well students support their positions and how substantial a response they present.

Feedback should be constructive and deal only with the team's strengths and weaknesses. Judges are asked not to be cruel and always to end with a positive statement.

The students are judged on a scale of 1–10 (1–2 = poor, 3–4 = fair, 5–6 = average, 7–8 = above average, 9–10 = excellent) on each of six criteria: understanding of basic issues, ability to apply constitutional knowledge appropriately, reasoning, use of supporting evidence, responsiveness to questions, and group participation.

The judges keep their score sheets until the end of the competition in order to change scores in comparison to other teams they see later. Before completing the score for each team, each judge must award a score of up to 100 points for the group's overall performance (0–69 = below average, 70–79 = average, 80–89 = very good, 90–100 = excellent). This score is to be used only as a tie breaker in the event that two teams have the same raw score.

The scoring is not sophisticated; it is a simple addition, with no attempt at averaging, so the cumulative scores can go up into three figures. The system is simple and transparent now but might need weighting if "We the People . . ." were to become a model for assessment of history/social studies within the schools.

The winners from each congressional district proceed to the state-level competition, and the state winners compete in the national competition held in Washington, D.C.

The students I saw competing in a congressional district competition were nervous. Their speech halted, and their voices cracked. One girl was in tears a few moments before the competition began be-

cause she had dropped her notes in the restroom, and they were wet.
"Uhms," "Y'knows," and "likes" filled dead air. Although the students' ineptness as speakers reflects the pervasive lack of training in
oral discourse in schools today, their responses were frequently in-
telligent and well thought out.

The questions asked were scholarly and required serious analysis
in order to respond fully to the issues addressed—for example: What
are the basic ideas of classical republicanism? How was James Madison's view of republicanism reflected in the Constitution? In a republican government, if there is a conflict between the common
welfare and an individual's rights, what considerations should be
taken into account in deciding which should come first? In their
4-minute prepared statement, the students I watched began by saying
that classical republicanism relies on the civic virtue of its people. In
attempting to define the common good, James Madison said that a
government that protects each individual's natural rights is protect-
ing the common welfare. One student said, "In republicanism the
common welfare is superior to individual rights, and when individual
rights are violated, then the government must step in and place controls on those people who are violating those rights."

There was less coherence in the 6-minute period of response to
spontaneous questions. The students were nervous and unable to
make the leap to contemporary issues. They chose as their example
of the conflict between the common welfare and individual rights the
issue of gun control, but could not analyze the arguments for each
side. "Gun control represents this problem. Some people say it is a
violation of their rights not to allow them to have guns, but others
say that because of random violence everybody's rights must be protected and controls must be placed on guns." At no time did the
students express an opinion on which way they thought the issue
should go and support it. Pressed by the role-playing judges, one
student simply said, "It's a problem, but the NRA has so much power
that no one can get [the laws] changed."

Another student showed rather more grasp of the issues in the unit
on federalism. Asked in the 6-minute follow-up period, "Is the system of checks and balances currently working? Were the anti-
Federalists correct in their fear of a strong federal government? For
example, in the current Gulf situation who has the right to declare
war—Congress or the president?" the student replied extemporane-
ously, "While Congress is the only body which can officially declare

war, the Constitution provides the president with the power to set up the inevitability of war by ordering troops to the Gulf."

In response to a follow-up question asking how to increase voter turnout, one member of the group responded, "More education about the government and how it works would help people understand how deep their responsibility is. I know that this class has taught me more than I ever knew before and that without it I probably would not want to be involved in politics either."

I watched a district-level competition. By the time the teams compete in the national in Washington, D.C. (usually in congressional office buildings), their sophistication and analytical ability have noticeably increased. But, since more students compete at lower than at higher levels of the competition, the implications for teaching cover a wide range of schools than just those of winning teams.

"We the People . . ." is almost a type case of performance assessment. It is a direct demonstration of students' ability to do what we expect after studying the Constitution and the Bill of Rights: explain their history and background and apply them to other times and situations. The requirements for working in teams and the involvement of the community are not typical of performance assessment, but a good argument could be made that they should be.

The competition has tapped a powerful incentive for students by combining competition with community involvement. One of the U.S. education system's most insidious failings is its lack of ability to make education "real" for the average student. There will always be students who strive to succeed academically for reasons having little to do with school—pride, emphasis on education at home, or a desire to go on to university or college. For the majority of students (even those who do succeed), however, high school is like doing time until they can get out and get a job or go on to college.

But all of the team members, not just the academic stars, take the competition seriously. In the weeks before the competition, they meet outside school, spend hours in law libraries researching issues, and rehearse answers to hypothetical questions. The competition galvanizes their energy as usually only sports and other adolescent preoccupations can. They want to do well before important adults.

The competition also reveals the shortcomings of the kind of teaching these high school students have experienced for more than ten years. The 4-minute prepared statements were notably better than the answers to questions in the follow-up period. The students were also much stronger in recalling facts than in applying concepts to different situations. When asked about the origins of the doctrine of natural rights in the eighteenth century, they covered their inability to deal with the question by referring to the historical facts about the writing of the Constitution. Is it possible that ten years of multiple-choice testing and the teaching that prepares for it by stressing memorization of facts from textbooks has caused these deficiencies?

We do not need to speculate about another shortcoming in the students' responses because we know that oral communication is ignored in schools. (Under the influence of the whole-language movement, speaking and expressing opinions orally are beginning to return as part of the literacy curriculum in elementary schools.) If students are not part of extracurricular groups like debating teams or theater, they receive no training in how to speak before a group. During the "We the People . . ." competition, students struggled for words, lacking the resources that training would have given them. The competition specifically forbids scoring on the students' oral abilities now, but the organizers might want to capitalize on the message the competition sends to the schools by reconsidering that policy.

The competition and the preparation for it have lasting effects on the students' learning. Teachers assert that the knowledge learned from the curriculum and the competition is drawn on all year. One teacher responded when asked if her students quickly forget the material once the competition is over, "Oh no, it becomes a background for the Advanced Placement U.S. history class. Over and over they refer back to such concepts as civic virtue or right to revolution in order to explain and put in context certain historical and modern events."

The competition has enormous potential as a model for the evaluation of history/social studies and government classes. It is the most imaginative and well-organized social studies assessment I know of—more impressive than current ideas at the state level. It promotes students' responsibility for their own learning, makes teachers into guides rather than authorities, gives the subject a "real-life" importance for students, and allows the students to experience the stimulation of healthy risk. Performing in front of distinguished members of the community may be thrilling, but it can also be terrifying. The fear of failure and desire for success are magnified, and students are asked to take a real risk. They rise to the occasion. The attempt strengthens them and provides them with an experience to fall back on. "That was the worst thing I've ever had to do, and the best," said one student.

The mystery is why "We the People . . ." has not been seized as a model. The evaluation is faithful to the intent of social studies and government: understanding the Constitution's origins, how it works, and its application today. The Center for Civic Education is not proprietary about the competition and would like to see it adopted on a large scale.

The competition asks for teamwork, otherwise neglected in school, but a vital feature of the working world. It would not be hard to get individual scores from the team's work; students could write individual essays based on the questions in the prepared and extemporaneous portions. Their cooperation could also be judged by checklists filled out by both teachers and students, as is proposed in the Connecticut high school mathematics and science assessments, also designed for groups.

If a model such as the "We the People . . ." competition were adopted and community members became expected members of evaluation teams, the schools would go a long way to solving their public relations problems. Rather than telling the public about the schools, the community members would learn for themselves and also take some responsibility by writing comments for teachers and students.

Some inspired state testing director ought to realize the potential of the design for assessing history/social studies and work with the Center for Civic Education staff to adapt it for a statewide assessment. In its present form, with the requirement for whole class involvement and presentation by teams, it works well as program assessment, which is usually the scope of statewide assessment. But it would not be hard to derive individual student scores with some additional information, which would make the competition useful also as an individual student assessment.

The competition is already roughly standardized, since the same questions are asked in order to make fair comparisons. It would require some technical scrutiny to make the scoring reliable; producing an acceptable system would not be impossible. Drawing the program and the competition into the educational system would ensure the formation of a feedback loop between assessment and curriculum. Because "We the People . . ." is voluntary now, the students of only a few teachers—those with the energy to reach out for stimulating programs—get the benefit of measuring their learning against real-life standard. It seems to be another case of the rich getting richer. Learning in history/social studies certainly needs the information that this assessment could provide to all teachers and students.

The Odyssey of the Mind

The Odyssey of the Mind has been in existence for a dozen years as an adjunct, noncurricular activity in members schools.[8] There is an annual fee for membership. The objective of the organization is to develop students' creativity by setting them problems that can be solved only in groups and by applying knowledge and skills from a variety of disciplines. Clearly, these aims are consonant with desires expressed by business and industry executives for employees who can think flexibly and work cooperatively. The business community has enthusiastically supported the Odyssey of the Mind.

Competitions are held in four divisions, from kindergarten through college. An adult coach takes care of logistics such as meeting places and gives some training in divergent thinking, but the coach is strictly prohibited from helping the team with its competition project.

As soon as they decide to enter the competition, the teams begin in their school meetings to deal with problems like this one: Divisions II and III (grade 6–12) were asked in 1989 "to design and produce a transportation system consisting of five battery-powered vehicles carrying costume parts to each of the five, six, or seven teammates. Costume parts will arrive just in time to change the team's appearance. Vehicles will run in paths that will allow vehicles to crash into one another if their movements are timed incorrectly." Those are the only instructions, leaving plenty of room for creative interpretation as the team members prepared over a few months for the competition. The teams could spend no more than $75 on materials and equipment in their presentation and could take no more than 8 minutes for the final version.

In the same year, another division (K–12) was set the problem of designing and constructing "a balsa wood and glue structure that will balance and support the greatest weight for its specifications. The structure must measure 8 to 8½ inches in height and may not exceed 15 grams in weight. The score will be determined by the pounds of weight supported per gram weight of the structure." The elementary divisions (K–8) were asked to "create a fable and perform the team's interpretation of how a moral came into existence." They could spend only $50 on costumes and equipment and had 8 minutes to perform.

There is a maximum score for these long-term problems and additional points for enhancement or stylistic elegance in the solution. At the competition itself, each team must solve a problem on the spot, with judges alone allowed in the room with the team.

These Odyssey of the Mind group problems are models for interdisciplinary integrated assessments. There is irony in the observation that although 6,000 schools throughout the world (more than 200 schools in California alone) now participate in the Odyssey of the Mind, the U.S. schools do not seem to have connected the competition to the teaching and learning core of the school and seen in it a model for accomplishing the purposes of education.

The examples in this chapter have provided some idea of the creativity that can be found in and around our schools. Hope for American education is justified if everyone concerned—teachers, parents, students, administrators, legislators—acknowledges this creativity and seeks to promote it in every school and every classroom. Business as usual will not do; there are already a number of ways to steer it in a new and more productive direction.

5

Portfolios

I am very proud of what was written in my portfolio. I'm not being conceited, I just didn't know that people thought I could write OK. If anything, I thought I was an underachieved writer but now I realize that I am the same as everyone else and that makes me happy.

—California student[1]

In one of the increasing number of journals for teachers devoted to using portfolios, which are springing up around the country, there is a list of thirty-five purposes for portfolios (Figure 5.1).[2] Each—from "to replace competency exams" through "to connect reading, writing, and thinking"—is a legitimate and praiseworthy reason.

The multiplicity of purposes for portfolios seems to give permission for free interpretation. Possibly because portfolios appear to be both easy to use and unrestricting and also possibly because of the eagerness with which they have been embraced, "portfolio" seems to spring most easily to the lips of state superintendents and politicians when they want to invoke alternatives to multiple choice. It is, perhaps, difficult to raise enthusiasm for "open-ended questions" or "manipulative skills assessments"—they do not fit well into speeches—but portfolios sound exotic enough to raise interest and at the same time are sufficiently well known not to be a threat.

And they are well known. No other form of performance assessment is as widespread as portfolios. They are used from kindergarten through graduate school. Several universities and colleges use the

These thirty-five purposes were developed by California English/language arts teachers and printed in *Portfolio News* (Winter 1990). I am responsible for dividing them into classifications.

1. *As a teaching tool*

—to provide students ownership, motivation, a sense of accomplishment, and participation
—to involve students in a process of self-evaluation
—to help students and teachers set goals
—to build in time for reflection about students' accomplishments
—to individualize writing instruction
—to provide more reasons/opportunities to write
—to set up an apprenticeship situation
—to connect reading, writing, and thinking
—to serve as a vehicle for publication
—to aid in parent conferences
—to give importance to daily writings
—to extend the amount of time devoted to practice in writing

2. *Professional development of teachers*

—to study curriculum and effective teaching practices
—to allow for better staff communication
—to reduce the paper load
—to identify school strengths and needs for improvement
—to examine writing in different disciplines
—to build a sequence in writing instruction
—to establish an esprit de corps within departments and faculties
—to account for curriculum implementation
—to assess curriculum needs
—to foster professionalism and collaboration
—to evaluate the kinds of assignments given students
—to accommodate schoolwide projects: artwork, math graphs, writing from community, parents, teachers, custodial staff, and others

3. *Assessment*

—to serve as an alternative to standardized testing
—to serve as a college application/high school placement vehicle
—to replace competency exams
—to serve as a grade or end-of-year culminating activity
—to provide program evaluation
—to supplement or substitute for the CAP
—to serve as a vehicle for changing the schools' conversation with the public

4. *Research*

—to observe growth in second-language students
—to examine growth over time and progress in students' writing
—to validate how students learn a new language
—to look at revision/process

Portfolio News, published by Portfolio Assessment Clearinghouse, c/o San Dieguito Union H.S. District, Encinitas, CA 92024.

FIGURE 5.1 Purposes for Portfolio Assessment

portfolio method for conducting undergraduate writing classes, and one or two ask for portfolios from students seeking admission. It is probably true to say that every one of the thirty-five purposes is being pursued in these projects, and in one or two cases, all thirty-five at once.

Portfolios began with the need to carry around samples of artwork to show prospective buyers. The metaphor has been retained in the physical appearance of the majority of samples: they are collections of work in a binder or folio. The exceptions are audiotapes and videotapes, either as portfolios or additions to them, and other artifacts. Portability seems to be of the essence; portfolios are meant to accompany a student or be passed along to the student's next teacher.

The feature that defines a portfolio and differentiates it from a folder or collection of work is the selection mechanism. Based on the purpose or purposes, pieces are included to demonstrate progress toward a stated aim. A portfolio is a subset of all work done; something must be rejected for it to be constructed. Portfolios can be used in any academic discipline; English/language arts, creative writing, and mathematics portfolios are now widespread, and science portfolios are beginning in California and in Pittsburgh, Pennsylvania.

The major virtue of portfolios is that they can be designed to function simultaneously as a teaching tool and as an assessment medium. Portfolios are more likely at the moment to be used to inform the student of progress and to provide feedback on the teacher's instruction, without being graded, although scored assessment is being developed, as in Vermont's mathematics portfolios. In one case (Advanced Placement Studio Art), it is well established. They can in fact be used for all of the purposes I cited in chapter 1: as the basis for student grades, as feedback to teachers about the success of teaching techniques, for placement or career decisions, for accountability, and as stimuli to improve teaching by providing a model of desirable practice.

PORTFOLIOS FOR PROFESSIONAL DEVELOPMENT OF TEACHERS

Among the devotees of portfolios who write articles on their use, there are two camps: those who see portfolios as primarily a teaching tool and those who see them as an assessment instrument, and never the twain shall meet, apparently.[3] The thirty-five-item list in figure 5.1 has been categorized to show that in fact there are four distinct classes of purposes, and perhaps more. The number of camps is only two, because "professional development" and "research" do not arouse passions as "teaching" and "assessment" do.

Professional development, however, is one of the major benefits of portfolios. In a California junior high school, teachers designed portfolios to contain evidence of student writing in all subjects.[4] During the early part of the summer, the teachers met in groups to grade the contents of the portfolios; that is, they graded the separate pieces of work included in the portfolios, not the collection as a whole. Since the graders were not those who had taught the students (although they were members of the group; they disqualified themselves from reading their own students' work), the grading session turned into a professional development session as teachers debated standards and exchanged teaching ideas. The teachers noticed the different quality of writing a student produced in one class as opposed to another, which led to a deeper understanding of purposes and contexts for writing. Surprisingly, in this school some students were producing more interesting and livelier writing in history/social studies classes than in English/language arts. This observation led to the discovery that history teachers were giving students a more thorough preparation for each writing assignment than the English teachers had assumed was needed.

Research into portfolios also has benefits beyond increases in knowledge. The junior high school described in this chapter is a research site for Arts PROPEL, a collaboration among the Pittsburgh public schools, the Educational Testing Service (ETS), the Collaboratives for Humanities and Arts Teaching (CHART) funded by the Rockefeller Foundation, and Harvard University's Project Zero (founded by Howard Gardner, who developed the theory of multiple modes of intelligence cited in the description of the New York ESPET grade 4 examination in chapter 3). Arts PROPEL is intended to last five years, bringing together researchers from the Educational Testing Service and Project Zero with school personnel in order to find out how portfolios work in teaching the arts—mainly the visual arts, music, and creative writing. The researchers have interviewed students and teachers in order to document the project, and they conduct regular meetings with groups of teachers to assess progress and to design additional approaches.

Information about learning processes is pouring forth from the research. The portfolios permit the observation of what Dennis Palmer Wolf, a Project Zero senior researcher, calls "the footprints of a work," documenting the cognitive and affective shifts, the ups and downs, as the composition of a play, a poem, or a painting proceeds.[5]

The research potential is also important for the development of the growing body of teacher-researchers—teachers (often participants in the National Writing Project) who undertake to account for a phenomenon in their own classroom or school. There are the beginnings of a teacher-research literature, as teachers write up what they have found from working, frequently with the assistance of a college or university researcher. Portfolios are obvious raw material for teacher research. To some extent, every teacher who uses them in the classroom or who takes part in a portfolio evaluation session is doing research, for the experience cannot do otherwise than increase the stock of knowledge about students and their learning processes.

WANTED: CLEAR DEFINITIONS

The multiplicity of purposes that portfolios can serve means that it is important to define the term at the beginning of a project. Test publishers are beginning to market portfolio systems, which include videotapes to introduce the system to the teachers, teachers' manuals, student portfolios with record-keeping information already printed on the inside, and even boxes to store the portfolios in. The kits leave the teachers no room for their own ideas; they are simply following a preset pattern, like technicians. These systems might not even be called portfolios by those who believe that a portfolio is essentially rooted in an individual teacher's or student's purposes.

Another example where definitions must be clear comes from the Senior Institute of Central Park East Secondary School. It calls its culminating activity, which earns the student a graduation diploma, a "portfolio," although it has fourteen components, including science experiments and "physical challenge." Another example: the South Brunswick New Jersey early childhood observation system (to be described in chapter 6) is called a "portfolio," probably because of its portability, but it does not contain student work alone and its contents are standardized for all teachers using it.

HOW PORTFOLIOS CAN WORK

To illustrate how portfolios can help students reflect on their own learning and therefore begin the process of learning to assess themselves, we will look at the experience of a teacher, Kathryn Howard, of Reizenstein Middle School in Pittsburgh, who wanted her students to develop the ability to judge their own work.[6] She thought portfolio evaluation had the potential to make students responsible for their own learning, her primary purpose. But she also wanted to affect the class so that the room itself changed shape. The students would not expect to be sitting in rows facing her desk and the blackboard but clustering in groups or absorbed in comparing versions of their work. She wanted to involve parents as well.

A Junior High Class Learns Self-Assessment

Howard teaches an eighth-grade writing class, where she assigns critical essays about readings, as well as creative writing. She found that inducting her students into the use of portfolios took a year and went through five phases. The process brought about a shift in the relationship among teacher, students, and the activities surrounding writing, just as she had intended, although she had not anticipated the feelings accompanying the change.

The major obstacles at first were the students' expectations, based on their former experiences in learning writing. They expected to be able to "write it and forget about it" in one shot. Their criteria were superficial, confined to good or bad spelling, whether the papers were clipped together, poor handwriting, and similar qualities. They defined success in writing class as completing an assignment without making errors. They had no personal investment in their writing: it was assigned, it was corrected, and it was thrown away.

When Howard began the portfolio process by asking the students to read their work aloud to a partner, a group, and a whole class and respond to questions about it, they were at first nonplussed. They had no response to such questions as, "What did you like about the piece?" "What were you thinking about when you wrote that particular sentence [paragraph]?" "What would you like to know more about?" As far as possible, they had not thought at all while writing.

After a prolonged oral phase, during which students not only began to consider the questions but also to regard each other as sources and coaches, Howard asked for a written reflection. She posed two questions only: What is done well in your writing? What needs to be improved?

Carefully structured questions are a feature of good portfolios. In the process of beginning to appreciate complexity, students should not be overwhelmed by questions that are too broad. Their attention should be focused on aspects of the topic, with the understanding that other aspects will receive attention at other times.

These two questions are the foundation of reflection on one's own work. Students are being trained to assess themselves, surely a central aim of education. Taking responsibility for one's own learning, working at developing self-critical capacity, and trusting one's own judgments are central to a definition of adult behavior in a sophisticated society. They are the habits expected by the students' future employers. And beyond preparation for work, these habits are the basis for a satisfying life as a citizen and lifelong learner.

The process of written reflection began unpromisingly in Howard's class. The students reverted in writing to the helpless superficiality they had at first displayed when asked to respond orally. Some simply repeated the teacher's comments on their work. Others asked her what they should write. But six months after the process began, the students were ready to construct a portfolio of their writing to that point.

The portfolio began with a piece of writing important to the student. The teacher took no part in the students' selection of the piece, for she wanted to see what was important to them. If they could not decide, they worked with a classmate. Then they responded to questions, shown in figure 5.2, developed to guide portfolio selection by teachers and an Educational Testing Service researcher who has been working with portfolios since the early 1980s.[7] Several encouraging developments emerged from the answers to the questions: students worked cooperatively, not competitively; they began to talk seriously to one another about their "pieces of work," using the argot of the portfolio world; they began to understand that both form and content are meaningful, so that changing order is also changing meaning; and some—by no means all—began to rely on their own judgment, so that A papers were not automatically chosen for the portfolio.

The next step upset the students' expectations again: they were asked a month later to choose for the portfolio a satisfying piece of work and an unsatisfying one. This assignment caused distress, be-

Thinking About an Important Piece of Your Own Writing

- Why did you select this particular piece of writing? (Why does this piece stand out from your other work?)

- What do you see as the special strengths of this work?

- What was especially important to you when you were writing this piece?

- What have you learned about writing from your work on this piece?

- If you could go on working on this piece, what would you do?

- What kind of writing would you like to do in the future?

- Now that you have looked at your collection of writing and answered these questions, can you identify a particular technique or interest that you would like to try out or investigate further in future pieces of writing? If so, what is it?

FIGURE 5.2 Questions Guiding Selection for the Portfolio

cause they had seen the portfolio as an opportunity to display success; they were reluctant to understand it as a record of development. Development necessarily includes failure, a truth difficult for students to accept. Two interesting results emerged: the students acquiesced so long as *they* decided what was unsatisfying (they were beginning to trust their own judgments), and they occasionally reclassified the piece they had chosen earlier as "most important" into "unsatisfying."

At the end of the school year, after several more writing assignments, the final portfolio was assembled. It contained two pieces, one satisfying and one unsatisfying, which could have been written in the month or so since the last selection; a written reflection on each piece, listing qualities that the student noticed about each; and a personal statement about the year's work in learning to write, including a self-evaluation of the student's strengths and weaknesses as a writer.

The year's work resulted in concrete evidence of each student's progress and also began the shift in relationships that Howard had originally aimed at. By the end of the year, the students understood that writing is a complex interaction of form and content, where meaning guides choices; that they, as students, must be responsible for their own learning; and that the teacher is a coach, not a dictator. The portfolio method was a powerful vehicle to bring about these changes. One year, however, is too short to consolidate such a shift. It can be wiped out too easily in a subsequent grade of unreflective teaching.

Involving Parents in the Portfolio Process

Howard added another innovation. At the beginning of March, she sent home with each student a folder of his or her work (not a portfolio in the sense of a selected group of work but everything) and asked each student's parents what they noticed, enjoyed, or were concerned about in their child's writing. The questionnaire in figure 5.3 guided their responses.

This was a pioneering move of some significance (and also fulfills another of the purposes for portfolios categorized in figure 5.1, "changing the means of communication with the public"). The change in writing instruction from an emphasis on correctness to the primacy of meaning and the process required to communicate it has

Student _____
Reader _____
Date _____

Please read everything in your child's writing folder, including drafts and commentary. Each piece is set up in back-to-front order, from rough draft to final copy. Further, each piece is accompanied by both student and teacher comments on the piece and the writing process. Finally, the folders also include written questionnaires where students write about their strengths and weaknesses as writers.

We believe that the best assessment of student writing begins with the students themselves, but must be broadened to include the widest possible audience. We encourage you to become part of the audience.

When you have read the folders, please talk to your children about their writing. In addition, please take a few minutes to respond to these questions.

• Which piece of writing in the folder tells you most about your child's writing?

• What does it tell you?

• What do you see as the strengths in your child's writing?

• What do you see as needing to be addressed in your child's growth and development as a writer?

• What suggestions do you have that might aid the class's growth as writers?

• Other comments, suggestions?

Thank you so much for investing this time in your child's writing.

FIGURE 5.3 Parent Portfolio Review and Reflection

not met with widespread understanding or approval among the general public, including parents. They tend to judge school by their own experiences in the classroom, so that to them, the value of writing is chiefly, sometimes solely, in the neat handwriting, accurate spelling and punctuation, and idiomatic English.

Furthermore, parents by and large (of course, there are exceptions, but these are justifiable generalizations on the basis of research and observation) regard the teacher as the authority in the classroom and find it hard to understand why students should be talking to each other. An Asian parent in California complained to a principal that he did not want his child in cooperative learning groups; he sent his child to school to learn from the teacher because the teacher knows everything and students know nothing.[8]

In addition to these factors, at the age of 14 students are beginning to put space between themselves and their parents. (To teenagers, if your mother likes it, you know it's awful.) But teachers need the support of parents even if students do not think *they* do. Bringing the student's work into the home in the portfolio and asking for written comments is an astute political, as well as educational, move. By this time in the year's writing experiences, the students in Howard's class were hungry for a bigger audience; they wanted more people besides their peers and the teacher to read their work. Including the parents adds another dimension to assessment—a third party, neither teacher nor student, assessing progress. Moreover, it is another variation on a theme that seems to be emerging as a side benefit of performance assessment: the interest and involvement of the community outside the school, for example, the parents in Bozeman's Longfellow Elementary School art assessment and the community members in the "We the People . . ." competition.

Howard's experiment was extremely popular among parents. With only two exceptions in a class of thirty-five (one response came from an older sister acting as a surrogate parent), all returned the forms with comments. The parents varied widely in their estimation of the pieces and in their answers to the questions. The strengths in the writing produced thirty-four different answers, with "vocabulary" and "expresses feelings/openness" at the top, with seven mentions each. The responses to the question about needs to be addressed produced another divergent group of replies, with "vocabulary" at the top, with eight mentions. The suggestions to help the class grow as writers ranged from "more reading" to "use letters to the editor," "have writers visit the class," and "publish a newspaper."

The process was completed when the students brought back the portfolios and then completed their own questionnaire (figure 5.4). The responses had their own pathos: "My mom learned more about the way I think"; "My parents now know that I do take my work seriously and that I can be creative sometimes"; "The thing that surprised me most is that she really liked it."

Most of you seemed to respond very positively to the experience of having your parents and/or others in your family read your writing folders.

Please take a few minutes now and respond to the following questions about your experience.

- What do you think your parents learned about you as a writer as a result of their reading your folders and discussing them with you?

- What did you learn about yourself as a writer as a result of your discussion with your parents?

- What surprised you most about the discussion?

- What suggestions do you have that might improve your discussion with your parents about your writing?

FIGURE 5.4 Student Response to Parent Reflection on Portfolios

Although no other collections of students' work were sent home formally to parents, it was apparent that during the rest of the year, parents had become part of the process for a number of students. They would mention that they "asked my mom" or "asked my dad" when explaining why they made changes. With the enlargement of the students' circle of readers, they began to understand that writing is a social process and needs input from different kinds of readers if it is to grow and flourish.

The Variability of Judgment

The experience of Howard and her students illustrates how the use of portfolios extends the meaning of assessment. The students' own assessment of their work now affects their grade, since the information from the portfolio is the basis for their grade. They are being trained in making choices for which they will be held responsible, and they are assessed in the progress they make as a result of that training. Furthermore, everyone involved in the process—students, teachers, and parents—experiences the variability of judgment, and they are not bothered by it.

This is important. The psychometric community has influenced the perception of educational evaluation so strongly that a judgment, expressed in a number or grade, is expected to be universally valid and reliable. It should be "right" in all circumstances and for everybody. It takes a little reflection to realize that education is alone as a social institution in requiring this of judgments. In most other arenas, we accept a range of opinions: critics of movies, plays, books, music, are not expected to agree absolutely. Because of the historical development of education in the United States, (to be sketched briefly in chapter 7), we expect a different standard of assessment than is normal in the rest of our lives. The portfolio process helps to remove the threat of different judgments, and therefore connects education to the real world again.

VERMONT'S STATEWIDE ASSESSMENT

Vermont had no tradition of statewide testing at all when it began developing its statewide assessment system in 1988. Like Connecticut and California, however, it recognized the crucial interdependence of teaching, learning, and assessment. Vermont developed a "Vision of a Third-Century Vermont School" in a series of focus sessions throughout the state. The vision sees the school as the focus of a learning community:

> School is no longer part-time, but a year-round opportunity to learn and relearn. School is not one place but a set of relationships among most of the individuals in the community, some of whom are teaching and some of whom are learning. . . . The teachers themselves are students of a very demanding profession. . . . Much of the leadership for the educational programs comes from teachers. They work together in teams. The teachers and administrators are constantly changing parts of the school, amplifying things that work, dropping things that don't.[9]

The Vermont assessment is an example of multiple evaluation; no single form of assessment is burdened with the responsibility of judging a student or a program alone. The technique has much to recommend it if it is used as a comprehensive evaluation at well-spaced, fairly long intervals rather than as an additive process.

The assessment of progress toward Vermont's vision will take the form of a tripartite assessment beginning in mathematics and writing at grades 4 and 8. Pilot tests took place in Spring 1991, and the program will be implemented fully in 1993. The three parts of the assessment are standard tests in mathematics and writing, which all students will take; portfolios of work in each subject;[10] and a "best piece" of work selected by the student in each subject. The uniform assessment in mathematics consists of multiple-choice and open-ended problems and uses items from the National Assessment of Educational Progress in order to compare Vermont's mathematics learning with that of the rest of the nation.

As in Connecticut and California, teachers are at the center of the process. They have served on Assessment Leadership Committees in both subjects, have piloted the assessments, and will participate in group grading for the writing sample and the "best piece" in both writing and mathematics. The portfolios will be evaluated by teachers in a pyramid of sampling in order to establish a statewide standard.

In early May 1991, a school's grade 4 portfolios in mathematics and writing were graded as a whole (not just their component parts) by the teachers under a team leader, using the group grading process. Team leaders then met later in May at a regional center and rescored a random 5 percent sample of their schools' portfolios (mixed so that no teachers scored portfolios from their own school). Next, at the state level, representatives of each region brought a 5 percent sample of their region's papers and scored them again. By this process, a statewide standard was established and then communicated to the state's teachers by examples of portfolios representing degrees of accomplishment so that teachers will know what standards they are shooting for.

When teachers score the portfolios, they can judge the quality of a school's program. In the writing assessment, they can tell whether students have been taught the writing process so they can develop self-assessment skills; in the mathematics portion, they will be able to determine whether the students have been encouraged to conjecture, explore, look for patterns, and try a variety of approaches.

The state reviews of the portfolios are intended to be used for program evaluation, although the state department of education is encouraging their use routinely and is offering professional development workshops to mathematics and language arts teachers to help them understand the power of portfolios. The results will be reported as a narrative summary of a school's achievement rather than as a list of scores. The results of the portfolio and "best piece" evaluations will be combined with the results of the standardized test in order to give a comprehensive picture of Vermont students' achievements in mathematics and writing.

The mathematics portfolios will be assessed against stated criteria in task performance and problem solving, mathematical communication, and mathematical empowerment (disposition toward mathematics—how confident the student feels about using mathematics). These three abilities are highlighted by the NCTM's *Curriculum and Evaluation Standards for School Mathematics*. Figure 5.5 contains an example of how the components of problem solving have been defined, so that achievement can be described in several ways. Figure 5.5B describes each of the major categories applied to the seven examples of mathematical work provided (in 1991) by Vermont fourth and eighth graders. Note the difference in attention paid to portfolio contents as opposed to a multiple-choice item: a bubble is either right or wrong, and that's all there is to it. Each of seven portfolio pieces can be rated from 1 at the low end, to 4 at the high end. The kinds of activity are noted at the far left, and on the right

Student: _____ ID Number: _____ School: _____ Grade: _____ Date: _____ Rater: _____	A1 Understanding of Task SOURCES OF EVIDENCE • Explanation of task • Reasonableness of approach • Correctness of response leading to inference of understanding	A2 How – Quality of Approaches/Procedures SOURCES OF EVIDENCE • Demonstrations • Descriptions (oral or written) • Drafts, scratch work, etc.	A3 Why – Decisions Along the Way SOURCES OF EVIDENCE • Changes in approach • Explanations (oral or written) • Validation of final solution • Demonstration
ENTRY 1 Title: _____ P I A O Puzzle Investigation Application Other			
ENTRY 2 Title: _____ P I A O Puzzle Investigation Application Other			
ENTRY 3 Title: _____ P I A O Puzzle Investigation Application Other			
ENTRY 4 Title: _____ P I A O Puzzle Investigation Application Other			
ENTRY 5 Title: _____ P I A O Puzzle Investigation Application Other			
ENTRY 6 Title: _____ P I A O Puzzle Investigation Application Other			
ENTRY 7 Title: _____ P I A O Puzzle Investigation Application Other			
OVERALL RATINGS →	**UNDERSTANDING OF TASK** FINAL RATING [1] Totally misunderstood [2] Partially understood [3] Understood [4] Generalized, applied, extended	**HOW – QUALITY OF APPROACHES/ PROCEDURES** FINAL RATING [1] Inappropriate or unworkable approach/procedure [2] Appropriate approach/procedure some of the time [3] Workable approach/procedure [4] Efficient or sophisticated approach/ procedure	**WHY – DECISIONS ALONG THE WAY** FINAL RATING [1] No evidence of reasoned decision-making [2] Reasoned decision-making possible [3] Reasoned decisions/adjustments inferred with certainty [4] Reasoned decisions/adjustments shown/explicated

COMMENTS:

FIGURE 5.5A Vermont Mathematics Portfolio: Profile Worksheet

A4 What – Outcomes of Activities	B1 Language of Mathematics	B2 Mathematical Representations	B3 Clarity of Presentation	CONTENT TALLIES
SOURCES OF EVIDENCE • Solutions • Extensions – observations, connections, applications, syntheses, generalizations, abstractions	**SOURCES OF EVIDENCE** • Terminology • Notation/symbols	**SOURCES OF EVIDENCE** • Graphs, tables, charts • Models • Diagrams • Manipulatives	**SOURCES OF EVIDENCE** • Audio/video tapes (or transcripts) • Written work • Teacher interviews/observations • Journal entries • Student comments on cover sheet • Student self-assessment	Number Sense – Whole No./Fractions (4) Number Relationships/No. Theory (8) Operations/Place Value (4) Operations (8)
				Estimation (4/8)
				Patterns/Relationships (4) Patterns/Functions (8)
				Algebra (8)
				Geometry/Spatial Sense (4/8)
				Measurement (4/8)
				Statistics/Probability (4/8)
				TASK CHARACTERISTICS

WHAT – OUTCOMES OF ACTIVITIES	LANGUAGE OF MATHEMATICS	MATHEMATICAL REPRESENTATIONS	CLARITY OF PRESENTATION	EMPOWERMENT COMMENTS
FINAL RATING [1] Solution without extensions [2] Solution with observations [3] Solution with connections or application(s) [4] Solution with synthesis, generalization, or abstraction	**FINAL RATING** [1] No or inappropriate use of mathematical language [2] Appropriate use of mathematical language some of the time [3] Appropriate use of mathematical language most of the time [4] Use of rich, precise, elegant, appropriate mathematical language	**FINAL RATING** [1] No use of mathematical representation(s) [2] Use of mathematical representation(s) [3] Accurate and appropriate use of mathematical representation(s) [4] Perceptive use of mathematical representation(s)	**FINAL RATING** [1] Unclear (e.g., disorganized, incomplete, lacking detail) [2] Some clear parts [3] Mostly clear [4] Clear (e.g., well organized, complete, detailed)	Motivation Flexibility Risk Taking Reflection Confidence Perseverance Curiosity/Interest Value Math

A1. *Understanding of the task.* In order to solve a problem you must understand the task. Understanding can include an appreciation of relevant information, being able to interpret the problem, understanding key questions that push for clarification.

A2. *Quality of Approaches, Procedures, Strategies.* Most problems have multiple ways in which they can be solved including, among others, simple guessing and checking, systematic listing, using some form of manipulative, using Venn diagrams, using grids to record possible combinations, using formulas, or applying algorithms.

A3. *Why the Student Made the Choices Along the Way.* Good problem solvers are constantly checking their assumptions, reflecting on decisions, analyzing the effectiveness of strategies, checking for exceptions, and verifying results in other ways. These skills may be the most critical components of good problem solving.

A4. *What Decisions, Findings, Conclusions, Observations, Generalizations the Student Reached.* Mathematics is no longer simply about finding the answer to an exercise. The issue is not what did you find, but what does it mean.

B1. *Language of Mathematics.* Mathematics is a language and students gain power in their ability to communicate with one another as they grow in their facility with the language. The goal is to help students become more proficient in the use of mathematical vocabulary, notation, symbols, and structure to represent ideas and to describe relationships.

B2. *Mathematical Representations.* Beyond terminology and notation, communication power in mathematics comes from being able to communicate information through graphs, charts, tables, diagrams, models and some types of manipulatives. Visual information often communicates information more powerfully than pages of text.

B3. *Clarity of Presentation.* The presentation of ideas is at the core of this criterion and it is an essential element of portfolio based tasks. The importance of oral and written communication skills demands that they be assessed. Students must be able to organize their thoughts and present them to others in a format that is organized, coherent, and sufficiently detailed to allow another to follow the student's thinking and conclusions.

FIGURE 5.5B Vermont Mathematics Portfolio: Explanation of Criteria the portfolio readers make notations of the math skills embedded in these activities. Students are likely to take a serious approach to learning math if adults spend this much time and thought evaluating their products.

The "overall ratings" chart at the bottom is a summation of the student's mathematical achievements. Looking at a sample of a school's portfolios and their scores on each category, the teachers will be able to target their teaching toward comprehensive mathematical abilities.

It was to be expected that the first batch of portfolios scored in May 1991 would demonstrate the need for change in teaching. In fact, 40 percent of the portfolios could not be scored on the profile worksheet because the work submitted consisted of conventional problems and worksheets, not puzzles, investigations, or applications. This is not bad news. We should expect the first examples of performance assessment to reveal clearly where improvement is needed, because the assessments are designed to do so.

The final report on a school or school district's performance will be in two parts: one reviewing and assessing portfolios and the other summarizing the assessment of the "best pieces," which will be scored individually against a scoring guide worked out at the state level by the teachers' leadership group. These reports from all over the state will be aggregated at the state level and also used as the basis for Vermont School Report Day. In each school district, the community will gather on a fall day to hear reports on local schools' progress and also to visit classes and see how children are learning. It is the idea of the New England town meeting applied to education.

A NATIONAL MODEL:
ADVANCED PLACEMENT STUDIO ART

Vermont's mathematics assessment is still developmental and may go through some modifications as it is pilot- and field-tested. At the other extreme, there is a portfolio assessment established on the national level that has been operating successfully for almost twenty years: the College Board's Advanced Placement Studio Art examination, called a "portfolio evaluation."

The Advanced Placement (AP) Program was instituted by the College Board in 1955; "Its examinations are designed and administered by the Educational Testing Service. The Advanced Placement Program is intended to give students appropriate credit and placement in college on the basis of satisfactory performance in college-level examinations taken while in high school. The examinations are scored by groups of university and college faculty, with some high school teachers, so that one of the results of the AP program is a penetration of the school-university barrier. Within the next few years, the AP program may become the model for university admissions procedures; an unspoken and so far unconsidered consequence of the switch to performance assessment in schools must be a change in what is acceptable for admissions.

In 1990 there were twenty-nine Advanced Placement examinations in fifteen disciplines, from art through physics and Spanish. All of these examinations, with the exception of studio art, consist of a multiple-choice portion and a free-response portion. Some, such as music and foreign languages, include the use of audiotapes for both examination materials and students' responses. Even biology, chemistry, and physics require the writing of essays in the free-response portion.

The scores are scaled from 5, for highest achievement, down to 1, at the lowest. Postsecondary institutions subscribing to the AP program usually accept scores of 3 and up as evidence that the student has mastered the material, and in many cases this means that students are not required to take a comparable course in college. Theoretically, a student who was successful on sufficient AP examinations could enter college or university as a sophomore and thus reduce both the time and expense needed to get the bachelor's degree. The AP examinations therefore provide a practical option for ambitious, hard-working students (frequently intending to become doctors) who want to cut the costs of a college education. Such students frequently spend their junior and senior high school years taking AP courses.

Studio art was added to the AP program in two stages: the general portfolio in 1972 and the drawing portfolio in 1980. The process is not called an examination but a portfolio evaluation. There is no multiple-choice or written portion.

Students submit three subportfolios within a portfolio, according to whether they are entering their work in the drawing portfolio or general portfolio evaluation. The drawing portfolio must contain six original works no larger than 16 by 20 inches; as many as twenty slides in a transparent plastic pack on a single theme concentration); and from fourteen to twenty slides in a plastic pack illustrating breadth, with no more than three slides each from twenty categories—such as, for example, use of perspective, basic geometric forms in different spatial positions, integration of human figures with backgrounds, works utilizing Cubist space, and studies of wrapped objects. A general portfolio is much the same, although only four works are required in the original work portion, films and videotapes may be submitted in the concentration section, and the breadth categories are drawing, use of color, design, and sculpture, with eight slides required in drawing and four each in the other categories.

Assessment is divided into the three sections, and eighteen judges look at all three in both divisions in the course of a week's work. The judges assign scores separately to each part, and the Educational Testing Service weights and scales them to produce the 5 through 1 ratings sent to the student and the college.

The logistics of scoring any of the AP exams are formidable since this is a national program. The numbers of examinations submitted have been growing since 1955, reaching 464,000 for all subjects in 1989. Furthermore, the scoring and reporting of ratings have to be completed between May, when students take the examinations, and August, when colleges need to record the grades so that students can be placed appropriately. Teams of readers (the evaluators) assigned to each of the twenty-nine examinations meet for a week of grading on a university campus, usually on the East Coast in order to remain close to the Educational Testing Service offices in Princeton, New Jersey. Approximately 60 percent of the readers are college faculty who teach the courses that AP examinations would replace and 40 percent are high school teachers. The high school teachers can be invited to serve as readers only after students in their classes have been taking AP examinations for three years.

Judging Art Portfolios

The main issue in studio art portfolio evaluation is the sheer physical bulk of 4,500 portfolios, all submitted in standard manila portfolios mailed to the participating schools by the Educational Testing Service. The material must be displayed all at once, since the group—not the individual works—is to be evaluated. And how do you look at a plastic pages of slides?

The answer is a gymnasium for the original works, a room lined with light tables for the collections of slides, and a small army of young people with strong arms and quick legs. The gymnasium is filled with tables lined up across the floor with a central aisle. On each table, the six drawings or four pictures by each candidate are laid out with about 2 feet of space between each. Identifying material accompanies them. The rows are divided into threes, right across the room, and three readers are assigned to each three rows. Each looks independently at every portfolio in the three rows, so that each portfolio gets three grades. Disagreements beyond a certain point are resolved by the chief reader, who is always a college or university faculty member.

As soon as the three readers have finished their three rows, the helpers repack the original works into the appropriate portfolios and set out new ones. It will take two days for the entire set of 4,500 to get on to the tables, be judged, and be repacked. The process moves so efficiently that it sometimes looks like a wave motion. There is an air of concentration, even reverence, in the huge space. If anything has to be said, it is whispered. Most of the time there is only the sound of the air-conditioning system and the soft tread of the readers as they move along, pause, write, and move a few more steps.

Meanwhile, in other rooms, some judges are hunched over the lighted screens looking at the concentration and breadth collections. The collections are viewed twice, with reconciliation if the grades are too far apart. To avoid staleness and declining sharpness in judging, the readers alternate between looking at the general and the drawing portfolios, the concentration and breadth slides.

At the end of the judging, after grades have finally been assigned, the portfolios, with their contents restored, are returned to the students.

This system, so efficient now, has evolved over the years. At one time, the original works were displayed on the floor, since there seemed no other large space, but the placement resulted in backaches for everyone—readers and helpers alike. Viewing pictures from head height is also unjust to them as art. Even looking at them on tables is not perfect, although it is the way in which teachers and students see them most often in the course of art instruction. For a while after floor viewing was abandoned, the portfolios were piled on tables, and the readers took out the contents of each, reviewed them, and put them back. The process was fraught with danger to the artwork and to the reader's temper; the artworks slipped off the tables on to the floor, and the reader dropped papers trying to retrieve them.

Criteria for Judging Studio Art

At the beginning of the grading of the art portfolios is a standard-setting session. A number of portfolios are put before the assembled readers, roughly illustrating all the possible scores. Looking at the variety in the general examination (not the drawing, which is a little more limited) at first inspires despair. How can you compare a collection of four photographs with four oils, or collages, or Sister Corita–like serigraphs? There are book illustrations, drawings in all media, even paper constructions that open like books with illustrations on each page. The first-time viewer panics at the thought of judging the quality of the portfolios. After a few minutes' discussion, however, the task becomes much easier than it looks at first for experienced art teachers to assign a numerical grade. According to Walter Askin, professor of art at the California State University Los Angeles, who was chief reader in the early 1980s, "There are more things that join us together than separate us. You can make those judgments as accurately as you can in mathematics or in writing or in any other subjects. These other subjects frequently have much more difficulty than we do in the visual arts in agreeing on standards."

Readers must choose not what they like but what should be expected of college-level accomplishment. Askin pointed to the many different factors involved in making the evaluations; for example, there may be formal factors—texture, design, technical mastery of the medium—in relation to subject matter, but sometimes there is no subject matter, so the formal elements have to carry the load. Essentially the judgment is made on the basis of experience. "What you're really after is a mind at work, an interested, live, thinking being. You want to see engagement. Recognition of it comes from long experience, and you intuit it." Askin pointed out that this is also true in other subject matters—an assertion that would chill the blood of psychometricians who would like the criteria to be explicit, overt, reliable, and related to the grade one for one.

Askin continued; "You get a sense for copied work, a sense when there's engagement, when inspiration, belief, direct involvement are present or absent." He believes that teachers make all the difference: "Sometimes I thought we were grading teachers as much as students." Some teachers bring out the best in their students; other teachers get good results, but their students are engaged strictly on a technical level. The teacher will assign failsafe assignments, which the student performs perfectly. But the thinking is the teacher's, not the student's, and the result is lifeless.

"A bright mind can learn to paint and draw well," says Askin. "The best student artists I saw probably became surgeons, because many students take all the AP courses they can, including studio art, in order to cut a year out of college. Students flourish where there are good high school teachers."

The types—the portfolios chosen to exemplify each grade—remain on display at the side of the room as standards for comparison when raters get stymied. Disagreements among raters are handled by making them as open as possible. Askin worked on the principle that it's better to see disagreement than keep it hidden. The group of readers talks through problem cases, although there are fewer of those than might be expected. When disagreements arise, more experienced readers are asked to work with their colleagues and compare the portfolio at issue with the types.

In June 1990, a walk among the tables produced the impression that a number of portfolios in the general examination had three good works and one poor one. Askin said that the unbalanced portfolio is just as common in the opposite direction and no more common than two good and two less accomplished. As with all other qualitative grading, there is a variety of ways to earn a single score.

In the concentration section, raters look at the plastic packs propped against the light and then check what the student has written. Students choose their own concentration and must explain it on a standard form; they must describe the sources of their ideas, the influences on them, and the technical assistance they received while working on the project. Examples of concentrations from the 1990 general portfolio were a collection of slides of jewelry designed in Japanese style; a series of copies of famous depictions of women; explorations of various media, such as drawing with a pen, using color entirely without drawing, or using texture as the design; and variations on a theme, such as a discotheque or the three kinds of Greek columns.

The breadth collection is assigned a separate grade for each of the categories required. It is intended to show how the students have stretched themselves beyond the medium or material with which they are naturally successful. It may be that the breadth collection shows the effects of teaching, as opposed to inborn talent, although this would need careful research. In the general portfolio, students do not choose their own media but must submit examples of drawing, color, design, and sculpture, all carefully prescribed. The sculpture submission, for example, must consist of two views of two different sculptures.

Here perhaps more than in the other two sections it becomes obvious that there are multiple paths to a single grade. The best breadth collection would show some level of accomplishment in all four areas, but that is rare. One or two may be outstanding and the sculpture pedestrian, let us say. Or there may be a pervasive lack of balance in all areas. The qualities sought are necessarily on a high level of abstraction to accommodate the different media.

The three sections of a student's portfolio are weighted to arrive at a maximum composite number. The chief reader's job is to convert these numbers into the reporting scale for AP examinations.

Why Is It Accepted?

The Advanced Placement studio art examination exemplifies solving the logistical problems of a national performance assessment and at the same time doing justice to the nature of the material. It is the only national portfolio examination and the only portfolio examination I know of that attempts a single grade for the whole portfolio, as opposed to grading the contents individually. (Vermont will be evaluating the whole of its writing portfolios but has established no track record yet.) If subjective grading is as big a threat as administrators and legislators say, then the grading of AP studio art should be controversial. But it does not seem to be.

The apparent acceptance of the grading scheme may be attributed to a number of factors. One is the prestige of the College Board and the Educational Testing Service. Whatever method of grading and scoring they use, it seems not to be questioned. The same phenomenon affects the acceptance of the Scholastic Aptitude Test (SAT). Despite the facts that the SAT is unrelated to curriculum, tends to correlate with socioeconomic status rather than educational accomplishment, and does not clearly predict college performance, it is an icon of American education, and the Educational Testing Service is identified with it.

A second factor is widespread ignorance of the methods of educational assessment. It is not only the general public that lacks knowledge; members of the educational community also do not know the meaning of "multiple choice," "norm referenced," "criterion referenced," "holistic grading," "performance assessment," and the other jargon of educational evaluation. This is no one's fault. Historically functions in American education have been rigidly divided. Teachers did not expect to know the technical details of assessment; they expected them to be taken care of by test publishers and psychometric experts, who would be contacted by the school district's administrators. The administrators, in turn, trusted the test publishers, and especially the doyen of the corps, the Educational Testing Service. Thus, it is not surprising that questions about the grading of AP studio art do not seem to arise.

Third, the nature of art is not conducive to objective evaluation. It is impossible to imagine a multiple-choice test for AP studio art. For this examination, the Educational Testing Service has refined the jury method of judging works of art, where collective judgment substitutes for objectivity. The jury method is widely accepted in other fields—sports, ballet, music, and drama competitions, for example—and is also the accepted means of judging art competitions.

The final reason that there seems to be no opposition to AP studio art's portfolio assessment is a chilling one: art is not important in American education. Jack Bledsoe, an art teacher at Walter Johnson High School in Montgomery County, Maryland, referred to art in passing as "one of the minor subjects" in high school. Since the toughening of graduation standards in states and school districts, with their demands for more units in English, mathematics, science, and social studies, there is no time for electives, and art has been squeezed out. It does not seem essential, and as workplace skills receive increasing emphasis, its plight is likely to worsen. Because art is considered a frill, how it is assessed apparently does not matter. This is a sad state of affairs, not the least because it hampers the widespread application of the portfolio method of assessment. If AP evaluated writing, mathematics, biology, or physics by reading students' portfolios, it would be regarded as a model to be followed across the country.

For these reasons, there is no controversy about the grading of AP studio art. Alice Sims-Gunzenhauser, the ETS coordinator for AP studio art, reported that she has responded to perhaps twenty telephone calls about the 1990 examination, not a high rate of dissatisfaction. Some calls were from parents complaining that their children were penalized or disqualified because the teacher had not given students the right instructions.

All students taking AP examinations are asked to complete a response form sent to each student with the examination. Most answers question a single item but rarely dispute results. In unusual circumstances, an examination will be rescored, but this is extremely difficult with AP studio art because the portfolio would have to be recalled after it has been sent back, and there is a risk that it might be tampered with before resubmission. One student who had received an art scholarship was upset at receiving a 1 and insisted on a rescoring, no matter how much trouble it caused. The result of a laborious process was a 2.

Effect on Students and Teachers

My conversations with teachers and students, whether the latter earned a 5, a 3, or a 2, revealed no dissatisfaction with the grading process. Some teachers are eager to join the annual panel of readers, but others are so busy with teaching and their own lives as artists that they prefer to trust their colleagues in colleges and other high schools.

The art teachers I observed and talked with had striking confidence in their ability to motivate, manage, and cajole adolescents and awaken them to their own potential. Teachers and students were focused on the experience of preparing for the examination, showing the now-familiar pattern of responding to the assessment with appropriate teaching. They saw preparation for AP studio art as the students' responsibility. The teachers had an easy relationship with their students; they were capable of informality and even affection, but they did not indulge lack of discipline. The teachers see their teaching as forming character. Angry at one boy's persistent absences, one teacher told him, "Just because you have an excused absence doesn't mean you're excused from the work." The student was asked to come in after school for three days to make up the time, a condition harsher than the school's absence policy.

The teachers believe, with Walter Askin, that art can be taught; inborn talent is nothing without effort. Talent will add to a person's ability to judge what has to be done to improve a product, but talent also needs instruction. They share Askin's belief that a bright mind can learn the techniques of art, and all used a technique they believe is essential to the development of artistic ability: they teach their students to criticize each other's work constructively. They make the class into a critical circle for the benefit of the students. In the classes I observed, these criticism sessions are so well designed and the students learn to communicate so skillfully that the students are disappointed in the quality of criticism when they go to college or university. "Please teach these students how to critique," wrote one former student from college to Jack Bledsoe, the Montgomery County, Maryland, art teacher.

Bledsoe paces the students' production of their portfolio items so that they do not run into a time crunch during the last few weeks of preparation. They must have twelve slides done for their concentration or breadth section by Christmas. He also recommends that they save a few dollars a month toward the $65 fee. He insists that students choose their own concentration topic and explain it coherently: "That's when they hate me the most. I won't do it for them. They whine and cry until they've got it figured out." Some of the concentrations his students have chosen (and successfully defended) include diving figures, architectural designs, shadows, and night scenes.

Bledsoe will not predict his students' scores and finds he cannot do so. He is not present during the final assembly of the portfolios and their packing into the oversized folders for transport. He points out that other AP teachers (such as his wife Donna Bledsoe who reads AP English examinations for the Educational Testing Service) can do nothing to help while their students are taking the examination. The final selection of the portfolio's contents is equivalent to the written examination, so he leaves it entirely to the students.

Studying art for the AP assessment has almost therapeutic effects on some students. One of Bledsoe's students preparing for the AP portfolio assessment in 1991 is a paraplegic. Bledsoe has cut down the scale of his productions from the usual 16 by 20 inches so that the student can physically manage them. An art therapist comes into his class at intervals, and Bledsoe discusses with her the violent images that some students use repeatedly in their work, but he does not pry or probe. He does not comment when a student draws his girlfriend in a bathrobe or when syringes and fat drops of black blood appear compulsively in a student's work.

Students in AP studio art classes generally refute the current impression that high school students do not care about their work. When provided with something to care about for themselves, an appropriate environment, and a teacher they want to please, they rise to the highest expectations set for them.

PORTFOLIOS: POTENTIAL AND PRECAUTIONS

Portfolios are the most flexible form of performance assessment. They are easy to set up because they require as little or as much as you want to put into the project. A portfolio project can be put in place by a teacher working alone, a number of teachers within a school, a whole district, or a state or a national program, as in the case of AP studio art. They can be adapted to whatever purpose seems important, provided that the purpose is clear at the outset. And the amount of information they can provide about teaching and learning approaches infinity. The surface has only been scratched so far.

A portfolio packs a tremendous punch in terms of turning around student attitudes, teachers' ways of working, and, ultimately, the school's understanding of its function. Like other performance assessments, but with much less fanfare because it is not cumbersome, the portfolio can help bring about a change in the model of U.S. education.

Portfolios can fulfill any and all of the purposes for educational assessment. The success of the AP studio art program disarms criticism. The fact that the results are delivered in the same form as other AP grades possibly conceals this success but also argues in favor of the essential soundness of the procedure. The Educational Testing Service is renowned for its psychometric rigor and would not countenance an assessment that did not meet its standards.

But portfolios should be handled with care, precisely because they seem to be all things to all situations. If used for accountability, their production must be standardized, and there must be careful attention to the reliability of readers. The charge of subjectivity, of wanton and unchecked personal judgment, hovers over portfolios. The next chapter will focus on subjectivity in the context of teacher judgments and will suggest ways in which subjectivity can be both honored and modified.

6

Teachers and Assessment:
Privilege and Responsibility

The tests go from part to whole, and our programs go from
whole to part. Those tests are basically for basals, and to
assess these kids that have learned whole language by
basals—it makes no sense at all.

—South Brunswick, New Jersey, teacher[1]

In a two-part television series on educational assessment aired in
February 1990, a physics teacher in a school belonging to the
Coalition of Essential Schools is shown assessing a student in physics
by listening and watching as the boy describes a body in motion,
drawing graphs on the blackboard. The scene contrasted vividly with
a paper-and-pencil multiple-choice test and provoked the response
from a number of viewers: "What's so new about that? Teachers
have been informally assessing their students like that forever." Exactly the point. But why don't we accept their judgments?

Teachers' assessments form by far the greatest proportion of assessment experienced by students, but it is not uniformly of high
quality and is not standardized. To earn public confidence as a vital
component (perhaps the basis) of a high-quality assessment system,
teachers' judgments have to be supported by evidence and attain
some comparability.

Educational assessment is never free of judgment, no matter what form the assessment takes—a hard truth for the public and education professionals to accept. Tests bought from companies that supply the material and then report the results in neat numerical rows and columns seem untouched by human judgment. In these cases, it is convenient to forget that judgment was used in the choice of the items and that judgment decided which bubble would count and which would not, and hence what the score would be. The people exercising the judgment are too far out of the picture to have faces and personalities, so it is easy to act as if they do not exist.

When judgment happens on site or close by, it becomes suspect. The education community has a moral responsibility to enlighten the public about the relationship between judgment and assessment and explain what is involved in a responsible judgment on a child's achievement and potential. Two Illinois researchers say; "One of the biggest problems we will have to address is how to get the general public to understand the limitations of test scores (and assessment data generally); at present, the American public is unfortunately all too credulous about standardized test scores."[2]

The problem is especially acute in the perceptions of some minority groups. An African-American school board member in California had the following to say at a conference where her school district was being urged to adopt performance assessment:

> The reality is the public doesn't believe us. Most of us are from a test-oriented culture and our minds compare. We don't think about differences, we think about better, and less than. . . . With a normed test you know that some subjectivity has gone into the development of the instrument, but then in the final result you know what the answer is. When you start talking about some of the assessment you want—portfolios—it's all subjective. It begins subjective and it ends subjective. . . . I want to know, is this A or B? I want to know, is my child above the fiftieth percentile? Is my child at grade level? Can my child read?[3]

Large-scale assessments for at least two of the three major purposes for assessment—deciding students' destinies and accountability—have to be reported in numbers or by letter grades, as this school board member says. Most of the reasons are practical, based on the uses to which assessments are put: admissions officers in selective colleges and universities have to depend on scores, public accountability requires numbers as a shorthand guide and for comparison, and federal financial allocations, from Chapter 1 through scholarships, function according to cutoff points. For elementary and secondary schools, the fact that the postsecondary sector is implacable in its dependence on numbers for selective admissions—SATs, ACTs, GPAs, first, second, or thirteenth in the class—makes numbers a practical imperative. The barriers between educational sectors are generally permeable only to numbers. In the late 1960s and early 1970s, the University of California at Santa Cruz experimented with narrative assessments but had to modify its practice when its graduates found they could not gain admission to graduate schools without numerical grades.

And there is psychological and philosophical justification for the use of numbers. The human psyche has a hunger for ordinality, for ranking and ordering. We assign numbers in order to rank, and we rank compulsively. Organizing by prioritizing is nothing more than grading importance and urgency: I am going to do this first, that second, and the other third because that is how important each is to me. Attempts to disguise this ordinal passion are usually doomed, as the school board member made clear.

BEING CAREFUL WITH NUMBERS

Judging is a teacher's professional responsibility. Whether this essay is a 3 or a 4 or whether this answer has enough in it to make it acceptable—a 1—or not quite enough—a 0—are questions demanding judgment informed by expertise, understanding of the reasons for the assessment, and knowledge of the use that will be made of the results. Numbers constitute the external sign that a judgment has been made according to a value system.

While conceding all this, we still have to remember that the discreteness of numbers can be cruel. They are only as good as our intentions in using them. Numbers are misused, for example, when they result in tracking students into remedial and vocational classes and therefore out of the academic core.[4] The National Commission on Testing and Public Policy cites a particularly tragic case in its 1990 report, *From Gatekeeper to Gateway*; a Hispanic woman was prevented from becoming a teacher because she failed one test by one point—this in a country that has too few Hispanic teachers for a burgeoning population of Hispanic students.[5]

Misuse is always present as a possibility, and there have to be safeguards as well as flexibility. But the school board member's remarks seem to reveal a trust in numbers that errs in the other direction. If numbers are reported, her remarks imply that she is satisfied; she does not inquire whether the process that produced the numbers is deleterious to authentic learning. She seems to imply that a number on a reading test is a more reliable indicator of children's ability to read than observing them or listening to them read aloud.

The widespread acceptance of test scores as indicators of quality rests on the same assumption. Schools are judged (and houses sold by real estate agents) in one school district rather than another on the basis of test scores. But these numbers do not mean that children can read, write, think, or apply what they have learned; they mean that the children got high scores on those tests.

It is unreasonable to expect that this blind faith in numbers alone will yield to argument or persuasion about the poor quality of teaching driven by multiple-choice testing, despite what researchers like Carol Ascher say: "These standardized tests have so driven the curriculum that they limit what teachers teach. The practice is especially notable in low-income schools where drilling was always a more prevalent form of instruction."[6]

The school board member and the public at large will have to experience the effects of better teaching and learning by seeing that children benefit. Convincing them can be hastened by including community leaders and parents in the process of change, as the Pittsburgh teacher did by sending home the students' language arts portfolios; as the Bozeman, Montana, school has done by including parents as interviewers in their art assessment; and as the "We the People . . ." competition has done by asking community members to act as judges.

The problem can also be alleviated by ceasing to depend on a single test for assessments with important consequences. As I have advocated throughout this book, multiple assessments provide fairer judgments on which to base a student's future. Even minority parents who distrust a teacher's judgment should not object to a combination of grades, portfolios, and scores on performance assessments (some of them collective) in addition to multiple-choice tests.

Teachers who participate in the assessment process increase their professionalism. Public confidence in one's judgment is a professional's expectation; it is hard to imagine doctors, lawyers, or public accountants functioning without respect for their judgment. In the case of teachers, the respect has to be earned.

One vital consequence of trusting teachers' judgments has been largely overlooked: the objective of all educational evaluation must be to produce students who can assess themselves. They cannot do this unless they see teachers judging responsibly, since students learn from their teachers as models. At the moment, students experience their teachers' judgments in the classroom but then see them pushed aside in favor of judgments external to the school—published tests, the SAT, the ACT. If we want students to become adults capable of assessing their own performances as workers and citizens, we must support the judgments that teach them self-assessment—those of their teachers—and not overrule them.

THE PRIMARY LANGUAGE RECORD

Teachers need ways of establishing their authority as evaluators of their own students in their own classrooms and having that judgment count for more than a classroom grade. One way is to bolster judgment with as much verifiable information as possible, typically by preparing a written record. Falsification may still be an issue, but if records are made on the spot while the student activity is going on, there is less opportunity for deception, whether intentional or unconscious.

A number of elementary schools in the United States are experimenting with a formalized record developed in England called the Primary Language Record (or, in its across-the-curriculum expansion, the Primary Learning Record).[7] Currently this produces a narrative evaluation of students' progress, but experiments with some versions of the Primary Language Record are underway to devise a scale so that numbers can be assigned to stages of achievement. The purists (like those who believe that portfolios should be used for reflection, not assessment) will object that those who use educational evaluation should learn to read narrative assessments, but that does not work, for both practical and psychological reasons. The best we can expect in educational assessment is a combination of descriptive and numerical assessments. In looking at the Primary Language Record as a sensitive method of collecting rich and productive information about children's progress in literacy, I am not suggesting that it is necessarily preferable to performance assessments that produce numbers. I am describing it here as a model for increasing the value of teachers' judgments by supporting them with reliable information.

The essence of the Primary Language Record is a pair of forms, one of them a summary of the other (or others), that record a child's progress and experiences in developing literacy. Despite appearances from such a bald statement, this is not simply a bells-and-whistles version of a report card, or the records which are called "cumes" (for "cumulative records"). These forms are a means of capturing students' progress as it happens, strengthening teaching, and adjusting the instructional program to the child.

The Primary Language Record was developed in the schools of the Inner London Education Authority (ILEA) before its demise in 1989 and was extensively field-tested before it was formalized and published. The schools where it was tested and is now used routinely contain a mixture of children and languages that rivals the schools of Los Angeles (where as many as 100 languages are represented in the student body of Hollywood High School) or of New York City. The children in London schools have immigrated from parts of the old British Empire, although a surprisingly large number come from the Middle Eastern countries, also represented in American city schools.[8]

The Primary Language Record consists of two forms. One, on beige paper, has four pages, which are completed over a year. The second, a white form, also has four pages and is intended to produce the raw material for the beige form. Entitled "Observations and Samples," teachers use it to make notes as they observe the child's progress from kindergarten through elementary school. The beige form is the cumulative record that summarizes all the white forms filled out in the course of the school year but also includes interviews with the parents and the children themselves.

The White Form: Formative Assessment

The teachers use the white forms constantly during their teaching (figure 6.1). I have seen them reaching out almost automatically to their desks or into their pockets when they see something they especially want to record—perhaps a child who was apparently unaware of print picking up a book on her own and staring fascinated at the page, or two children cooperating to tap out a story on the classroom computer for the first time.

About three times a semester, the teacher listens to each child reading individually and fills out a checklist while the child is read-

Observations and Samples (Primary Language Record)

attach extra pages where needed

Name: **Year Group:**

1 Talking & listening: diary of observations

The diary below is for recording examples of the child's developing use of talk for learning and for interacting with others in English and/or other community languages.

Include different kinds of talk (e.g. planning an event, solving a problem, expressing a point of view or feelings, reporting on the results of an investigation, telling a story ...)

Note the child's experience and confidence in handling social dimensions of talk (e.g. initiating a discussion, listening to another contribution, qualifying former ideas, encouraging others ...)

The matrix sets out some possible contexts for observing talk and listening. Observations made in the diary can be plotted on the matrix to record the range of social and curriculum contexts sampled.

LEARNING CONTEXTS	SOCIAL CONTEXTS				
	pair	small group	child with adult	small/large group with adult	
collaborative reading and writing activities					
play, dramatic play, drama & storying					
environmental studies & historical research					
maths & science investigations					
design, construction, craft & art projects					

Dates	Observations and their contexts

© CLPE/ILEA 1988, 1989

FIGURE 6.1 White Form of the Primary Language Record

2 Reading and Writing: diary of observations
(reading and writing in English and/or other community languages)

Date	Reading
	Record observations of the child's development as a reader (including wider experiences of story) across a range of contexts.

	Writing
	Record observations of the child's development as a writer (including stories dictated by the child) across a range of contexts.

Figure 6.1 (Continued)

3 **Reading Samples** (reading in English and/or other community languages)
to include reading aloud and reading silently

Dates			
Title or book/text (fiction or information)			
Known/unknown text			
Sampling procedure used: informal assessment/running record/miscue analysis			
Overall impression of the child's reading: • confidence and degree of independence • involvement in the book/text • the way in which the child read the text aloud			
Strategies the child used when reading aloud: • drawing on previous experience to make sense of the book/text * playing at reading * using book language * reading the pictures * focusing on print (directionality, 1:1 correspondence, recognition of certain words) • using semantic/syntactic/grapho-phonic cues • predicting • self-correcting • using several strategies or over-dependent on one			
Child's response to the book/text: • personal response • critical response (understanding, evaluating, appreciating wider meanings)			
What this sample shows about the child's development as a reader. **Experiences/support needed to further development.**			

* *Early indicators that the child is moving into reading*

FIGURE **6.1** (Continued)

4 Writing Samples (writing in English and/or other community languages)
'Writing' to include children's earliest attempts at writing

Dates			
Context and background information about the writing: • how the writing arose • how the child went about the writing • whether the child was writing alone or with others • whether the writing was discussed with anyone while the child was working on it • kind of writing (e.g. list, letter, story, poem, personal writing, information writing) • complete piece of work/extract			
Child's own response to the writing.			
Teacher's response: • to the content of the writing • to the child's ability to handle this particular kind of writing • overall impression			
Development of spelling and conventions of writing.			
What this writing shows about the child's development as a writer: • how it fits into the range of the child's previous writing • experience/support needed to further development			

Please keep the writing with the sample sheet

FIGURE 6.1 (Continued)

ing. Also about three times a semester, the teacher examines a piece of writing by the child, fills out a checklist, and files the writing with the white form—in effect, a progress portfolio. The checklist for the reading sample requires the title and type of the book the child has chosen (the choice may be guided but never overruled) and the language the child will read in. If the teacher cannot read, say Bengali or Urdu, a community member or school aide listens to the child reading. A child in transition from the community language to English may try reading in English and, of course, will not be expected to attain as high a level as might be possible in the native language. The listener checks on the white form the assessment method to be used: informal assessment, "running record," or "miscue analysis"—techniques for recording how the child reads while the reading is in progress. The listener then records an overall impression of the child's reading: confidence and degree of independence, involvement in the reading, and the way in which the child read aloud.

The Primary Language Record is based on the whole language approach to reading, which centralizes meaning, even while using every device from phonics to pictures to help the child read. The whole language approach to literacy introduces children to the strategies that accomplished readers use. If you think about what you do when you do not understand a passage or an unknown word, you will probably find that you reread the passage, look back over a few pages to find a clue to the word's meaning in the context, look at an illustration, sound out the word and see if it sounds like another word you know, and if all else fails, look it up in a dictionary. Teachers using the whole language approach show children that they can use these strategies and model them for the children as they read stories aloud.

Miscue analysis and its derivative, the running record, provide teachers with symbols to mark against the text to record where the child is having difficulty. Miscue analyses and running records chart children's progress in learning reading strategies. For example, they distinguish between mistakes indicating that the child does not know what is going on in the book and those which show that the child is following the story but may not be decoding each word exactly. The distinction between these two situations can be seen in this example: if a child substitutes the word "home" for "house" in the sentence "he went into his house," the child understands the context and has decoded a single word incorrectly; if the child substitutes the word "horse," then the child doesn't know what is going on but has tried to decode each word.

The next series of questions on the white form focuses on these strategies: drawing on previous experience to make sense; using semantic, syntactic, or grapho-phonic clues; predicting; self-correcting; and using several strategies or trying only one. Very young children on the threshold of reading are observed for their ability to play at reading, "read" the pictures, or focus on print. The child's response to what has been read is noted, and the final item asks the teacher to summarize what the sample shows about the child's development as a reader and suggest the next steps.

When the white form is being used for these periodic assessments, it is kept in the teacher's lap while the child sits comfortably on an adjacent chair or pillow. The child is usually so absorbed in the book that the teacher's quick scribblings go unnoticed. The form restricts verbosity because the answer boxes are not big enough for more than one or two words. When the child's reading time is over, the teacher takes a few moments to fill out the final item.

Logistically, the teacher can give sustained attention to single children only if there is assistance in the classroom. English primary classrooms frequently contain as many as thirty-eight children, but each school can call on a corps of adults who function as aides, especially in communities where many different languages are spoken. In any case, the amount of time devoted to each child is a few minutes in the earliest grades and not more than 15 at even the highest elementary grade. The response to a writing sample does not have to be written during class time, although the form asks about the circumstances surrounding the composition of the piece (how the writing arose, whether the child worked alone or with others or talked about it during the writing), which require observation.

The other parts of the white form ask for dated observations on the child's talking and listening, reading, and writing. Again these are intended to be back-of-the-envelope notes, not elaborate or formal expositions.

The Beige Form: Summation

The beige form (figure 6.2) has three parts, to be completed at the beginning, middle, and end of a school year. The first part records not only the usual formal information but also the languages the

Primary Language Record

School	School Year

Name	DoB Summer born child ☐
	☐ Boy ☐ Girl

Languages understood	Languages read
Languages spoken	Languages written

Details of any aspects of hearing, vision or coordination affecting the child's language/literacy. Give the source and date of this information.	Names of staff involved with child's language and literacy development.

Part A To be completed during the Autumn Term

A1 Record of discussion between child's parent(s) and class teacher

Signed Parent(s) _____   Teacher _____

Date _____

A2 Record of language/literacy conference with child

Date _____

© CLPE/ILEA 1988, 1989

FIGURE **6.2** Beige Form of the Primary Language Record

Part B   To be completed during the Spring Term and to include information from all teachers currently teaching the child.

Child as a language user (one or more languages)

Teachers should bear in mind the Authority's Equal Opportunities Policies (race, gender and class) in completing each section of the record and should refer to *Educational Opportunities for All?*, the ILEA report on special educational needs.

B1 Talking and listening

Please comment on the child's development and use of spoken language in different social and curriculum contexts, in English and/or other community languages: evidence of talk for learning and thinking; range and variety of talk for particular purposes; experience and confidence in talking and listening with different people in different settings.

What experiences and teaching have helped/would help development in this area? Record outcomes of any discussion with head teacher, other staff, or parent(s).

B2 Reading

Please comment on the child's progress and development as a reader in English and/or other community languages: the stage at which the child is operating (refer to the reading scales on pages 26-27); the range, quantity and variety of reading in all areas of the curriculum; the child's pleasure and involvement in story and reading, alone or with others; the range of strategies used when reading and the child's ability to reflect critically on what is read.

FIGURE 6.2 (Continued)

B2 (continued)

What experiences and teaching have helped/would help development in this area? Record outcomes of any discussion with head teacher, other staff, or parent(s).

B3 Writing

Please comment on the child's progress and development as a writer in English and/or other community languages: the degree of confidence and independence as a writer; the range, quantity and variety of writing in all areas of the curriculum; the child's pleasure and involvement in writing both narrative and non-narrative, alone and in collaboration with others; the influence of reading on the child's writing; growing understanding of written language, its conventions and spelling.

What experiences and teaching have helped/would help development in this area? Record outcomes of any discussion with head teacher, other staff, or parent(s).

Signature of head teacher and all teachers contributing to this section of the record:

FIGURE **6.2** (Continued)

Part C To be completed during the Summer Term*

C1 Comments on the record by child's parent(s)

C2 Record of language/literacy conference with child

C3 Information for receiving teacher
This section is to ensure that information for the receiving teacher is as up to date as possible. Please comment on changes and development in any aspect of the child's language since Part B was completed.

What experiences and teaching have helped/would help development? Record outcomes of any discussion with head teacher, other staff, or parent(s).

Signed: Parent(s) _____   Class Teacher _____

Date _____   Head Teacher _____

To be completed by the Summer half-term for 4th year juniors.

FIGURE 6.2 (Continued)

child speaks and/or reads and writes and the names of the school personnel who will be involved with the child's language and literacy development. This is already a hedge on a single teacher's judgment because all the teachers or aides listed will have input.

The two boxes under these formalities exemplify the genius of the Primary Language Record. They record first a discussion about the child's language development with the child's parents and then a discussion with the child. The parent discussion is qualitatively different from the usual parent conference: the teacher is asking for the parent's help in understanding the child. Great care is taken in London schools to make the situation nonthreatening, with community members translating for a parent who cannot speak English, and strict attention paid to punctuality because of the child care arrangements that must be made to free some parents. After the discussion, the teacher writes a summary of the conversation while the parent is still there and asks the parent to read it (or listen to a translation). The parent then signs the statement.

When American teachers are told about the parents' essential role in the Primary Language Record, they usually ask how the parents are persuaded to come to the interview. In London schools, the parents of most children come willingly. Only one or two in a classroom are not supported by a parent, grandparent, relative, or older sibling. There seem to be two causes for the high rate: the interview is nonthreatening—the parents are there so that their perceptions and views can be heard—and the word travels around the community quickly when the school makes a welcoming gesture. American schools invite parents to back-to-school nights and open houses, but these events tend to raise fear and anxiety in parents whose memories of school are not happy ones. Other contacts also may seem negative, for schools tend to summon parents only when something is wrong. There are exceptions, of course, in the United States (academic booster clubs of parents, for example), but asking for parents' observations of the child's intellectual development does not seem widespread as a way to involve the parents with their children's education.

The interview with the child extends the picture of the child's reading, writing, listening, and watching preferences (favorite television programs are mentioned often). The essence of these interviews is that they are nonjudgmental. The objective is to understand the child, so that literacy experiences can be targeted to broadening, deepening, or beginning, as needed.

The central double spread of the Primary Language Record summarizes the child's language abilities during the central part of the school year. The teacher (or teachers) summarize from the white forms the observations and their responses to the reading and writing samples. For each major division of language use—speaking and listening, reading, and writing—the teachers respond to this question: "What experiences and teaching have helped/would help development in this area? Record outcomes of any discussion with head teacher, other staff, or parents." Professional judgment is clearly called for and also bolstered by discussion with others.

The final page of the Primary Language Record is a mirror image of the first page. At the end of the year, the parents are invited to comment on the center pages and what they report of the child's progress, and the child also comments on his or her learning for the year. The last box contains information intended for the teacher who will receive the child next year, especially including any developments since the middle of the year. The question about possible help for problems is repeated, this time for the child's general achievement in language arts. Everyone concerned signs the Primary Language Record: the parents, all the teachers who worked with the child, and the head teacher (principal). The beige form, the white forms, and the writing samples then go with the child to the next teacher and also provide input for the child's report card, since language arts is only one part of the child's educational program.

The Primary Language Record has been designed to establish that the teacher is a member of a team, thus militating against perceptions that judgment is free and unconstrained. The existence of the notes, as well as the summaries, also adds objectivity. If there is a question of unfair judgment, the records can be produced. Because they were made at the time of the observation, they have authenticity. The teacher's judgment is therefore not arbitrary, since it is subject to refinement by both colleagues and records.

A secondary benefit of the Primary Language Record is that it perceptibly improves teaching. A head teacher said, "It really stops the teachers talking so much and makes them listen," an observation confirmed by the teachers themselves. Since the teacher must record evidence of progress on the white form, the evidence is sought. The teachers learn about their students by observing and listening and also learn about the effects of their teaching.

OTHER OBSERVATIONAL TECHNIQUES

The Primary Language Record succeeds because it is a team product, it doubles as assessment and as a guide to practice, and it focuses attention on what children can do. Other kinds of observation based on checklists are not so acceptable to teachers, even in England. The English National Curriculum adopted in 1989 has a complicated assessment component that includes teacher observations of students' performing Standard Assessment Tasks (SATs, by coincidence!). The intention is to verify that the standards of the National Curriculum are being met by seeing whether children can perform standard tasks.

These tasks, however, are also intended to be embedded in instructional units. English primary schools organize their teaching and learning by theme and topic rather than by discrete subject areas. The Standard Assessment Tasks pilot-tested in spring 1990 were also thematic, but the themes did not necessarily fit with the topics already in progress in the school, which alienated the teachers because they had to prepare special materials for the tasks. Already put off, they were asked to conduct the lessons and observe the students and fill out checklists at the same time.

The classroom management problems overwhelmed even teachers used to well-disciplined English children. A teacher with thirty-eight 7 year olds and only occasional help finds it difficult to work with a separate group on a Standard Assessment Task, no matter how well behaved the children are in their little uniforms. (Tiny boys wear ties and grey tailored shorts, the girls blue and white dresses, or blouses and jumpers.) At one school, the researcher who escorted me and I were both greeted with obvious relief as adult help. During the course of the day I administered one of the Standard Assessment Tasks by sitting with a group and assessing the children on speaking and listening.

The structure of the checklists was as much to blame as the classroom management challenge. The teachers found the detail irritating. They would repeat: "You know your own children, don't you?" The difference is in the orientation; checklists that focus on subject matter or skills ask teachers to compare their students with an exterior standard: did the students show they understood a concept? But observation material like the Primary Language Record asks teachers to pay attention to the student and record what they hear and see. It is not a simple matter of collision between the roles of teacher and evaluator that makes the checklists irritating, for teachers perform both roles all the time; it is a matter of being in control of what to observe.

CHECKLIST OBSERVATIONS IN CLEVELAND, OHIO

Teachers in U.S. schools have similar classroom management problems with observations and checklists. I heard the reactions that follow from elementary teachers in the Cleveland, Ohio, area who were experimenting with science modules developed as part of a National Science Foundation project. They all tried to use the checklists while observing the children's activities in science. Teachers who always use cooperative learning (in which students work in groups on projects) had no difficulty with observation because they had learned how to redirect their energies from supplying information to acting as coach. Other teachers stole time from reading lessons to observe groups of children doing experiments and manipulations at the side of the room while the other children read; they filled out the checklists later since they were already doing two things at once. Some teachers found it impossible to observe and help the children do the activities simultaneously. One or two said basically the same thing as the English teachers: they knew which children could do the tasks and at what level and felt that checking off all the details on the checklist was superfluous.

Most of them agreed with the teacher who said, "I can't be doing that, checking off on a checklist of kids' names, while I need to be answering questions or monitoring what's going on. It's not as if it's one skill; it's six different areas you're supposed to be checking." They needed aides, assistants, or a situation in which they could act only as observers and not combine their roles. One experienced teacher said: "I had pairs of students working with lighted candles heating metal. One girl kept teasing her partner by pulling the candle away from him. When I got to them, the candle was about a centimeter away from her nose. You know, I can't be doing a checklist while that's going on."

Critics should be reassured by teachers' unwillingness to fill out checklists in these circumstances. It shows the seriousness with which they take their professional responsibilities. They are concerned not only with safety (a classroom basic) but with the quality of attention they are giving to both the instruction and the observation checklist.

They are not willing to shortchange either their teaching or their obligations to assess performances. The teachers also want to observe what is happening in the child's development, not what someone else thought would be important.

THE SOUTH BRUNSWICK
EARLY CHILDHOOD PORTFOLIO

At least three states—Georgia, North Carolina, and Missouri—now have early childhood assessment programs using multiple measures and including teachers' observations. That they were not directly influenced by the Primary Language Record points to a confluence of ideas about the assessment of children. There has been a strong revulsion against paper-and-pencil multiple-choice tests for young children.[9] North Carolina outlawed them for kindergarten and grades 1 and 2, which led to the development of observational profiles of students. Six school districts in Alaska are experimenting with forms of these assessments, with the assistance of the Alaska Department of Education. Considering the speed at which performance assessments are mushrooming, there may be many more now at the state and district levels.

South Brunswick, New Jersey, has developed an early childhood assessment system that is based on the Primary Language Record (although with considerable modifications by teachers) and is moving toward quantification. South Brunswick Township is a county school district located halfway between the universities of Princeton and Rutgers. The township contains six elementary schools (K–6) and in all six the kindergarten and grades 1 and 2 are participating in the assessment as a matter of district policy. Grade 3 will be added as the cohort of children moves up in the school.

The assessment system is referred to as portfolio assessment, although it consists of much more than "portfolio" may bring to mind. Its origins are eclectic; it is heavily influenced by the Primary Language Record but has additional elements, one especially developed by an Educational Testing Service researcher in nearby Princeton. Like the statewide early childhood assessments in North Carolina, Missouri, and the Alaskan districts, the South Brunswick portfolio was developed primarily by teachers, who examined programs like the Primary Language Record and Reading Recovery, a remedial reading program developed in New Zealand, and then designed what they needed. The portfolio undergoes reassessment and revision each summer in workshops for teachers.

The portfolio is used to adjust instruction for each child, in conferences with parents and other adults who work with the child, and to assess the child's growth over time. It guides individualized instruction and allows the measurement of student growth over time, as opposed to a single-point evaluation.

Like the state assessments I have cited (California, Arizona, Maryland) South Brunswick's move toward performance assessment began with new forms of curriculum and instruction. The school district administration gave teachers the task (willingly accepted, it should be said) of researching and implementing a "developmentally appropriate" early childhood education curriculum. "Developmentally appropriate" curriculum is based on a view of the young child (before grade 3) as a natural learner whose methods of learning differ from those of older children and from one another. Young children learn by doing and performing, have a low tolerance for boredom, and live in the literal world. The assumption behind developmentally appropriate teaching is that the more methods of teaching are tied into the developmental stages of children, the more effective those methods will be in imparting knowledge and skills to children. The result in South Brunswick was a wholesale move to this type of curriculum and teaching in grades K–3.[10]

In language arts, developmentally appropriate instruction implies the whole language teaching method, an eclectic approach to developing literacy that uses the child's own language and experiences, employs any means necessary—including phonics and word recognition—to get children reading on their own, introduces "real" books (not basal readers) to children, frequently by reading aloud to them, and focuses on meaning, not on encoding and decoding skills. The children do not learn to read from basal readers, which are textbooks where the vocabulary is carefully controlled and the stories are correspondingly bland; they do not fill out workbooks where they are asked to circle the *m* or the *p*, and are not given spelling lists to memorize.[11] Teachers use Big Books, outsize books with large print that everyone in a circle of about ten children can see, as the teacher reads and points to each word and each picture. South Brunswick early childhood programs now extend the whole language approach to mathematics and are developing an addition to the portfolio to chart math learning.

As a natural consequence of a new approach to teaching, a new assessment was needed. Since all testing exercises an influence on what is taught and how, it was clear that developmentally appropriate teaching could be thwarted by an emphasis on the discrete knowledge and skills required to succeed on machine-scorable, multiple-choice tests. With the help of the researcher who introduced the South Brunswick teachers to the Primary Language Record, they developed instruments during summer workshops, field-tested them in their classrooms, and then modified them.

The portfolio caused a good deal of distress in the school year 1989–1990 because the paperwork load seemed overwhelming. Teachers made the same kind of complaints that I heard from the Cleveland, Ohio, teachers about observation checklists. But as one teacher said, "South Brunswick truly is a teaching district," and the administration responded to complaints by scheduling a summer workshop to revise the portfolio before it was used in first grade. Revisions were proposed and tried until both kindergarten teachers who had used the portfolio and the grade 1 teachers who were scheduled to use it were satisfied that it was workable.

Like the London schools where the Primary Language Record is used routinely, South Brunswick elementary schools manage to provide more than one adult in each classroom using the portfolio. This involves some sophisticated financial maneuvering, so that the budget has not been exceeded.

Details of the Portfolio

The portfolio consists of eight parts for kindergarten and Grade 1:

1. *Self-portrait.* The child is asked to draw a self-portrait, which is then affixed to the portfolio (or even drawn directly on the manila folder). The exercise is repeated at the end of the year. The exercise, which is not formally evaluated, provides an objective record of how the child's self-concept and eye-hand coordination develop over a year.

2. *Child interview.* A teacher or other adult in the classroom writes down answers the child gives in response to questions about favorite activities, television watching, reading, and the literacy activities of others in the home.

3. *Parent questionnaire.* Unlike the Primary Language Record, this is not filled out during an interview with the parents but is sent home

for parents to fill out before their first conference with the teacher. It asks parents about their child's reading interests so the parent may develop a working relationship with the child's teacher.

4. *Concepts about print.* This brief test is administered by reading two specially adapted books with the child. It assesses the child's concepts of print before learning to read. Children are asked to point to the front and back of the book, to show where the story begins, to indicate the direction in which print is decoded, and to explain the meaning of question marks and periods (if the child is sufficiently advanced). The book includes pages printed upside down and with the print running in the reverse direction.

The test has a dual function: it is part of the portfolios, but it is also a nationally normed test, part of the mandated package of tests for kindergarten children in New Jersey, which is used to identify children in need of compensatory education. Using it as part of the portfolio kills two birds with one stone.

5. *Word Awareness Writing Activity (WAWA).* This activity records the level at which children begin to comprehend the rules of forming words. The WAWA (which is also the name of a convenience store chain in New Jersey, not entirely by coincidence!) gives the teachers a means of documenting children's growth in connecting the sounds of words with their appearance in written form. The teacher asks the children to write a word after hearing it repeated and used in sentences. The children are reassured that they are not expected to know the spellings but are expected only to try to render in writing what they hear. Children's progress is recorded in five stages: precommunicative—random letters or scribbling; semiphonetic—some sounds represented by letters; phonetic—letters used appropriately for major sounds; transitional—some evidence of awareness of spelling patterns; mostly correct—ten out of thirteen words correct. This test was developed by the ETS researcher in order to demonstrate that there is a natural progress toward spelling, so teachers and parents should not be alarmed at scribbles and "invented" spelling.

6. *Reading sample.* This one-to-one reading assessment allows the teacher to estimate how each individual child is dealing with print. The teacher is required to take a reading sample and document it with analysis three times a year but can administer additional assessments if the child seems to be having difficulties. One form for recording a child's reading growth is photocopied directly from the Primary Language Record. There are two forms the teacher may

choose from when administering the reading sample: the running record or miscue analysis.

The running record can be administered on a known book or an unknown book depending on the information the teacher wants. Using a known book reveals to the teacher how well the child makes use of reading strategies (what to do with an unknown word, how to use the context to infer meaning) and is used with children in the early stages of reading. Using an unknown book reveals the child's ability to integrate reading strategies effectively and shows a movement toward independent reading. The running record provides a means of recording what a young child is thinking and doing while reading.

The miscue analysis is used with children who can read independently, that is, students who are self-correcting and reading fluently. For a miscue analysis, the book must be unknown to the student. The teacher records the miscues using an accepted code and then analyzes them for clues to the student's instructional needs.

7. *Writing sample.* This is a sample of a student's free writing. It is unedited by the teacher, but the teacher may provide a written "translation" if invented spelling and sketchy syntax make it difficult to read easily. One of the forms for recording a child's writing growth is photocopied directly from the Primary Language Record.

8. *Class record.* This is the only element in the portfolio that is not a part of the child's individual record. It is a class profile enabling the teacher to identify children who may need extra attention in certain areas. The record is a one-page matrix, with yes-no answers to five questions: Does the student pay attention in large and small groups? interact in groups? retell a story? choose to read? write willingly? The teachers use copies of the class record at regular intervals to adjust their class instruction, as opposed to the individual attention they give each student.

The portfolio is a legal-sized, accordion-pleated folder, filled with manila folders marked with the names of each element in the portfolio. There is one portfolio for each teacher and an individual one for each child, filled with manila folders for the collection of materials and copies of interviews and tests. Teachers keep the collection near their desks. "'I just run to it when there's a question about a child—it's right there in a milk crate," one teacher said.

Each teacher's portfolio also contains optional observation sheets that can be attached to the reading and writing samples if the teacher thinks more observation is necessary. When a child is having difficulty, the teacher is expected to keep detailed records of the child's activities, thus making it less likely that a child will be lost in the system.

The portfolio provides teacher, parents, and school administrators with both individual and group information on the literacy development of students. Students are observed interacting in the classroom, problem solving, reading aloud, and writing. Numerical grading is not used, and the impact of mandated multiple-choice testing is reduced to a few sessions of familiarization with number 2 pencils and "bubbles" before the annual New Jersey tests are given.

The Portfolio as a Guide for Teaching

The enthusiasm for the portfolio among the early childhood teachers in South Brunswick is striking. Assessment to these teachers is part of teaching. In fact, I found it difficult in conversation to focus them on assessment at all. "I don't think the portfolio's for grading but for me to teach them what they need to know. And I know what they need, because it's all there in the portfolio," said a young teacher. The portfolio provides "tangible proof of what you're talking about," the observations made in the classroom. She uses it for referrals to the student assistance team, a child study group consisting of a psychologist, a social worker, and a counselor; conferences with parents; to improve her own teaching; to know exactly the weaknesses and strengths of each child; and to identify children who need special attention.

The teachers thought that norm-referenced, multiple-choice testing was not useful to them because it does not assess development in whole language. The epigraph to this chapter summarizes their view. They regarded the New Jersey–mandated tests as irrelevant more than as obstacles. They realize that parents accept the multiple-choice scores as the authoritative evaluation of their children, but they believe that the portfolios could become replacements for multiple-choice tests if parents understood how they function.

Using the portfolio, teachers find it easy to identify the learning strategies of each child and consequently to develop activities that will stress the student's strengths while providing practice and help with weaknesses. In the past, teachers have taught and assessed primarily verbal and logico-mathematical learning, but the portfolio allows them to understand and support other kinds of learning styles.

It gives them information on which to base classroom activities. In one kindergarten room, I watched a small boy thoroughly enjoying himself alone at the paint table, smearing paint all over his hands, making handprints on paper, and then covering the entire sheet with paint. The teacher said what she had learned about the child from using the portfolio indicated that he had not had the opportunity to play freely with messy, squishy materials (unlike many of his middle-class peers), so she was letting him catch up.

Using the Portfolio

In a first-grade class, another teacher characterized her teaching as continuous assessment and response to the information it provides. She organizes her teaching so that she can use the portfolio as an integral part of instruction. At one point in the morning, she settles the class down and then calls children one by one to her table for individual conferencing. She can see half of the class (about ten children out of twenty-one) every day from 10:30 to 11:10 A.M., since some children require only 2 minutes of her time and others require 10. She may see three children together if all are reading the same book, to ask them to retell the story or to respond to some events in it. During this time, the portfolio assessments take place.

The teacher and the adult aide in the classroom, who assists for an hour each morning so that the teacher can see the students individually, always keep dated class record sheets at hand to make observational notes. About once a month, these notes are summarized for each child and put into the child's folder. They are used for two main purposes: for conferences with parents and to pull together impromptu groups of children who may all be having the same difficulty so that they can be helped simultaneously.

The teacher sat at a round table in a corner of the classroom, so that children coming for individual attention did not lose their connection with the class. (Children in elementary school frequently object to being pulled out from their peer group, even if the activity is intended to help them). The teacher asked each child to read and then made a running record as they did so. The children then responded to comprehension questions about what they read.

One child was superficially proficient in reading, but the running record revealed that he was decoding rather than reading for meaning, that he went back to the beginning of phrases he misread rather than correcting them on the spot, and that he did not seem to be enjoying the story. The teacher made notes to talk with the child's parents about his reading experiences at home. Another child was at a much less advanced stage of reading but was beginning to recognize words and understand that he could look at other places in the book to find the same words in a new context.

The portfolios make it possible for South Brunswick teachers and administrators to approach creatively a sore point in early childhood education, retention—keeping a child back for another year of the same class. Research clearly shows that retention is harmful to children, but there is a widespread belief that children should not go to the next grade until they have mastered the material taught in the present one.[12] When the time comes for retention decisions in South Brunswick kindergartens and first and second grades, the portfolio record is consulted to see if the child has made progress. If progress can be shown, the student is promoted on the assumption that every child develops at his or her own rate and there is nothing to worry about until the child reaches the third grade, since individual children are so variable in development. If no progress is apparent, the child is promoted but is identified for compensatory education.

The South Brunswick administration is characterized not only by its visionary dedication to teachers but also by its hard-headedness about evaluation. Recognizing that the observation portfolio will remain a valuable teaching and conference aid but not become accepted as an assessment tool if its results are not translated into numbers for public use, the administration has initiated a process of using the portfolios to assign a number on a "literacy scale" to each child at certain points, probably the end of each year of early childhood education. The Educational Testing Service researcher and two colleagues are involved in the process, which will produce such detailed descriptions of what a 5, 4, 3, 2, or 1 means that people outside the South Brunswick district will be able to apply the scale. The group has looked at many literacy scales (including one developed by the Center for Language in Primary Education in London, which produced the Primary Language Record) but intends to develop its own with the Educational Testing Service, since the evidence contained in the South Brunswick portfolio seems richer than that supporting other scales.

MODERATION: HOW OTHER COUNTRIES SUPPORT TEACHERS' JUDGMENTS

An important motivation for increasing the reliability and objectivity of teachers' judgments is to cut down on the amount of testing. The National Commission on Testing and Public Policy estimates that "at some grade levels a student may have to take as many as seven to 12 such tests a year."[13] If teachers could adjust their standards to those set by state authorities (or university admissions offices or national authorities), students could be spared from so many occasions of formal assessment.

In other countries, teachers take part in a process called moderation which is a way of collectively establishing and maintaining standards. It may be as simple as exchanging 10 percent of examination papers with another school district to check that standards are the same, or it may resemble a group grading standard-setting session. The moderation systems in Sweden and in the Australian Capital Territory (around Canberra) combine centralized testing with student grades to produce a grade for each student according to a nationwide (or territory-wide) standard and also to assist teachers in standardizing their own grading.

In Sweden, teachers' grades are standardized by comparing them to the results of tests developed by the National Board of Education: "The standardized tests are used for assessing the achievement of the total population taking the same course. . . . Their chief purpose is to enable the teacher to compare the performance of his own class with that of the total population and adjust his marking scale according to the outcome of the testing."[14]

All Swedish schools award "marks" or grades on a five-point scale, with 3 being the average performance. (Swedish education is unified under the Riksdag or Parliament and the National Board of Education. The small size of the school population makes unity less difficult to achieve than it might be in another countries; there are about 1 million students in elementary and secondary school—fewer than in the New York City School District.) In the regular elementary and secondary school, no marks are required before the final two grades, when decisions are made about whether students should go on to upper secondary school and what courses they should take there. Marks are used in upper secondary school for admission to the universities.

Standardized tests (which correspond to our assessments, since they are not multiple choice) are prepared by the National Board of Education for elementary and secondary school, where they can be used voluntarily by teachers, and for upper secondary school, where they are compulsory. After the students have completed the test, the teachers grade the standardized tests, using detailed scoring guides provided by the National Board of Education. About one-third of the tests are randomly selected to be sent to the National Board of Education, which works out a series of norms from this corpus of tests. The teacher awards marks on the five-point scale, adjusting the grades to the norms sent by the National Board.

The all-important final grade, used for making decisions about the student's future, is first established by the teacher using all the information available about a student's performance: written work, test scores, and classroom observations. These yield a preliminary ranking for the class, from which the teacher works out a mean for comparison to the norms established by the National Board. If the means and the distributions agree, the preliminary marks are probably in line with national standards. If they are not, the teacher has to do some adjusting.

The final step is a class conference, which is attended by the head (the principal), the assistant head, and all the teachers who teach that class of students—that is, the teachers of English, Swedish, mathematics, science, history, and so on for that grade. The purpose of the class conference is to make final decisions on the mean and distribution of marks for these students in each subject, using the National Board of Education's standards and the relative achievement of other classes in the same subject. "A teacher who wants to retain noticeable differences between test results and preliminary marks has to convince the class conference that there is a valid reason for doing so," says the official description. Thus, Swedish students can be fairly confident that their marks would be about the same no matter what school in what part of the country they attended.

The teacher's position in the Swedish assessment system is different from that of U.S. teachers; the judgments are not overruled but adjusted. Indeed, according to *Assessment in Swedish Schools*, "The individual teacher is solely responsible for the marking. No educational or legal authority can alter a given mark, or force a teacher to do so."[15] The class conference is a persuasion session. It is safe to assume that since the system has been in operation for a number of years (most of this century, according to the history accompanying the description), there are few surprises. The standards will largely have been internalized by the teachers, especially since they themselves were students in the system before they became teachers. The teachers are the center of the grading system; the tests are explicitly designed to help them maintain standards, not to show them how wrong they were about the children's achievements.

In the Australian Capital Territory, an administrative unit surrounding Canberra, the capital (much like Washington D.C.), there are two kinds of moderation, each dependent on the other: statistical moderation and "social" moderation, which is much like group grading.[16] They are used in a high-stakes assessment, to determine which students are admitted to the Australian National University at the end of their secondary education.

The social moderation comes first. The Australian Capital Territory education authority arranges for groups of teachers from different schools but teaching the same subject to meet and discuss their grades. There are usually twenty or so teachers in a group, which might represent five schools in a densely populated area or twenty schools in another area. The object of their work is to standardize their grades among themselves, so that students from different schools get more or less the same grade for the same kind of work. The grades can be based on written examinations, and usually are, but there may be other inputs, such as portfolios and observations. They proceed much like a group grading the writing assessments of the CAP—establishing prototypes to indicate the features that must be present for each grade.

The results of these meetings are forwarded to the central education authority in the forms of individual grades for students and a class mean. There they are combined with the results of the Australian version of the SAT (much the same as ours but with an essay and more emphasis on subject matter knowledge). This statistical moderation converts the teachers' grades to the same mean and standard deviation as the national score, so that the final score represents the score and the grade on the same scale.

For our purposes, the important part of the procedure is the social moderation, which, like the Swedish marking system, is built into the teacher's professional duties and is paid for accordingly. It is not something added on for a little extra pay, as group grading frequently is in the United States. In the Swedish and Australian systems, the teachers are expected as professionals to care about the quality of their judgment and seek to make it as standardized—and authoritative—as possible.

The Swedish and Australian models are worth exploring to see whether they could translate into a useful system for the United States. One extra wrinkle would make the Australian scheme especially helpful and eliminate one occasion of testing for the students: the students could take a statewide test—like the Arizona writing assessment, for example—and it would be scored as it is now by regional groups of teachers. At the same time, the language arts teachers in a district would score the tests themselves in groups. They could score a random sample so that the task does not become overwhelming. Then they would compare the scores given by the regional groups (accepted by the state as the official scores) to their own. They would adjust their scores to correspond with the state scores, and, I hope, also adjust the grades they assign during regular classroom teaching. They would have a strong answer to students and parents who complain about "hard grading": this is the standard established by the state.

Such a scheme has the possibility of becoming the basis of the U.S. national assessment, proceeding upward in a pyramid from state to regional to the national level. Teachers would be where they should be—at the center of the process.

7

How American Education Got into the Testing Trap

Although it is not new to include thinking, problemsolving, and reasoning in *someone*'s school curriculum, it is new to include it in *everyone*'s curriculum. It is new to take seriously the aspiration of making thinking and problemsolving a regular part of a school program for all of the population, even minorities, even non-English-speakers, even the poor.[1]

There is a rich variety of ways to assess students' achievement and the quality of programs in schools. We can assess students while they do what we hope they will do: read and make sense of what they read in writing, solve problems we should think about while trying to use resources wisely, apply knowledge learned in one discipline and to the challenges of another, reflect on their own accomplishments and criticize them constructively, use historical knowledge to understand political and social conditions. We can even use assessments to help them do these things.

The question then arises: since these assessments seem only natural, why did we ever do otherwise? Why were American students ever subjected to the dull tyranny of the bubble? How did American education become slave to the spurious efficiency of norm-referenced, multiple-choice testing?

One part of it never did. From the beginning of the republic, the elite private education available to the children of the upper classes measured its students' progress through written essays, projects, and individual demonstrations of creativity and proficiency. A very few high schools in rich cities and suburbs also paid less attention to test scores than to students' performances. But the bulk of American public education was designed to provide workers for a mass production economy, and so its history is that of the factory model of schooling.[2]

The name is not as new and derogatory as it might seem. It was used as long ago as 1934, when Elwood P. Cubberly called American schools "in a sense, factories," and used the expression with pride.[3] The model still provides the underlying structure of the system, despite the fact that it is clearly dysfunctional in view of different global economic structure.[4]

The factory model was based on the assembly line, for the sake of simplicity and efficiency. The designers of the assembly line worked on these principles: reduce any process to its component parts; in sequence, add one or two components at a time; give each operator only limited responsibility; and inspect each stage of manufacture.

The factory model has governed U.S. public schools for so long that many of the buildings in which children learn—significantly called the "plant"—look like factories. What happens to them parallels the treatment of material on the assembly line as it is processed. Children, who are regarded as the raw material for the product, begin at one end of the plant and are sorted into "tracks" to be given different treatment.[5] They are given standard treatment in the form of workbooks and textbooks by technicians, the teachers. The technicians have no authority beyond the operation they are supposed to be performing—the low reading track in the second grade, for example. The authority rests in the plant's managers, the principal and administrators, and further up in the corporate headquarters, the superintendent and district administrators. They, in turn, are governed by a board of directors, the school board. There is even a regulatory agency in this model—the state department of education.

This is a broad characterization of the factory model, but certainly some schools almost exactly fit the description. Even more disturbing, many people, especially parents and grandparents who attended schools that were more or less like this, think this is the way school should be. They are unaware that the shape of schooling is dictated by the business and industry whose needs it serves. Those needs are different now from in the past.

THE NINETEENTH CENTURY

Ironically, the factory model began with a dream of the common school, which remains an unrealized ideal for U.S. education.[6] At the beginnings of the republic, common schools seemed a necessity, since a democracy requires citizens to be well educated if they are to discharge their civic responsibilities. *Citizens*, however, was a restricted term; it did not include slaves, indentured servants, or women.

The schooling available to those defined as citizens in the later eighteenth and early nineteenth centuries already showed a bifurcation that later would become a rift. There was private education based on the model of the British and French school systems of the time; the teaching and learning consisted almost exclusively of the Latin and Greek classics, and essay writing and oral presentation were the media of instruction and examination. Performance assessment was the norm.

During the nineteenth century, the teaching and learning broadened to include the classics of English literature, and even science was studied as these subjects began to spread into the universities. Like their counterparts today, the teaching and learning at these elite private schools was driven by the universities for which they were preparatory. They taught to the test—the entrance examinations at Harvard, Yale, and Princeton—but it was a test worth teaching to.

Public schools, usually supported by townships, taught reading, writing, and a little arithmetic. Memorization of poems and passages was a major feature; many one-room schoolhouses in developing western settlements resounded to recitations of Shakespeare and Milton, although there is doubt as to how much was understood as well as memorized. These schools, which we remember from pictures of the Norman Rockwell type, were a rite of passage for the students, who knew that their lives would be spent on the farm or, later, in the factory. The schools were taught largely by young women, graduates of the normal schools and land-grant colleges that sprang up after the Morrill Acts, first passed in 1860 and then extended in 1890, and were notorious for pointless repetitions of simple skills.

The split between public and private education began to widen toward the end of the nineteenth century. Two major factors simultaneously brought this about: the flood of immigrants and the development of the industries served by their labor. Immigration in the final decades of the nineteenth century was proportionately greater than it is now; although numerically the United States now admits more new people each year, the number entering the country then constituted a higher percentage of the population. At the same time, the United States was claiming its place as a world industrial power. It needed workers who would be able to follow orders and perform efficiently—human machines. The public school system expanded rapidly to meet the demand by providing a minimal education—the basics of literacy and computation—regarded as necessary for the job. It was a utilitarian schooling that commonly terminated at the fifth grade level. The ideal of a citizenry educated to participate in the political process was buried in the rush to provide workers.

While the immigrant children were learning just enough to make them useful in factories (stuffed into overcrowded classrooms taught by young women whose knowledge was not much greater than their own), the elite studied the classics in private preparatory schools and went to the Ivy League universities and the other universities founded during the nineteenth century by industrial philanthropists.[7] Theirs was an education intended to produce leaders who could make decisions; public education prepared future factory workers to take orders.

IQ TESTING

At the time of World War I, this division, based on economic realities and social prejudice, suddenly received the blessing of science. Academic psychology, led by H. H. Goddard and Lewis Terman, took the tests developed by Alfred Binet in France and developed the concept of IQ, which in 1916 was used to screen U.S. Army recruits, with devastating results for the children of Eastern and Southern European immigrants.[8] Stephen Jay Gould, who skewers the widespread belief that these tests were "scientific" in his book *The Mismeasure of Man,* carefully points out that Binet himself regarded his tests as practical guides for the identification and improvement of children needing special help. Binet's tests were diagnostic, not prescriptive. But Binet's careful delineation of the capacities of his test was lost in the rush to justify "scientifically" labeling subpopulations. The purpose of intelligence tests is still widely misunderstood. They do not measure innate ability but mental capacity at a certain point in a child's life and should be used cautiously in the context of other information about the child.

All such caution was thrown to the winds when Terman developed his intelligence test at Stanford. Prejudice now had science on its side. Gould quotes from Terman's 1916 book, *The Measurement of Intelligence:*

> The tests have told the truth. These boys are ineducable beyond the merest rudiments of training. No amount of school instruction will ever make them intelligent voters or capable citizens. . . . They represent the level of intelligence which is very, very common among Spanish-Indian and Mexican families of the Southwest and also among negroes. . . . Children of this group should be segregated in special classes and be given instruction which is concrete and practical. They cannot master abstractions, but they can often be made efficient workers, able to look out for themselves.[9]

Terman and his colleagues were not without critics even at their moment of triumph. In 1923, Terman and Walter Lippmann engaged in an acrimonious debate in the pages of the *New Republic*. In one of the last exchanges, Lippmann clarifies his position in a ringing statement:

> I hate the impudence of a claim that in fifty minutes you can judge and classify a human being's predestined fitness in life. I hate the pretentiousness of that claim. I hate the abuse of scientific method which it involves. I hate the abuse of scientific method which it involves. I hate the sense of superiority which it creates, and the sense of inferiority which it imposes.[10]

Unfortunately, the apparent simplicity and efficiency of the IQ tests was too attractive to politicians and decision makers, who gave educators more than enough support to overwhelm the objections of Lippmann and others who have argued that the tests are invalid, unscientific, and unfair.

ATOMIZATION AND SEQUENCING

At the same time as intelligence testing was beginning to dominate education, Taylorism, the decomposition of a production task into incremental steps, was bringing assembly lines into the factories. Taylorism was reinforced by academic behaviorism, a theory of cognitive psychology holding that psychological functioning is definable in terms of overt behavioral manifestations. It denies the reality of mental activities that can be inferred and explained in their own terms. A major tenet of behaviorism is stimulus and response theory (based on Pavlov's famous dog experiments), which reduces human action to a series of responses to favorable or unfavorable stimuli.

Stimulus-response theory has obvious implications for teaching: break down a subject into units, and then provide rewards for learning the material and punishments for not learning it. Children could be led up a ladder of achievement from one rung to the next, as they acquired one bit of information—or portion of a skill presented as a bit of information—and then the next. Of course, tests could measure where a child was on the ladder and insist that the child should not attempt to climb higher until the lower level skill was mastered.

These two principles, atomization and sequencing, account for the workbooks in reading that take children through letters, then words, and then sentences; for the sequence in mathematics that forbids estimation, application, and use of calculators until basic arithmetic (even long division) has been mastered; and for the textbooks dumbed down according to readability formulas.[11]

Tracking and multiple-choice testing have shared their history in American education. They reinforce each other; tests shunt students into tracks, where the instruction fits them to score predictably on achievement tests and thus apparently to validate the tests.

Operating with the support of "science" in its pedagogical principles, its selection mechanisms, and its production schedule, the factory model of schooling reached its zenith along with the American corporation to which it supplied human machines. Robert B. Reich says:

> Thus did America's grammar schools and high schools at midcentury mirror the system of mass production. Children moved from grade to grade through a preplanned sequence of standard subjects, as if on factory conveyor belts. At each stage, certain facts were poured into their heads. . . . As in the mass-production system, discipline and order were emphasized above all else.[12]

Order in learning meant proceeding from skills—phonics in reading, circling the *m* and the *p* in lists of words, for example—to knowledge. Children could not be expected to understand ideas until they had mastered "basic skills." Unfortunately, the tracking that goes along with the assembly-line model kept some children from ever encountering any ideas.

The American ideal of the common school receded further. For most students, common schooling meant that all students entered a single door in the morning but then separated into tracks and never mingled again throughout the day. In most secondary schools, there were three tracks—college bound, general, and vocational—although there were many local variations. Students maintained their tracks even in physical education, driver education, and performance classes in the name of efficient scheduling. In elementary schools, students were divided according to reading and mathematical ability. Groupings might be disguised by whimsical names like "Bluebirds" and "Robins," but no one (least of all the children) was deceived.

For a good part of the period, the factory model worked. It produced three levels of workers: the college-track students were prepared for the public universities (the elite took most of the places in the Ivy League), the general-track students were ready for the clerical jobs necessary as U.S. business boomed, and the vocational students became the manual workers, feeding the assembly lines while the United Stats still had them.

Some aspects of public education began to change after World War II in the period Reich calls "midcentury." Graduation from high school became an expected event. Before the war, only 50 percent of students graduated, a number that the unemployment of the 1930s pushed up from 29 percent in 1920. Until the late 1950s, high schools were regarded as preparation for postsecondary institutions and in many cases were directly controlled by them.

In the late 1960s U.S. education was stirred up by the response to *Sputnik*, the Soviet Union's triumph in space, and went through the upheaval of the New Math. This experience of failure in innovation has lessons for the reformers of the 1990s. The New Math was imposed from outside the school system by university professors, who perceived that current mathematics pedagogy was misrepresenting the subject and consequently holding back the achievement of American students in mathematics. They were quite right. America's dismal performance on international comparative tests during the 1980s is ample vindication of the mathematics professors' perception. However, they did an extremely poor job of selling the New Math to the teachers and to the parents, who tried to help their children with homework and found that their own training of thirty years before no longer applied. Innovations in elementary and secondary schools cannot be imposed from outside; they must be thoroughly understood and "owned' by teachers before they have any chance of success.

The New Math died unmourned amid the turmoil of the 1960s and 1970s, when politics seemed to invade American schools as never before. Yet despite political success in getting schools desegregated, the basic structure remained the same. Schools were integrated but still tracked. Children might be bused to achieve racial balance, but minority children and the increasing number of limited English-speaking immigrants were proportionately overrepresented in the remedial tracks and even special education classes.

TESTING TRIUMPHANT

Achievement testing, like IQ testing, was an integral feature of the factory model. It functioned as quality control and operated by sampling just as it did with manufactured goods. Quality control is maintained by random sampling of products, backed by statistical formulas that prescribe the number of items that must be sampled in order to draw conclusions about the entire batch. Norm-referenced, multiple-choice test items are assumed to be proxies for the student's learning of a body of information; a high test score means not just that students know the answers to the questions but know all or most of what they have been taught.

In its heyday in the 1960s and early 1970s, testing was enormously aided by the increasing use of technology in the testing industry. As computers, scantrons, and similar machines became cheaper and easier to use, norm-referenced, multiple-choice testing became almost universal. These were the years when it was argued that writing ability could be tested by multiple choice.

The test publishers were in the best of business situations; they had a captive and growing market and an increasingly efficient technological means to supply it. Between 1955 and 1986, the dollar volume of sales of tests at the elementary and secondary level grew by 400 percent and are probably now about half a billion dollars a year. This figure is cited by the National Commission on Testing and Public Policy in its 1989 report, *From Gatekeeper to Gateway*, which also supplies a startling indication of the increase in testing during the middle years of the century: in the *Education Index*, which lists educational articles and books published in a year, the average number of column inches needed to cite articles on curriculum barely doubled in the fifty years between 1930 and 1980, but the number of inches needed to cite articles and books on testing increased thirty-five times.[13]

During this midcentury period, there were occasional voices crying in the wilderness against multiple-choice testing. In 1948, some far-sighted psychologists pointed out that what they called the "elementalistic" method of assessment mispresented reality:

> The "real" test of a football player is playing in a real football game . . . and therefore the best way to assess a football player is to confront him with the necessity of playing in a simulated football game which includes as many components of the real game as possible. This assumption, a commonplace to laymen, is not without novelty in the field of psychological testing.[14]

Banesh Hoffman wrote *The Tyranny of Testing* in 1962 with a preface by Jacques Barzun, which now seems ironic: "As the present book shows, it is the testers who are on the defensive, fighting a rearguard action against the irresistible force of the argument which says that their questions are in practice often very bad and in theory very dangerous."[15]

Other protests against the bubble came from the open education movement, which advocated an approach to early childhood based on the child's exploration of a friendly environment. The Workshop Center for Open Education published a lively series of articles on the inappropriateness of multiple-choice testing in the early 1970s, and the Association for Childhood Education International issued position papers written and edited by Vito Perrone in 1975 and 1976. The North Dakota Study Group, headed by Perrone, continued to meet, write, and publish articles throughout the 1970s, and 1980s, but like the other groups that protested against multiple choice—notably the Center for Fair and Open Testing, commonly called FairTest—they were essentially on the fringes of American education. Despite their wise and cautious warnings, the juggernaut of testing rolled on. It would take much more powerful voices—those of business and industry, who depended on the school system for workers to maintain American competitiveness—to slow the testing engine.

Meanwhile, the form of tests became the form of teaching, especially for minority children overrepresented in the lower tracks. Teaching is still testing for these children. Subjects—even reading and writing—are dissected into pieces of information that will fit the multiple-choice format. Never mind thinking—that will only slow down the response time; never mind applying concepts or connecting learning to everyday life—the point is to get the scores up:

> In kindergarten, the children . . . practice filling in circles with big crayons—a knack that will be handy when they mark the answer sheet on a standardized test.
>
> In first grade, as the children learn to read, the blackboard is covered with questions about vowel sounds and consonants—written in the multiple-choice format that is a staple of standardized tests.
>
> By second grade, the children spend many afternoons in a special class on taking tests. They practice spelling, arithmetic, and more basic tools, such as heeding directions and learning not to panic.
>
> It is not until third grade that these students actually will confront the standardized exam that every . . . schoolchild must take.[16]

In a New York School, "Children are taught how to guess intelligently by eliminating unlikely choices. They work on science and social studies passages like those on the tests. They practice filling in answer bubbles."[17]

Teachers do not like teaching in this way, but their objections are pushed aside—or never heard—by administrators, school board members, and even parents, who only want to see scores go up.

A NATION AT RISK

Dissatisfaction with the effectiveness of American education was seeping into the national consciousness in the 1970s. In 1979, a U.S. Department of Education with a cabinet-level secretary was authorized by Congress (although it was almost strangled in its infancy in Ronald Reagan's administration). Education was becoming a national concern, as opposed to a state and local matter.

In 1983, a report that fixed public attention on the schools was published, and it took a national perspective. With *A Nation at Risk*, issued by the National Commission on Excellence, the inadequacies of American education were publicly acknowledged. "If an unfriendly foreign power had attempted to impose on America the mediocre educational performance that exists today, we might have viewed it as an act of war."[18] At the time, it seemed as if greater effort on everyone's part would solve the problem, but in fact *A Nation at Risk* was the death knell of the factory model.

The world had changed, but American education had not; *A Nation at Risk* simply drew attention to this fact. In the years after World War II, American business had traversed a great arc from supremacy over world commerce in the 1950s to debtor status in the 1980s. Largely because of U.S. generosity to the defeated after World War II, competitors such as Germany and Japan (and later Korea and China) learned how to produce as well as the Americans and then went beyond mass production to the international networks Robert B. Reich calls "enterprise webs." In the new world order of production, a corporation may have an American name, but parts of its products will be manufactured in countries on several continents. Its "brain" will be the "symbolic analysts" who collectively design products, solve problems, and extend ideas.

In addition, the days of the assembly line, while not entirely gone, are numbered. Instead of the atomization of tasks and processes, production is increasingly organized, as it is in the Motorola plant outside Chicago, by teams of workers. These teams, which include all levels of workers from machine operators through designers, cooperate to produce the part or solve the problem necessary for the end product to be competitive. Discipline and order are much less emphasized in the running of these teams. They have been replaced by analytical ability and cooperation.[19]

In the late 1980s, all aspects of American education came into question—testing among them. American business and industry discovered it needed a different kind of worker—one who could manipulate the sophisticated symbols necessary to play the new global economic game. Movements began to restructure American schools, to professionalize teachers, to reshape curricula in the direction of concepts and applications, and to reform testing. "Beyond the Bubble," the title of several conferences held beginning in October 1988 by the CAP, became a rallying cry. A rush of articles on alternatives to the bubble flooded the education press in 1989 (especially the April 1989 issue of *Educational Leadership* and the May 1989 issue of *Phi Delta Kappan*, which have both become indispensable texts). The issue of testing and its unforeseen and unwanted effects on children's learning began to interest the press. Banesh Hoffman, Jacques Barzun, and Vito Perrone suddenly began to seem like prophets.

THE OBSOLESCENCE OF THE FACTORY MODEL

In a world for which it is inappropriate, the factory model is obsolete for a number of reasons.

---

1. Business and industry leaders realized that the education system was not producing the kind of workers they needed.[20]

The teams of problem solvers and global webs need workers who can think, as the chairman of the Xerox Corporation, David T. Kearns, wrote as part of a vision statement for American education:

> The modern employee must be more highly educated, better informed, more flexible than ever before. He or she must be, because what we're paying for is the ability to think, to solve problems, to make informed judgments, to distinguish between right and wrong, to discern the proper course of action in situations and circumstances that are necessarily ambiguous.[21]

Systems, however, will always try to meet a new challenge within their existing framework until it becomes obvious that a new system is needed. The factory model of education responded in the only way its practitioners knew: by adding "thinking skills" to the existing program in the form of "kits" or extra units. Higher-order thinking skills (HOTS) became the fashionable topic of workshops at educational conferences and the advertising focus for manufactures of educational materials in the late 1980s. Teachers complained about the added burden of having to teach thinking, as well as everything else. To them, it was another bolt that had to be installed as the assembly line passed them. The bankruptcy of the model is obvious from the absurdity of assuming that children have to be taught to think and that "thinking" can be taught separately from any other human activity.

2. The theoretical basis of the factory model in behaviorism was superseded by a different theory of cognition. The human mind is now seen as learning differently, proceeding in the opposite direction form that posited by the behaviorists.

That something was wrong was sensed by a number of prominent psychologists who, toward the end of World War II, cooperated on a holistic assessment of Office of Strategic Services personnel. In 1948 they produced a book, *Assessment of Men,* which now reads like an early manifesto for the new cognitive psychology:

> The main body of psychology started its career by putting the wrong foot forward. . . . Instead of beginning with studies of the whole person adjusting to a natural social environment, it began with studies of a segment of a person responding to a physical stimulus in an unnatural laboratory environment.[22]

Since they wrote, cognitive psychologists have developed theories in which understanding is a whole, not an accumulation of parts. We approach new information with mental schemata into which we insert what we learn. The mind does not process bottom up, as the behaviorists and Taylor imitators believed. The acquisition of information is not additive. Instead we process top down, adapting what we learn to our schemata and at the same time modifying those schemata with the new material. The result is that thinking cannot be decomposed into its elements. Skills are best learned in the context of understanding concepts.

The revolution in thinking about cognition was, like so many other scientific developments in this century, a gradual accumulation of evidence by different researchers, growing to the point at which the entire field recognizes that a fundamental change has taken place and must be acknowledged. Among these researchers are John Bransford and his colleagues at Vanderbilt University and David Rumelhart and his group at the University of California, San Diego, as well as the numerous groups concerned with the development of artificial intelligence. If you want to make a machine that can think like a human being, clearly you have to find out first how a human being thinks. Howard Gardner summarizes "top-down" processing in this way:

> But researchers have come to appreciate anew that human subjects do not come to tasks as empty slates: they have

expectations and well-structured schemata within which they approach diverse materials. . . . The organism, with its structures already prepared for stimulation, itself manipulates and otherwise reorders the information it freshly encounters—perhaps distorting the information as it is being assimilated, perhaps recording it into more familiar or convenient form once it has been initially apprehended.[23]

The implications for the classroom are clear: the mind is not a wiped slate, children think whether we teach them to or not, and skills can and should be learned within the context of meaningful information. There is no additive process between the individual letters and the reading of a sentence; instead, the letters gain their meaning from the sentence as a whole.

Phil Daro, director of the California and the American Mathematics Projects, gave a vivid example of the role of parts and wholes in knowledge at the first "Beyond the Bubble" conference in California in October 1988. He asked how many people in the audience could sing A above middle C. The response was blank embarrassment from the audience. Then he asked how many could sing "Twinkle, Twinkle, Little Star," and almost everyone could. They could sing A above middle C without any trouble when the isolated skill was embedded in a larger task. Daro advocated applying the same principle to learning in general: instead of basals and worksheets, literature and writing; instead of algorithms in mathematics, problems and puzzles. In each case the necessary skills will be acquired in the framework of the whole. Sylvia Farnham-Diggory clearly agrees:

> The fundamental point is that instruction should begin with comprehensive, important, long-range projects within which basic skills training is embedded. This approach is diametrically opposed to the path of most traditional education, where basic skills are taught first, in more or less isolated ways, before a child is thought to have the foundation for more complex learning enterprises. In fact, our minds work the other way round.[24]

In mathematics, two prestigious national groups, the NCTM and the Mathematical Sciences Education Board (MSEB) of the National Research Council, have incorporated schema-based cognition into their recommendations for teaching mathematics:

Research in learning shows that students actually construct their own understanding based on new experiences that enlarge the intellectual framework in which ideas can be created. . . . Mathematics becomes useful to a student only when it has been developed through a personal intellectual engagement that creates new understanding. Much of the failure in school mathematics is due to a tradition of teaching that is inappropriate to the way most students learn.[25]

A similar movement toward conceptual, personalized, and meaning-oriented teaching can be documented in all the traditional disciplinary areas. Testing experts have also become conscious of the need to change their picture of the mind's activities. Robert J. Mislevy of the Educational Testing Service sums up the situation as "the application of twentieth century statistics to nineteenth century psychology."[26]

News about the change in cognitive psychology has not spread to the general public or to teachers who were trained before the conceptual approach was widely accepted. Parents expect their children to bring home workbooks and are disturbed when they see the "developmental spelling" documented by the South Brunswick portfolio observation. They think teachers should be drilling their children to spell correctly. I have answered telephone calls from elementary mathematics teachers protesting against the National Council of Teachers of Mathematics' *Curriculum and Evaluation Standards* on the grounds that problem solving and statistics are not developmentally appropriate for young children, who, they say, should be learning the "basics." The old atomization and sequencing approach is not even seriously ill, let alone on its deathbed, in U.S. schools. Despite the thoughtful reconsideration of testing exemplified by Mislevy's work, atomization and sequencing still underlie commercial norm-referenced, multiple-choice testing. David Deffley, the president of CTB/Macmillan/McGraw-Hill, which produces the CAT, said in spring 1990 on a nationwide television program on educational assessment, "We believe that there are skills students must master before they can begin to learn content."

---

3. The two strands of education in the United States have come together as a consequence of the changes described. What was once reserved for the elite private schools—high academic standards, thoughtful teaching and learning, cultural experiences in breadth and depth—is now necessary for everyone.

Robert Reich calls it the "education of the symbolic analyst" and points out that "our best schools and universities are providing a small subset of America's young with excellent basic training in the techniques essential to symbolic analysis."[27] Now every school in the United States has to provide this training for every child.

Ironically, the need for an expensive retooling of American education comes at a time when the country's economic circumstances are weakened for many reasons, not the least of which is the nation's new status as a debtor nation. It is the entire system of American education that must be changed; no single component is a panacea. But the professional development of teachers, the infusion of technology, the longer school day and school year, the addition of health and welfare personnel to school staffs—all needed to bring elite private school standards to public schools—will cost billions of dollars. Only farsighted legislators at the state and national levels will understand that it is a price that must be paid if the educational system is not to sink into irrelevance.

---

4. A new population of students with different needs, abilities, and value systems is now in the schools.

I am not speaking only about the non-English-speaking immigrants who are flooding into the schools of the Southwest, the Atlantic coast, and Chicago. In California, for example, the traditional Anglo population became a minority in the state's schools in 1988. The immigrant populations do not all present the same challenge. Some Asian immigrants, for example, adapt well to the factory model of schooling once they have learned the language sufficiently. Other immigrants have no experience of schooling in their own countries; they have no cultural expectations but a great deal of fear and apprehension of failure.

Although the immigrants are perceived, especially by teachers and administrators, as an almost impossible obstacle to overcome, in some ways their problems are not different from those of the traditional population. Teachers frequently say they are baffled by the attitude of students, even the youngest elementary children, no matter whether they are immigrants, African-American, Hispanic, Asian,

Asian-American, or Anglo. Many of these children will not sit quietly and fill out worksheets; they will do only what they want to do. Teachers blame the parents, who are frequently both working (or there is only one parent in the home) and have little time for their children. The children seem to have no childhood; they are responsible for a great deal at early ages. They carry their own keys, look after siblings, prepare meals, put themselves to bed, get themselves up in the morning, and find their own transportation to school. It is hardly surprising that as students, these children do not want to do the trivial tasks the teacher sets them; they are used to autonomy and responsibility.

A writer who taught for a year in a New York City junior high school described her average students in these words:

> But their academic successes were so few, and their emotional and social problems so overwhelming, that school long ago stopped being a place to learn. It was, first and foremost, a place to act out—to explode, to play and shout and rant, to vent all their anger and confusion about life at home and the world around them.[28]

The disconnected, unmotivated student is found not only among the lower socioeconomic groups where physical existence is a struggle. The dropout rate is rising in middle-class and even upper-class institutions, and daily absence rates are routinely between a quarter and a third of any school's population.

Children at all levels of American society are different from children twenty, ten and even five years ago. Their parents were the first generation who grew up entirely under the influence of television. The children, the ones in school (and frequently out of it), are the true inhabitants of Marshall McLuhan's global village. For them, television is background; life without it unimaginable.

But what distinguishes these children from their parents is the huge amount of stimulation available in their environment. Advertising is ubiquitous, even in school; music bathes them in rhythm heard from radios and cassettes constantly—sometimes in the classroom, from teachers who play music as background, hoping to create an atmosphere congenial to students; and consuming is their preoccupation as they accumulate whatever clothing and equipment are the current fad. Whole sections of the clothing and entertainment industries are devoted not only to interesting school-aged children in their products but to keeping them restlessly searching for whatever is new.

For this generation of children, school as an academic institution—as opposed to a social gathering place or a sports club—can compete with these stimuli for their attention only if it offers access to something they want, such as admission to a prestigious college or university. It could offer the opportunity to construct meaning from their fragmented experiences, as I pointed out in advice I wrote for U.S. Secretary of Education Lamar Alexander on his appointment.[29]

School has little power to involve the majority who do not care about admission to the Ivy League; there is always some university or community college they can attend, and performance in school has nothing to do with employability for those who go directly from school to work.[30] On the second count, the factory model of education offers no tools to help students understand and control the hugely overstimulating environment in which they are growing up.

The school cannot change the conditions of the students' lives, which make them so different from students in previous generations. Instead, schools must change how they approach their job.

WANTED: A NEW MODEL OF SCHOOLING

The 1980s were a time of ferment in U.S. education as these four factors—the demands of business and industry, a better understanding of how children learn, the need for an elite education for all, and a different kind of student in American schools—gradually and unevenly entered the national consciousness:

- Business and industry leaders produced report after report calling for better-qualified graduates.
- Educational researchers reported on the effects of practices such as tracking and retention in grade.
- Reports were written on college-bound and non-college-bound students.
- All minorities received attention in yet more reports.
- Specific levels of education, especially the middle or junior high schools, were examined.
- Conferences were held on effective schools, discipline, higher-order thinking skills (HOTS), restructuring, and performance assessment.

- State departments of education issued subject-matter guidelines and frameworks.
- Bills were prepared in state and federal legislatures.
- The governors and the president stepped onto the merry-go-round in the September 1989 summit that in early 1990 produced the national goals for education.

The prescriptions vary, but all agree that the schools must change.

Curiously, one might almost say all agree—except the schools. It is not entirely true to say this, but it is defensible to compare the vast amount of writing and speaking around and about the schools with the reality that the schools go on much as before. My own rough estimate is that real change has happened in about 1 percent of American schools at this point—maybe 750 out of the 75,000 or 80,000 public schools in the United States.

Change is advocated largely by people who have a different kind of professional expertise from that found in schools. Educators do not trust reformers who have no practical experience and who do not face the constraints they perceive shackling them in the form of school board members, parents, administrators, and students, characterized by school personnel as reluctant, ill prepared, and often recalcitrant. Teachers and administrators frequently perceive their position in a failing enterprise to be someone else's fault—even the students' fault for not being interested in learning. Without getting into the issue of teacher preparation, the training of most teachers and administrators has prepared them only to play their roles on the educational assembly line. More is being asked than they have been trained to supply.

The factory model is self-contained to the point where it takes an almost fanatical degree of energy to burst out from the inside. For example, getting teachers together to talk about a possible change, or even to find out how colleagues in a subject area treat a topic, can seem an insurmountable problem since there is no paid time for such meetings. Some union contracts specify 7 hours in the school building for teachers and strongly discourage, if not forbid, any time spent at the school without additional pay. Currently there are 2.3 million teachers in U.S. schools (over 1.5 million of them in elementary schools), and most are likely to be there five or even ten years from now. While preservice teacher training is clearly important for the long-term health of the school system, the need now is for teachers already in the schools to feel the imperative to change.

Changing the model—even disseminating the idea of changing the model—is not just a matter of publishing a visionary description or talking about it at conferences, since conferences are attended primarily by administrators and members of the auxiliary organizations (such as the Council for Basic Education) that devote their time to chivvying the American school system into action. Changing the model means persuading school personnel to invest in the unknown, to put their energy into defending new practices to parents and students, and to row upstream against a current that apparently has everything in its favor—custom, support, tradition, economic structure.

Nevertheless, public education faces irrelevance, and perhaps worse, if radical change does not take hold on a large scale. Already choice schemes that place public and private schools in competition with each other are being implemented in a few cities: students are allowed to choose a private school, and a certain amount of money is paid by the public funds to that school to educate the students. The subordination of public to private education is not even the real threat; the threat is that the boredom and oversimplification of the factory model will make schools negligible in the fabric of society. The real education of workers will occur in their workplaces, and the schools will shrivel into inferior child care institutions. The vision of a common school that should prepare all citizens to participate proudly in a democracy will be extinguished.

This chapter began to asking how and why we got into this mess. We got into the testing trap because we built schools on the factory model. Public education was understood as preparation for a job in mass-production industry. Testing was seen as quality control, to be performed with the same efficiency as the delivery of instruction. It was—and is—an integral part of the model. What we learn from the history of schooling in the United States is that the system is a package deal; you buy all of it or none of it. Changing it means offering another package. For this reason, attempts to assess programs or students by using performance assessment without changing anything else in the system are doomed to failure. Performance assessment depends on a different relationship among students, teachers, and the topic of study. It has been consciously employed to bring about those changes in some cases. The way out of the testing trap is a model of education centered on student responsibility for learning, with teachers as coaches, not technicians, and with the emphasis on performance.

8

Next Steps

> I imagine good teaching as a circle of earnest people sitting
> down to ask each other meaningful questions. I don't see it as
> a handing down of answers. So much of what passes for
> teaching is merely a pointing out of what items to want.[1]

A *New Yorker* cartoon in a February 1990 issue makes a depressing comment on American education without saying a word. It shows a room with windows along one side and children seated at rows of desks, all facing a man leaning on a larger desk, and the man is saying: "Today, people, we're going to review our commitment to the planet." The reader does not have to be told that the scene is taking place in a school; the physical relationship of the parties, facing each other, and the "teacher talk" make it clearly recognizable.

By the end of the century, a school should no longer look like this. School should be unrecognizable to those who spent time in such classrooms. What a school should look like will depend on the problems the students are solving, the equipment they are using, and whether they need to be gathered in one place or are working, either singly or in small groups, in libraries, laboratories, document collections, or museums. The teacher will not be confronting the class or, I hope, be using the condescending language we all resented when we sat in those desks but will probably be hard to find: teachers will be working with one group or another or sitting at a terminal communicating with their students, wherever the students may be.

Delineating the details of new models of schooling is not my purpose, and I do not intend to continue dreaming. Excellent models of education have already been designed, and some are becoming reality.[2] My point is that performance assessment will be an integral part of new models of schooling, but—more immediately urgent— implementing it now will push along the development of those models.

There is no doubt of the urgency to get the nineteenth-century factory model retooled for the twenty-first century. But to summon the collective energy needed to implement just one part of it, performance assessment, we must have information about practical issues such as cost, responsible use, equity, and public understanding.

HOW MUCH WILL IT COST?

No one knows accurately how much performance assessments cost, partly because there is no accurate information about how much any form of educational assessment costs. When school district or state personnel put a dollar figure on evaluation, they may be counting only the cost of buying the test from the publisher, complete with reported results. The district or state education office typically will not include the costs of the testing and evaluation office maintained (in big school districts and in state departments of education) to oversee the administration of the tests or the time administrators spend with test salespeople and, later, their own colleagues to decide on a test. Nor will they include the teachers' time spent preparing students for the test—time that, on the admission of many teachers, is not spent "teaching" in the sense that they recognize.

But the costs of a testing and evaluation office, of consultants, and of teachers' time scoring assessments will be included in the cost of performance assessments because the work will be done in-house. When the cost comes out to be several times that of buying a test from a publisher, that figure is reported, but the basis for the comparison is forgotten or not recognized. The Educational Testing Service's 1990 Annual Report cites a state "with a strong commitment to educational assessment" that found that performance assessment would cost ten times more than the existing state program.[3] The basis for the alarming figure is not given.

Certainly performance assessments cost more to score and report because it costs more to pay people to read papers than to load up a machine with bubble sheets. Even if the costs of development were the same, the extra cost for scoring still makes performance assessment a more expensive proposition than multiple-choice examinations—no matter whether school systems buy them from a test publisher or develop them in-house.

But is the cost of scoring an assessment cost alone? When you pay teachers to score, do you just get reports back? As we saw from the example of the California writing assessment in chapter 2, the return is more than graded papers. The teachers understand more about what students need to know and be able to do. As they themselves say, scoring assessments is the best professional development they ever experienced.

The costs of scoring could just as easily be charged to professional development as to assessment. The same is true of developing assessment tasks in states, such as California and Maryland, where teachers are involved, and districts, such as South Brunswick, New Jersey, where the teachers modify the K–2 portfolio annually. Teachers who face the difficult question of finding suitable tasks, making them clear and fair to all students, ensuring that they do test what is valued, are probing into the heart of their professional concerns.

Thus, the question of comparative costs depends on what you want to count and where you want to put it in the budget. For performance assessment, but not for multiple-choice tests, some of the costs can be attributed to other parts of the budget, since working with performance assessment can replace other forms of professional development.

In any case, the basis of comparison must be clear before any figures are accepted, especially the frightening tenfold, thirty times, a hundred times claims that appear in the newspapers. Further, we really do not know what performance assessment will cost because there has not been enough experience with it yet.

One more point needs to be made about the cost of assessment: Americans want to get education on the cheap, and assessment is no exception. The public and legislators on all governmental levels want information but are unwilling to pay what it really costs. Dale Carlson, California Assessment Program director, has tried to draw attention to the disparity between needs and the money to meet them by calling for the "1 percent solution." He means that assessment might reasonably cost 1 percent of the state budget for California education, which would be twenty times more than it costs now. The situation is, if anything, worse in other states and at the federal level.[4]

CAN WE TRUST PERFORMANCE ASSESSMENTS?

The examples in this book have amply demonstrated that performance assessments are either good instructional material or motivate good instruction—or both. They have not as clearly demonstrated that they are reliable sources of information in terms of scores. Only the College Board's Advanced Placement Studio Art Portfolio Examination has a track record in providing individual student scores, although other performance assessments produce reliable scores on program assessments.

We certainly can trust group grading, in which standards are established by a consensus process and then applied by readers to student products (the art portfolios, essays, or written answers). The process and its variations are widely known and practiced and have been scrutinized by psychometricians for reliability. For example, the interrater reliability for the California Assessment Program writing assessments is about 90 percent in a single year. The Educational Testing Service has used group grading for the essay portions of the Advanced Placement examinations for almost forty years and has fewer complaints about it than about the multiple-choice portions of the tests.

Unresolved problems with group grading include reliability across years, as determined by rescoring papers from one year to another (some prompts are kept from year to year to make this possible), and the extended assessments designed for the Arizona and Maryland statewide assessment programs, where at the moment it does not seem clear how outside influences are to be controlled. (Perhaps they should not be, as Fred Finch of the Riverside Publishing Company, argued.)

Two developments will probably occur simultaneously. As psychometricians work with the scoring of performance assessments, including portfolios, they may suggest changes in their form in order to produce usable results. At the same time, expectations may be modified, so that the same degree of psychometric rigor is not required for all assessments.

We have two examples of such modifications: the Longfellow Elementary School art assessment in Bozeman, Montana, and "We the People . . . ," neither of which pretends to psychometric sophistication. Their designers chose the simplest method available to get comparative scores; judges assign scores, which are then totaled. There is no weighting, no scaling—just addition.

Neither of these scoring schemes would stand up to a moment's scrutiny from a psychometrician, but they do not need to. The purposes of each assessment are served adequately. The Longfellow Elementary School art assessment needs only to show that the Art in Action curriculum has produced growth in knowledge about art as demonstrated by ability to respond to pictures. The "We the People . . ." competition plays for high stakes only at the culminating national level, and even then the academic fate of individual students does not hang on the results.

Clarifying the purposes for which scores are needed and requiring only sufficient rigor for those needs would increase the variety of ways in which assessment information is reported. As Robert Linn has written, "An important outcome of the alternative assessment movement is that it challenges the education community at large to reconsider just what are valid interpretations of *any* kind of assessment information."[5] For example, a narrative report on a district's writing program based on student portfolios might be more valuable than laboriously calculated scaled scores. As the South Brunswick K–2 portfolio has clearly shown, observation reports can influence decisions about individual children more sensitively than test scores.

Performance assessments can be trusted to provide not just more information than the amount we now receive from norm-referenced, multiple-choice but information of a different quality; we want to know how well students are being trained for a complex world, and we can judge their progress only by their performance on complex tasks.

ARE PERFORMANCE ASSESSMENTS FAIR TO ALL STUDENTS?

We do not know. It would be premature to make any statements about equity until performance assessments have been part of a school or state program for at least three years. I stress "part of the program," because simply pulling out norm-referenced, multiple-choice testing and trying to replace it with performance assessments—without changing the school's teaching and learning—will not work. Moving to performance assessment must be seen as a shift in the entire system.

In chapter 6 I quoted the apprehensions of a San Diego City Schools Board member, who feared that performance assessments are scored subjectively and that children will suffer from the expectations of "racist" teachers. On the other hand, teachers in Navajo nation schools welcome the advent of the Arizona Student Assessment Program and its performance assessments because they think their students' achievements are misrepresented by norm-referenced, multiple-choice tests. A teacher in Chinle Schools told me, "I don't believe there is ever any evidence of what's really happening on our reservation because we're using the Iowa Test of Basic Skills. We're not satisfied with anything that's happening in evaluation at this point." A vivid picture of the distance between what the Navajo children can do and what the tests report is provided by Dorothy King, a consultant in Native American education in Chinle, in "Real Kids or Unreal Tasks: The Obvious Choice":

> The administrator flipped some more pages. "Sample: find the sentence that has the words in the correct order: A boy walks. Walks a boy. Boy walks a."
>
> "There's two of 'em," said Marie.
>
> "Show me," said the administrator. She pointed to the first two. "Where have you seen a sentence like that before?" asked the administrator.
>
> "At the video place—'Comes a Horseman.' Have you seen it?"
>
> "Yes," he mused. "It's one of my favorites." He turned the page. He was losing his enthusiasm.[6]

There is no evidence that the apprehensions of the African-American school board member or the hopes of Native American teachers will be fulfilled. Equity and fairness must always occupy the first rank in any education reform, but performance assessment is not in itself either fair or unfair, equitable or inequitable. It will have these qualities to the same degree as the personnel in the school system have them.

The best way to ensure equity is not to rush to conclusions too early and on too little evidence. Multiple choice has had half a century of dominance. A new system should at least be given a few years and systemic support before it is judged.

PUBLIC INFORMATION

Ignorance about education is widespread in the United States. To a certain extent, this ignorance has been fostered by an unfortunate conception of "professionalism" among educators. Being professional seems to mean developing a jargon that only the initiated can understand—like lawyers and doctors. But the language of education obscures communication between parent and teacher about the child's welfare.[7] Since children go to school every working day and go to the doctor only once a year routinely, the professional language of educators has proportionately considerably more impact on children than medical jargon.

The language of assessment is especially obscure (norms, stanines, grade equivalents) and places a barrier between educators and parents. Parents are so intimidated that they do not ask the questions they should about what the jargon or the scores mean or how they are arrived at. In some cases, this reluctance is reinforced by cultural differences when parents come from countries where there is a pattern of strong authority over schools and parents are not expected to question it; in other cases, they expect that school should be just the way it was in the past. They do not expect to understand what test scores mean; that is for the experts.

Add to this the curious division in public attitudes to the quality of schooling documented in annual surveys, especially the one conducted by the Gallup organization for *Phi Delta Kappan*, the monthly magazine for educators.[8] People think that schools in general rate only a "C," but their own local school is doing pretty well. This complacency, which stymies reform efforts, is an underlying factor in the calls for a national testing program. If people see how poorly even their own local schools do on national tests, then maybe they will wake up and do something about it, according to the theory.[9] It seems a bit like hitting someone over the head with a two-by-four to get their attention.

In general the public is uninformed about educational matters largely because of ingrained attitudes. The situation is not helped by the press, which shares those attitudes, especially about assessment. *Newsweek* published a special issue in September 1990 entitled *How to Teach Our Kids*, which included "A Consumer's Guide to Testing," by Tom Morganthau.[10] The article is based on an interview with a researcher at the Educational Testing Service—and that is all. Parents reading the article would have no idea that there are well-developed alternatives to what Morganthau calls "standardized" testing and that they need not go through the pain of learning what "stanines" and "percentile scores" mean. They are not told that multiple-choice testing affects teaching and learning.

Changing the model of education in the United States and the form of assessment it needs will depend crucially on informing first the press and, through it, the public. Parents and taxpayers need to be given enough information so that they can ask basic questions: How many tests will my child have to take this year? What kind of tests? How does the teacher prepare the class for the tests? What happens to the results? Do you know that you could assess my child's progress by using a portfolio? Has the school arranged for the teachers to attend a professional development session on different kinds of assessment techniques?

The cause of performance assessment—like school reform in general—needs the assistance of the most effective communication system in the United States: advertising. Reflect on the efficiency of advertising (on television, in newspapers and magazines) in changing attitudes about food, cars, and consumer goods, and consider its potential for educating the public about new ways of teaching and learning.

IS IT WORTH IT?

Who would pay to explain assessment to the public? The question provokes a profoundly disquieting answer: what we as a society will pay for is an indication of value, and it is obvious that we do not value education or its assessment highly. We do not value education because, like bridges and roads, it is the infrastructure for the economy and as such produces no wealth. We use advertising to produce revenue, not to call attention to infrastructure in trouble.

Those who urge schools to compete with each other for students are applying the model of economic competition from the industrial and business world, but it is the wrong model for education. We do not ask builders of roads and bridges to construct competing highways and provide choices among bridges. The standards for an economy's infrastructure are the degree to which it supports productive activities. Poor roads and bridges inhibit the movement of goods; an investment in the quality of transportation infrastructure is a necessary condition for the continued health of a competitive economy.

As we are constantly being told by business executives, national commissions, and education watchers, the United States must improve its educational infrastructure if it is to keep its seat at the global poker table. I have cited a number of these exhortations in this book but find it difficult to cite any speeches or plans to provide the money to pay teachers professional wages, to lengthen the school day and the school year, to provide extended care before and after school, to equip each classroom with the technology that is ubiquitous in offices and homes, and to continue the education of teachers in the same way as lawyers and doctors renew and refresh their knowledge. If education is as vital to the nation's economic future as everyone says it is, where is the political will to finance it adequately?

AMERICA'S GRAND VISION

The argument from competitiveness has a certain mean-spirited utilitarian flavor. Surely education is more than the production of workers, whether they work on an assembly line or at a terminal in the center of an enterprise web. While we have concentrated on arguments that will persuade business and industry to support the infrastructure on which they depend—that is, bottom-line arguments—we have forgotten to appeal to the idealism underlying the American public school system.

I do not want to conclude this summary of performance assessment as a promising component of an improved educational system without focusing on what we expect from schools.

American education began with a vision, which we should not allow to tarnish. The mandate of the U.S. school is unlike that of any other system: to make a working, voting citizen of every child.

It is healthy to step back and let the grandeur of this vision sink in. Other societies still do not recognize every child's right to a secondary education. The systems held up as models, chiefly the European and Japanese, separate their students into tracks early in their school lives, and therefore the high standards for which they are extolled are available to a subset of the students, not the totality.

Our own society used to make the same distinctions. But we now expect that everyone will be able to read the kind of literature that only the highly educated middle class used to read; to understand mathematics and science, which was unavailable outside a university only fifty years ago; and to follow sophisticated arguments about immensely complicated issues like the competing claims of loggers and owls in forests, of commerce and the earth's ozone layer, of a global economy and local civil rights. Progress toward this vision could accelerate with a financial investment commensurate with its scope.

The success of the American school should not be measured by the number of high scores on the SAT or the percentage of students above the national average but by its progress toward enabling every student to read good books, understand mathematics and science, and think analytically about public issues they will vote on. The economy needs well-educated students, but American society needs them even more.

Notes

Chapter 1:
FROM TESTING TO ASSESSMENT

1. Quoted in *Atlanta Journal and Constitution*, April 22, 1990, p. A1.

2. Richard Stiggins of the Northwest Regional Laboratory, Portland, Oregon (speech to a regional meeting of the Mathematical Sciences Education Board, November 1990). In his many articles and conference presentations, Stiggins has made a specialty of in-class teacher assessments and how to improve them.

3. Stiggins, "Revitalizing Classroom Assessment," "Assessment Literacy," and "Teacher Training in Assessment."

4. Forty-five states collect and report information on students' achievement scores, and thirty states have statewide minimum competency tests. All fifty states collect and report data that can be used for accountability, such as attendance figures, expenditures, and teacher credentials. See Office of Educational Research and Improvement, *Creating Responsible and Responsive Accountability Systems*.

5. Quoted in Livingston, Castle, and Nations, "Testing and Curriculum Reform," p. 24.

6. Cannell, *How Public Educators Cheat on Standardized Achievement Tests.* Schwartz and Viator, *The Prices of Secrecy*; a large number of newspaper articles, such as "Test Drills Put Scores before Schooling, Critics Say," and "Parents of First-Grade Girl Claim School Fudged on Test. Drill Methods, Pizza 'bribe,' Anger Coweta Couple," *Atlanta Journal and Constitution*, April 22, 1990, pp. A1, A14; and on the topic of perhaps illegitimate preparation for multiple-choice tests, *New York Times*, July 24, 1990, p. B1, and *Washington Post*, May 20, 1990. A scandal in South Carolina, where a teacher, Nancy Yergin, was fired for cheating by looking at the test before it was given was the subject of as

195

egment on CBS's "60 Minutes" in 1990. Yergin said that she had been told to cheat by her principal, Linda Ward, who denied the allegation.

7. National Commission on Excellence in Education, *A Nation at Risk.*

8. Ravitch and Finn, *What Do Our 17-Year-Olds Know?*

9. National Center for Fair and Open Testing, *Sex Bias in College Admissions Tests: Why Women Lose Out.* Much more than a discussion of gender bias in the SAT and the ACT, this book provides a comprehensive survey of problems with these tests and includes a bibliography. On the use of the SAT to judge the quality of schools, see "S.A.T. Scores Are In."

10. The complete references are found in chapter 7, where a brief history of American public schools touches on IQ testing.

11. Discrete exercises are used in Part 1, and passage-based exercises are used in Part 2. The reading selections in Part 2 exemplify scientific writing and descriptions of experimental results.

12. Heard at the annual conference on assessment held by the Education Commission of the States in Boulder, Colorado, June 1990.

13. Bloom, Madaus, and Hastings, *Evaluation to Improve Learning.*

14. Cannell, *Nationally Normed Elementary Achievement Testing in America's Public Schools.* After his successful attack on norming, Cannell went on to investigate cheating, and documented his findings in *How Public Educators Cheat.*

15. The research was reported in "Physician's Test Study Was 'Clearly Right.' "

16. Koretz, "Arriving in Lake Wobegon."

17. Fredericksen and Collins, "A Systems Approach to Educational Testing."

18. Hiebert and Calfee, "Advancing Academic Literacy through Teachers' Assessments."

19. Among recent articles testifying to the psychometric community's interest in performance assessment are: Mislevy, "Foundations of a New Test Theory"; Fredericksen and Collins "Systems Approach"; Fredericksen, "Notes on the Design of Future Assessment Systems"; Linn and Dunbar, "Complex, Performance-Based Assessment." In addition, Chester E. Finn, Jr., a former assistant U.S. secretary of education who believes in the power of testing to draw attention to the poor performance of American schools, referred in a public television interview to the present "rotten tests" on March 15, 1991.

20. Suen and Davey, "Potential Theoretical and Practical Pitfalls and Cautions of the Performance Assessment Design."

21. Shepard, " Why We need Better Assessments."

Chapter 2:
ASSESSING WRITING IN CALIFORNIA, ARIZONA, AND MARYLAND

1. *Arizona Essential Skills for Mathematics*, p. i.

2. Final report of the December 1989 California Education Summit (Sacramento: California Department of Education, 1989), p. 17.

3. Like much of the other information in this description of the CAP writing assessment, this material comes from handouts distributed by CAP personnel at conferences, including the CAP Technical Seminar, of which I am a member. The major published source is California Department of Education, *Writing Achievement of California Eighth Graders: Year Two*.

4. The Bay Area Writing Project began at the University of California, Berkeley, with the cooperation of school districts in the San Francisco Bay Area in 1973. It selected good teachers for its summer institutes so that they could share their best ideas for teaching writing and also develop their own writing. In 1977, the Writing Project began an expansion process that has now taken it across the United States (the National Writing Project) and to England, Australia, and Canada. It has brought about a revolution in writing pedagogy, partly by stimulating research into the psychological processes underlying the act of composing.

5. My experience as co-director of the UCLA Writing Project in 1977 gives me firsthand knowledge here.

6. For example, Wiggins, "Teaching to the (Authentic) Test," "Rational Numbers," and numerous speeches and presentations to conferences and seminars.

7. Arizona Department of Education, *Arizona Student Assessment Program Overview*, p. 26.

8. Arizona Department of Education, *Designing Curriculum*, p. 6.

9. Arizona Department of Education, *ASAP Overview*, p. 26.

10. This is based on my access to the Maryland assessments when I was a consultant to the Maryland State Board of Education. My report was published in *School Board News* 34, 1.

Chapter 3:
EXAMPLES OF PERFORMANCE ASSESSMENTS IN SCIENCE AND MATHEMATICS

1. From interviews conducted by Joan Boykoff Baron, director of the Connecticut Common Core of Learning Assessment, with students in San Antonio, Texas, in November 1989, reported in *Compact Dia-*

logue, newsletter of the Common Core of Learning Assessment, 1, 3 (November–December 1989), 5.

2. The description of the New York grade 4 ESPET is based on visits to Buffalo schools in May 1989, ongoing correspondence and conversations with Douglas Reynolds, Science Bureau chief of the New York State Education Department, and a visit to Albany when the scores were checked. Almost nothing has been written about the ESPET. Knowledge about it has been disseminated through appearances at educational conferences by Reynolds and regional coordinators.

3. Gardner, *Frames of Mind*, p. 129.

4. Berryman, *Who Will Do Science?*

5. *New York Times*, May 23, 1990, and *Education Week*, May 30, 1990: "Unlike the current tests, which are primarily multiple-choice, the proposed assessments would include a portfolio of a student's best work, a professional evaluation of a pupil's accomplishments, and examinations—'not limited to multiple-choice, standardized tests'—in the core subjects of English, math, science, and social studies."

6. National Council of Teachers of Mathematics, *Curriculum and Evaluation Standards*, p. 191.

7. California Assessment Program, *A Question of Thinking*.

8. *New York Times*, November 1, 1990, A1, A24.

9. The Connecticut examples come from materials distributed at Common Core of Learning Assessment Project Advisory Group meetings and at various conferences around the country, including especially the 1990 American Educational Research Association (AERA) annual convention in Boston.

10. Some of the following description comes from Davey and Rindone, "Anatomy of a Performance Task."

11. Robert Dorfman, professor emeritus of political economy at Harvard University, in a letter to the *New York Times*, February 10, 1991.

12. Steen, "Forces for Change in the Mathematics Curriculum."

Chapter 4:
GETTING STUDENTS, PARENTS, AND THE COMMUNITY
INTO THE ACT

1. "Central Park East Promise to Students," printed in all information and publicity material about Central Park East Schools, New York. The schools were founded by Deborah Meier, the first teacher to receive a MacArthur Foundation award. These statements are the "habits of mind" the Central Park East Schools teach as the basis of all learning.

2. There is an extended description of the Walden III Rights of Passage

Experience in Archbald and Newmann, *Beyond Standardized Testing*.
The exact nomenclature for these extended demonstrations of student
competence has not been established. They may be called "exhibitions"
or "portfolios," with each constituent part also called a portfolio.

3. See Cannell, *How Public Educators Cheat on Standardized Achievement Tests*, for further discussions of the secrecy issue.

4. I gathered information about the Longfellow Elementary School art
assessment in Bozeman on a visit to the school and through numerous
conversations with Campeau. As in the case of many of the other
examples in this book, there is no published description of the assessment.

5. These were described to me by Michael Fischer, Bureau of Social Studies Education, New York State Education Department. Publications are
available from the department in Albany, New York, especially *Guide
to Social Studies Program Evaluation* and *New York State Program
Evaluation Test in Social Studies*.

6. See note 5 in chapter 3.

7. Descriptions of the "We the People . . ." curriculum and competition
are available from the Center for Civic Education, 5146 Douglas Fir
Road, Calabasas, California 91302.

8. The program is organized by the Odyssey of the Mind Association, Inc.,
P.O. Box 27, Glassboro, New Jersey 08028.

Chapter 5:
PORTFOLIOS

1. Quoted in Murphy and Smith, "Talking about Portfolios," p. 25.

2. *Portfolio News* 1, 2 (Winter 1990), 3. Available from Portfolio Assessment Clearinghouse, c/o San Dieguito Union High School District, Encinitas, California.

3. "Editorial: Portfolios—Whose Definition?" p. 8.

4. The description here is based on verbal report given by Mary Ann Smith
and Sandra Murphy, who organized the junior high school portfolio
assessment as part of a Bay Area Writing Project program (San Francisco Bay Area) to explore portfolios as an assessment mechanism in
1988 and 1989.

5. Wolf, "Opening Up Assessment"; "Portfolio Assessment: Sampling Student Work"; a number of articles in *Portfolio*, the quarterly newsletter
of the Arts PROPEL project, available from Project Zero, 326 Longfellow Hall, Harvard Graduate School of Education, 13 Appian Way,
Cambridge, Massachusetts 02138-3752; and oral presentations at conferences and seminars throughout the country. Wolf is also the director

of the annual summer Institute on New Modes of Assessment, funded by the Rockefeller Foundation, at Harvard University.

6. Howard reported her process in an article entitled "Making the Writing Portfolio Real." My description is based on her article, interviews with her, numerous other reports from Project Zero, and also on conference presentations of the results of asking her students' parents to respond to their children's writing.

7. Camp, "The Educational Testing Service Writing Portfolio," "Direct Assessment at the Educational Testing Service," "Presentation on Arts PROPEL Portfolio Explorations," and numerous presentations at conferences and seminars throughout the country. Camp's papers can be obtained by contacting the Educational Testing Service in Princeton, New Jersey, 08541-0001.

8. Oral communication during one of my accreditation visits to California high schools, 1983–1988.

9. *Should These Be Vermont's Goals for Education?* pamphlet distributed throughout the state in 1989 and 1990.

10. Mills, "Portfolios Capture Rich Array of Student Performance."

11. Information about the Advanced Placement examinations and the Studio Art Portfolio Evaluations is available from the Advanced Placement Program of the College Board, Educational Testing Service, Princeton, New Jersey, 08541-0001. The description here is based on my visits to the scoring of the AP studio art portfolios in June 1990 and on extended conversations with staff and readers of the portfolios.

Chapter 6:
TEACHERS AND ASSESSMENT: PRIVILEGE AND RESPONSIBILITY

1. Interview at Deans Elementary School, South Brunswick, New Jersey, October 1990.

2. Pearson and Valencia, "Assessment, Accountability, and Professional Prerogative."

3. Shirley Weber, president of the Board of Education, San Diego City Schools, speaking to the Panasonic Partnerships Conference in Santa Fe, New Mexico, May 1990. Her complete remarks were printed in *Basic Education*, 35, 8 (April 1991), 3–5.

4. The literature on tracking is cited in note 6 in chapter 7.

5. National Commission on Testing and Public Policy, *From Gatekeeper to Gateway: Transforming Testing in America*, p. 5.

6. Ascher, *Testing Students in Urban Schools.*

7. The Primary Language Record was developed by Myra Barrs and Anne Thomas at the Center for Language in Primary Education, a component

of the Inner London Education Authority, before it was disbanded by Margaret Thatcher's government. The Primary Language Record is being tried in the schools of the Center for Collaborative Education in New York and in California under the auspices of the California Literature Project, as well as being the basis for the South Brunswick, New Jersey, portfolio assessment.

8. I watched the Primary Language Record being used in its pure form in a Southeast London school where the children were in different stages of English language proficiency, from native English speakers through speakers of Bengali, Urdu, Turkish, Arabic, Greek, French,and various African languages and dialects of the West Indies.

9. Among a large number of articles about early childhood testing are: Meisels, "High-Stakes Testing in Kindergarten"; Jervis, "Daryl Takes a Test"; Livingston, Castle, and Nations, "Testing and Curriculum Reform: One School's Experience."

10. South Brunswick's developmentally appropriate curriculum for early childhood education gained national attention when it was featured in a *Newsweek* article on children's learning, April 17, 1989.

11. A particularly fine example of the difference between testing based on an artificially contrived passage and that based on a literary work is to be found in Carol Chomsky, "Language and Language Arts Assessment," in Schwartz and Viator, *The Prices of Secrecy*, pp. 70–73. Chomsky compares a multiple-choice test taken from the California Achievement Test (CAT) reading comprehension series with a test she apparently designed, using a passage from *Charlotte's Web* by E. B. White followed by questions to which the students write short answers (or perhaps respond orally): "If selections from literature, along with open-ended questions, make up the data bank for comprehension testing, the message is that this is what reading is about. These are the books worth reading and exploring, these are the models of writing worth internalizing, emulating, and expanding on" (p. 73).

12. Shepard and Smith, "Flunking Kindergarten: Escalating Curriculum Leaves Many Behind"; Frymier, "Retention in Grade Is 'Harmful' to Students," p. 32.

13. *From Gatekeeper to Gateway*, p. 15.

14. National Swedish Board of Education, Information Section, *Assessment in Swedish Schools*, p. 10.

15. Ibid., p. 7.

16. There is no easily available written documentation of the Australian Capital Territory moderation system. The researcher who explained it to a meeting of the technical seminar of the California Assessment Program said that he had seen only one written description of the system—a guide for parents.

Chapter 7:
HOW AMERICAN EDUCATION GOT INTO THE TESTING TRAP

1. Resnick, *Education and Learning to Think*, p. 7.

2. This brief history of U.S. public education is based on ibid.; Daniel Resnick, "Minimum Competency Historically Considered"; Resnick and Resnick, "The Nature of Literacy: An Historical Exploration"; Lauren Resnick, presentation at the "Beyond the Bubble" conference in Sacramento, California, October 1988; Daniel Resnick, presentation at the Panasonic Partnerships Conference, San Diego, California, November 1989. The definitive history of U.S. public education is Cremin's trilogy, *American Education*.

3. Cubberly, *Public Education in the United States*.

4. According to Reich, *The Work of Nations*, twenty-first century capitalism will be based on the "enterprise web," in which groups of experts will sell their problem-solving skills, especially in microchip-based technology, to corporations, which will finance the project.

5. Tracking and its reliance on both aptitude and achievement testing have been thoroughly explored in two books by Oakes, *Keeping Track* and *Multiplying Inequalities*, and innumerable articles by John Goodlad Oakes and Robert Slavin. The research is summarized in my *Perspective*.

6. Cremin, *The American Common School*. Cremin says that independence produced "a vigorous demand for the universal education of the people—a demand conceived by its proponents to be at the very heart of republican society and government" (p. 29).

7. Smith provides a brief revealing history of the relationship between industrial philanthropy and the founding of universities in *Killing the Spirit*.

8. Please note that here the subject is intelligence testing, not achievement testing. The inadequacies of intelligence tests have been dissected in Gould, *The Mismeasure of Man*, perhaps the most accessible discussion of the subject; Block and Dworkin, *The IQ Controversy*; Lewontin, Rose, and Kamin, *Not in Our Genes*. Strenio, *The Testing Trap*, is partly an indictment and partly a survival guide to aptitude testing.

9. Gould, *Mismeasure of Man*, pp. 190–191.

10. The entire exchange is reprinted in Block and Dworkin, *The IQ Controversy*, pp. 4–44.

11. The imbecility of dumbed-down textbooks and how they get ruined further as learning tools by special interests has been summarized by Tyson-Bernstein, *A Conspiracy of Good Intentions*, and Tyson and Woodward, "Why Students Aren't Learning Very Much from Textbooks."

12. Reich, *Work of Nations*, p. 60.

13. National Commission on Testing and Public Policy, *From Gatekeeper to Gateway*, p. 15.

14. Office of Strategic Services Assessment Staff, *Assessment of Men*, p. 38.

15. Hoffman, *The Tyranny of Testing*, p. iv. Barzun referred to Hoffman's book in an op-ed article for the *New York Times*, "Multiple Choice Flunks Out," October 11, 1988.

16. *Washington Post*, May 20, 1990.

17. *New York Times*, July 24, 1990, p. B1

18. National Commission on Excellence in Education, *A Nation at Risk*, p. 5

19. *America's Choice: High Skills or Low Wages!* report of the Commission on the Skills of the American Workforce (Rochester, N.Y.: Nation Center on Education and the Economy, 1990), forcibly argues that American industry must adopt the team model of production and that American education should prepare workers for it. The report and Reich's *Work of Nations* complement each other.

20. See chapter 1 and note 11 in chapter 1 for a businessman's succinct summary of the situation.

21. Kearns and Doyle, *Winning the Brain Race*, p. 90. Kearns was appointed deputy secretary of education by Lamar Alexander, U.S. secretary of education, in March 1991.

22. Office of Strategic Services Assessment Staff, *Assessment of Men*, p. 466.

23. Gardner, *The Mind's New Science*, p. 126. Gardner's book is an exhaustive survey of developments in cognitive psychology since behaviorism.

24. Farnham-Diggory, *Schooling*, p. 5.

25. Mathematical Sciences Education Board, *Everybody Counts*, p. 6.

26. "Foundations of a New Test Theory" (paper published by the Educational Testing Service, October 1989), abstract.

27. Reich, *Work of Nations*, p. 233.

28. Sachar, "My Year of Living Dangerously," p. 47. These paragraphs describing the changed American student come from conversations with teachers; articles in *Teacher Magazine*; Freedman, *Small Victories*; Kidder, *Among Schoolchildren*; Johnson, *Teachers at Work*; Rose, *Lives on the Boundary*; and "School-Business Ties"; "Do We Care about Our Kids?" p. 40; McCormick, "Where Are the Parents?" and personal observations from visiting schools as part of accreditation teams and on research projects.

29. *Basic Education* 35, 6 (February 1991), 2–4.

30. Albert Shanker, president of the American Federation of Teachers, in his weekly advertising column "Where We Stand," in the *New York Times*, Sunday edition, frequently refers to the lack of consequence that education has for most students. Employers do not look at high school diplomas for qualifications, so students see no point in working hard in high school.

Chapter 8:
NEXT STEPS

1. Walker, *Meridian*, p. 188.

2. Deborah Meier's Central Park East Schools in District 4, Manhattan, and the schools in New York City that belong to the Center for Collaborative Education (founded with Meier's MacArthur Fellowship award) provide one model (see chapter 4); the schools in the Coalition of Essential Schools provide another. They both follow the principles of good education laid out by Sizer in *Horace's Compromise*. David Kearns and Denis Doyle offer a model for restructuring schools into a year-round magnet system, where students have choices about the kind of school they want and even the parts of the year when they will attend. *Winning the Brain Race*, pp. 40–41. Walden III, a public alternative high school in Racine, Wisconsin, is another small-scale model that has drawn national attention. See Archbald and Newmann, *Beyond Standardized Testing*. Schlechty describes the school as "knowledge-work organization" in his *Schools for the 21st Century*.

3. *Trustees' Public Accountability Report*, p. 6.

4. David Kearns and Denis Doyle make a related point about the miserable financing of educational research, which, like assessment, provides information about education: "The nation's research expenditures are less than one tenth of one percent of the national expenditure for education operations and capital outlay, which in 1987 was approximately $150 billion. . . . The U.S. Government spends more on agricultural research than it does on education research." *Winning the Brain Race*, p. 106.

5. Linn, "Complex, Performance-based Assessment," p. 23.

6. King, "Real Kids or Unreal Tasks: The Obvious Choice."

7. Barth, "The Flaw of Educationese," pillories the translation of desirable behavior into "skills": life skills, values clarification skills, self-esteem skills.

8. *Phi Delta Kappan* annual Gallup Poll on public attitudes to education, published in the September issue.

9. Calls for a national test have come from the President's Advisory Committee on Education; the National Education Goals Panel, organized by

the National Governors' Association to chart progress toward the national educational goals proclaimed by President George Bush in September 1989; Educate America, a private group founded by Thomas Kean, ex-governor of New Jersey, and Saul Cooperman, ex-superintendent of education of New Jersey; and the U.S. Department of Labor, the Secretary's Commission on Achieving Necessary Skills (SCANS), which advocates a national test of functional skills for the workplace. In addition, the National Assessment Governing Board is seeking expansion of the National Assessment of Educational Progress (NAEP) to make state-by-state and even district-level comparisons possible from NAEP data. A different approach to national assessment is being developed by the Learning Research and Development Center at the University of Pittsburgh and the National Center on Education and the Economy, under the leadership of Lauren and Daniel Resnick. They are working on a national examination system, not a single test, that would use performance assessments of the kind described in this book. See "An Examination System for the Nation," available from the Learning Research and Development Center, University of Pittsburgh.

10. *Newsweek* special issue (September 1990), 63–68. The editors of the special issue apparently did not refer back to their own files: "Not as Easy as A, B, or C," January 8, 1990 discusses the problems with norm-referenced, multiple-choice tests and features the Connecticut high school mathematics and science assessments in a separate box on p. 58.

Bibliography

American Association for the Advancement of Science (AAAS). *Project 2061: Science for All Americans.* Waldorf, Md.: AAAS, 1989.

Applebee, Arthur, Judith Langer, and Ina Mullis. *Crossroads in American Education: A Summary of Findings.* Princeton, N.J.: Educational Testing Service, 1988.

Archbald, Doug A., and Fred M. Newmann. "The Nature of Authentic Academic Achievement." In H. Berlak, ed., *Assessing Achievement: Toward the Development of a New Science of Educational Testing.* Albany, N.Y.: SUNY Press, forthcoming.

———. *Beyond Standardized Testing: Assessing Authentic Academic Achievement in the Secondary School.* Reston, Va.: National Association of Secondary School Principals, 1988.

Arizona Department of Education. *Arizona Student Assessment Program Overview.* Phoenix: Arizona Department of Education, 1990.

———. *Designing Curriculum.* Phoenix: Arizona Department of Education, 1989.

———. *ASAP Overview.* Phoenix: Arizona Department of Education, 1990.

———. *Arizona Essential Skills for Mathematics.* Phoenix: Arizona Department of Education, 1987.

Ascher, Carol. *Testing Students in Urban Schools: Current Problems and New Directions.* New York: Clearinghouse on Urban Education, Teachers College, Columbia University, 1990.

Askin, Walter. *Evaluating the Advanced Placement Portfolio in Studio Art.* Princeton, N.J.: College Board and Educational Testing Service, 1986.

Barrs, Myra. "*The Primary Language Record*: Reflection of Issues in Evaluation." *Language Arts* 67, 3 (March 1990), 244–253.

Barrs, Myra, and Anne Thomas. *The Primary Language Record Handbook*. New York: Heinemann Educational Books, 1989.

———. *Patterns of Learning*. London: Center for Language in Primary Education, 1990.

Barthe, Patte. "The Flaw of Educationese." *Basic Education* 34, 5 (January 1990).

Becoming a Nation of Readers. Washington, D.C.: U.S. Department of Education, 1985.

Berryman, Sue. *Who Will Do Science?* New York: RAND Corporation and the Rockefeller Foundation, 1983.

Block, N. J., and Gerald Dworkin, eds. *The IQ Controversy: Critical Readings*. New York: Pantheon, 1976.

Bloom, B., G. Madaus, and J. T. Hastings. *Evaluation to Improve Learning*. Baltimore: Johns Hopkins University Press, 1983.

California Assessment Program. *A Question of Thinking: A First Look at Students' Performance on Open-Ended Question in Mathematics*. Sacramento: California State Department of Education, 1989.

California Department of Education. *Writing Achievement of California Eighth Graders: Year 2*. Sacramento: California Department of Education, 1989.

Camp, Roberta. "The Educational Testing Service Writing Portfolio: A New Kind of Assessment." Paper presented at the National Council on Measurement in Education conference, April 1983.

———. "Direct Assessment at the Educational Testing Service: What We Know and What We Need to Know." Paper presented at the National Council on Measurement in Education conference, April 1983.

———. "Presentation on Arts PROPEL Portfolio Explorations." Seminar on Alternatives to Multiple-Choice Assessment, Educational Testing Service, Washington, D.C., March 1990.

Cannell, John Jacob. *Nationally Normed Elementary Achievement Testing in America's Public Schools: How All Fifty States Are above the National Average*. West Virginia: Friends for Education, 1987.

———. *How Public Educators Cheat on Standardized Achievement Tests*. Albuquerque, N.M.: Friends for Education, 1989.

Carnegie Forum on Education and the Economy. *A Nation Prepared: Teachers for the 21st Century*. Report of the Task Force on Teaching as a Profession. New York: Carnegie Corporation, 1986.

Chubb, John E., and Terry M. Moe. *Politics, Markets, and America's Schools*. Washington, D.C.: Brookings Institution, 1990.

Commission on the Skills of the American Workforce. *America's Choice:*

High Skills or Low Wages! Rochester N.Y.: National Center on Education and the Economy, 1990.

Commons Commission. *Who Will Teach Our Children?* Sacramento, Calif.: Commission on the Teaching Profession, 1985.

"Creating a Profession of Teaching: The Role of National Board Certification." *American Educator* 14, 2 (Summer 1990), 8–22.

Cremin, Lawrence. *American Education.* 3 vols. New York: Harper & Row, 1970, 1980, 1988.

———. *The American Public School: An Historic Conception.* New York: Columbia Teachers College, 1951.

Cubberly, Elwood P. *Public Education in the United States.* Boston: Houghton Mifflin, 1934.

Davey, Bruce, and Douglas A. Rindone. "Anatomy of a Performance Task." Paper presented at the American Educational Research Association Convention, 1990.

De Lange, Jan. *Mathematics, Insight, and Meaning.* Utrecht, the Netherlands: n.p., n.d.

"Do We Care about Our Kids?" *Time*, October 8, 1990, p. 40.

Duke, Daniel L., and Bruce Gansneder. "Teacher Empowerment: The View from the Classroom." *Educational Policy* 4, 2 (Summer 1990), 16–20.

Dyer, Henry S. *Parents Can Understand Testing.* Columbia, Md.: National Committee for Citizens in Education, 1980.

"Editorial: Portfolios—Whose Definition?" *Portfolio News* 1, 2 (Winter 1990): 3.

Edmonds, Ronald. "Effective Schools for the Urban Poor." *Educational Leadership* 37 (October 1979), 15–24.

Educational Leadership. Redirecting Assessment. 46, 7 (April 1989).

———. Cooperative Learning. 47, 4 (December 1989–January 1990).

Educational Testing Service (ETS). *Learning by Doing: A Manual for Teaching and Assessing Higher-Order Thinking in Science and Mathematics.* NAEP Report 17-HOS-80. Princeton, N.J.: ETS, May 1987.

Farnham-Diggory, Sylvia. *Schooling.* Cambridge: Harvard University Press, 1990.

Fredericksen, John. "Notes on the Design of Future Assessment Systems." Paper prepared for Educational Testing Service, Princeton, N.J., 1990.

Fredericksen, J. R., and A. Collins. "A Systems Approach to Educational Testing." *Educational Researcher* 18, 9 (1989), 27–32.

Freedman, Samuel J. *Small Victories: The Real World of a Teacher, Her Students, and Their High School.* New York: Harper & Row, 1990.

Frymier, Jack. "Retention in Grade Is 'Harmful' to Students." *Education Week*, December 6, 1989, p. 32.

Gardner, Howard. *Frames of Mind: The Theory of Multiple Intelligences.* New York: Basic Books, 1983, 1985.

———. *The Mind's New Science.* New York: Basic Books, 1985.

———. "Assessment in Context: The Alternative to Standardized Testing." In B. Gifford and M. C. O'Connor, eds., *Cognitive Approaches to Assessment.* Boston: Kluwer Academic Publishers.

Gendler, Tamar. "Testing What We Want to Measure." *Basic Education* 33, 1 (September 1988), 7–11.

Getty Center for Education in the Arts. *Beyond Creating: The Place for Art in America's Schools.* Los Angeles: Getty Center for Education in the Arts, 1985.

Glickman, Carl D. "Good and/or Effective Schools: What Do We Want?" *Phi Delta Kappan* 68, 8 (April 1987), 622–624.

Goodlad, John. *A Place Called School: Prospects for the Future.* New York: McGraw-Hill, 1984.

Goodman, Kenneth S., Yetta M. Goodman, and Wendy J. Hood, eds. *The Whole Language Evaluation Book.* Portsmouth, N.H.: Heinemann, 1989.

Gould, Stephen Jay. *The Mismeasure of Man.* New York: W. W. Norton, 1981.

Haberman, Martin, "Thirty-one Reasons to Stop the School Reading Machine." *Phi Delta Kappan* (December 1989), 284–288.

Hakuta, Kenji. *Mirror of Language: The Debate on Bilingualism.* New York: Basic Books, 1986.

Hiebert, Elfrieda H., and Robert C. Calfee. "Advancing Academic Literacy through Teachers' Assessments." *Educational Leadership* 46, 7 (April 1989), 50–54.

Hoffman, Banesh. *The Tyranny of Testing.* New York: Crowell-Collier Press, 1962.

Holmes Group. *Tomorrow's Schools: Principles for the Design of Professional Development Schools.* East Lansing, Mich.: Holmes Group, 1990.

Houts, Paul L., ed. *The Myth of Measurability.* New York: Hart Publishing Company, 1977.

Howard, Kathryn. "Making the Writing Portfolio Real." *Quarterly of the National Writing Project and the Center for the Study of Writing* 12, 2 (Spring 1990), 4–7, 27.

Jervis, Kathe. "Daryl Takes a Test." *Educational Leadership* 46, 7 (April 1989).

Johnson, Susan Moore. *Teachers at Work: Achieving Success in our Schools.* New York: Basic Books, 1990.

Kamii, Constance, ed. *Achievement Testing in the Early Grades.* Washington, D.C.: National Association for the Education of Young Children, 1989.

Kaplan, George. "Kappan Special Report—Pushing and Shoving in Videoland U.S.A.: TV's Version of Education (and What to Do about It)." *Phi Delta Kappan* 71, 5 (January 1990), K1–K12.

Kearns, David T., and Denis P. Doyle. *Wining the Brain Race: A Bold Plan to Make Our Schools Competitive.* San Francisco: Institute for Contemporary Studies, 1988.

Kidder, Tracy. *Among Schoolchildren.* Boston: Houghton Mifflin, 1989.

King, Dorothy F. "Real Kids or Unreal Tasks: The Obvious Choice." *Basic Education* 35, 2 (October 1990), 6–9.

Koretz, Daniel. "Arriving in Lake Wobegon: Are Standardized Tests Exaggerating Achievement and Distorting Instruction?" *American Educator* 12, 2 (Summer 1988), 8–15, 52.

Kulm, Gerald, ed. *Assessing Higher Order Thinking in Mathematics.* Washington, D.C.: American Association for the Advancement of Science, 1990.

Lewontin, R. C., Steven Rose, and Leon J. Kamin. *Not in Our Genes.* New York: Pantheon, 1984.

Linn, Robert. "Complex, Performance-based Assessment: Expectations and Validation Criteria." Paper prepared for the Center for Research on Evaluation, Standards, and Student Testing, University of California, Los Angeles, n.d.

Livingston, Carol, Sharon Castle, and Jimmy Nations. "Testing and Curriculum Reform: One School's Experience." *Educational Leadership* 46, 7 (April 1989).

McCormick, John. "Where Are the Parents?" *Newsweek*, special issue (September 1990), 54–58.

McEntee, Grace Hall. "When the Teacher Has to Choose: What If You're Told to Give a Test You Know Is Bad?" *Teacher Magazine* (April 1990), 8–9.

McKnight, Curtis C., F. Joe Crosswhite, John A. Dossey, Edward Kifer, Jane O. Swafford, Kenneth J. Travers, and Thomas J. Cooney. *The Underachieving Curriculum: Assessing U.S. School Mathematics from an International Perspective.* Champaign, Ill.: Stipes Publishing Company, 1987.

Massachusetts Advocacy Center. *Locked In, Locked Out: Tracking and Placement Practices in Boston Public Schools.* Boston: Massachusetts Advocacy Center, 1990. Mathematical Sciences Education Board. *Everybody Counts.* Washington, D.C.: National Academy Press, 1989.

Mathison, Sandra. "The Perceived Effects of Standardized Testing on Teaching and Curricula." Paper delivered at the American Educational Research Association's convention, 1989.

Meier, Deborah. "Why Reading Tests Don't Test Reading." *Dissent* (Fall 1981), 457–465.

———. "In Education, Small Is Sensible." *New York Times*, September 8, 1989.

———, and Ruth Jordan. "The Right 'Choice' for Teachers." *Teacher Magazine* (December 1989), 68–69.

Meisels, Samuel J. "High-Stakes Testing in Kindergarten." *Educational Leadership* 46, 7 (April 1989).

Mills, Richard P. "Portfolios Capture Rich Array of Student Performance." *School Administrator* 11, 46 (December 1989), 8–11.

Mislevy, Robert J. "Foundations of a New Test Theory." Paper prepared for Educational Testing Service, Princeton, N.J., n.d.

Mitchell, Ruth. "Counselor-Consultants' Workshops: A Guide for Workshop Leaders and a Handbook for Counselor-Consultants." Unpublished paper. For the Western Association of Schools and Colleges and the California State Department of Education, 1988.

———. "Another Failure for California Schools, Where 'A' Stands for Easy Accreditation." *Los Angeles Times*, March 26, 1989, pp. 3, 6.

———. "Authentic Assessment." *Basic Education* 33, 10 (June 1989), 6–10.

———. "The Teaching Fallacy." *Basic Education* 34, 4 (December 1989), 6–10.

———. Report. *School Board News* (Maryland Association of Boards of Education) 34, 1 (December 1990).

———. "Across Boundaries." *Basic Education* 34, 5 (January 1990), 14–16.

———. "Performance Assessment: An Emphasis on 'Activity.'" *Education Week*, January 24, 1990, p. 56.

———. "A Letter to Test Publishers." *Basic Education* 34, 8 (April 1990), 7–10.

———. "The English National Assessment: Some First Hand Observations." *Network News and Views* 9, 8 (August 1990), 79–85.

———. "Deukmejian Gets Dunce Cap for Spiking Innovative School Assessment Program." *Los Angeles Times*, August 19, 1990, M5.

———. "Maryland School Performance Assessment Program: Report to the Maryland State Board of Education." *School Board News* 43, 1 (December 1990).

———. "An Open Letter to Secretary Alexander." *Basic Education*, 35, 6 (February 1991).

Mitchell, Ruth, with Juan Francisco Lara. "The Seamless Web: The Interdependence of Educational Institutions." *Education and Urban Society*, Sage Publications, November 1986, 24–41.

Mitchell, Ruth, with Rick Eden. "Paragraphing for the Reader." *College Composition and Communication* (December 1986), 416–430.

Mitchell, Ruth, with Kati Haycock and M. Susana Navarro. *Perspective: Off the Tracks*. Washington, D.C.: Council for Basic Education, 1989.

Mumme, Judith. *Portfolio Assessment in Mathematics*. Santa Barbara: California Mathematics Project, 1990.

Murphy, Sandra, and Mary Ann Smith. "Talking about Portfolios." *Quarterly of the National Writing Project and the Center for the Study of Writing* 12, 1 (Winter 1990).

National Center for Fair and Open Testing. *Sex Bias in College Admissions Tests: Why Women Lose Out*. Cambridge, Mass.: National Center for Fair and Open Testing, 1989.

National Center for Improving Science Education. *Science and Technology Education for the Elementary Years: Frameworks for Curriculum and Instruction*. Andover, Mass., and Colorado Springs: Network, and the Biological Sciences Curriculum Study, 1989.

———. *Getting Started in Science: A Blueprint for Elementary School Science*. Andover, Mass., and Washington, D.C.: Network, 1989.

National Commission on Excellence in Education. *A Nation at Risk*. Washington, D.C.: U.S. Government Printing Office, April 1983.

National Commission on Testing and Public Policy. *From Gatekeeper to Gateway: Transforming Testing in America*. Chestnut Hill, Mass.: National Commission on Testing and Public Policy, Boston College, 1989.

National Council of Teachers of English (NCTE). *Report Card on Basals*. Urbana, Ill.: NCTE, 1988.

National Council of Teachers of Mathematics (NCTM). *Curriculum and Evaluation Standards for School Mathematics*. Reston, Va.: NCTM, March 1989.

National Endowment for the Humanities (NEH). *American Memory: A Report on the Humanities in the Nation's Public Schools*. Washington, D.C.: NEH, 1987.

National Governors' Association (NGA). *America in Transition—The International Frontier: Report of the Task Force on International Education*. Washington, D.C.: NGA, 1989.

National Research Council. Mathematical Sciences Education Board. *Everybody Counts*. Washington, D.C.: National Academy Press, 1989.

National Swedish Board of Education. *Assessment in Swedish Schools.*

Stockholm: National Swedish Board of Education, Information Section, c. 1985.

"Not as Easy as A, B, or C." *Newsweek*, January 8, 1990, 56–58.

Oakes, Jeannie. *Keeping Track*. New Haven: Yale University Press, 1985.

————. *Multiplying Inequalities: Effects of Race, Social Class, and Tracking on Opportunities to Learn Mathematics and Science*. Santa Monica: RAND, 1990.

Office of Educational Research and Improvement. State Accountability Study Group. *Creating Responsible and Responsive Accountability systems*. Washington, D.C.: U.S. Department of Education, September 1988.

Office of Strategic Services Assessment Staff. *Assessment of Men: Selection of Personnel for the Office of Strategic Services*. New York: Rinehart and Company, 1948.

Office of Technology Assessment. *Technology and the American Transition*. Washington, D.C.: U.S. Government Printing Office, 1988.

Ogbu, John. "Schooling the Inner City." *Society* (November–December 1983).

————, and Fordham, Signithia. "Black Students' School Success: Coping with the Burden of 'Acting White.' " *Urban Review* 18, 3 (1986).

Paulos, John Allen. *I Think, Therefore I Laugh*. New York: Columbia University Press, 1985.

————. *Innumeracy: Mathematical Illiteracy and Its Consequences*. New York: Hill and Wang, 1988.

Pearson, P. David, and Sheila Valencia. "Assessment, Accountability, and Professional Prerogative." In *Research in Literacy: Merging Perspectives: Thirty-Sixth yearbook of the National Reading Conference*, 3–16. National Reading Conference, 1987.

Pechman, Ellen. *The Child as Meaning Maker: The Organizing Theme for Professional Practice Schools*. Washington, D.C.: American Federation of Teachers, 1989.

Perrone, Vito. *Working Papers: Reflections on Teachers, Schools, and Communities*. New York: Teachers College Press, 1989.

————, Monroe D. Cohen, and Lucy Prete Martin, eds. *Testing and Evaluation: New Views*. Washington, D.C.: Association for Childhood International, 1975.

Phi Delta Kappan 70, 9 (May 1989).

"Physician's Test Study Was 'Clearly Right,' a Federally Sponsored Study Has Found." *Education Week*, April 5, 1989, pp. 1, 19.

Ravitch, Diane, and Chester E. Finn, Jr. *What Do Our 17-Year-Olds Know?*

A Report on the First National Assessment of History and Literature. New York: Harper & Row, 1987.

Reich, Robert B. *The Work of Nations.* New York: Alfred A. Knopf, 1991.

Resnick, Daniel. "Minimum Competency Historically Considered." *Review of Research in Education* 8 (1980), 3–29.

Resnick, Lauren. *Education and Learning to Think.* Washington, D.C.: National Academy Press, 1987.

———, and Leopold Klopfer, eds. *Toward the Thinking Curriculum: Current Cognitive Research.* Reston, Va.: Association for Supervision and Curriculum Development, 1989.

Resnick, Lauren, and Daniel Resnick. "The Nature of Literacy: An Historical Explanation." *Harvard Educational Review* 47 (1977), 370–385.

Rose, Mike. *Lives on the Boundary: The Struggles and Achievements of America's Underprepared.* New York: Free Press, 1989.

Rose, Mike. "School-Business Ties: The Unexamined Paradox of Past Performance." *Los Angeles Times*, April 22, 1990.

Sachar, Emily. "My Year of Living Dangerously." *Teacher Magazine* 2, 7 (April 1991).

"S.A.T. Scores Are In, and All of Education Is Judged." *New York Times*, September 9, 1990, p. 10.

Schlechty, Phillip C. *Schools for the Twenty-first Century.* San Francisco: Jossey-Bass, 1990.

Schwartz, Judah L., and Katherine A. Viator, eds. *The Prices of Secrecy: The Social, Intellectual, and Psychological Costs of Current Assessment Practice.* Cambridge: Educational Technology Center, Harvard Graduate School of Education, September 1990.

Shanker, Albert. "The End of the Traditional Model of Schooling—and a Proposal for Using Incentives to Restructure Our Public Schools." *Phi Delta Kappan* 71, 5 (January 1990), 345–357.

Shepard, Lorrie. "Why We Need Better Assessments." *Educational Leadership* 46, 7 (April 1989), 4–9.

Shepard, Lorrie A., and Mary Lee Smith. "Flunking Kindergarten: Escalating Curriculum Leaves Many Behind." *American Educator* 12, 2 (Summer 1988), 34–38.

———. "Synthesis of Research on Grade Retention." *Educational Leadership* (May 1990), 84–88.

Sizer, Theodore. *Horace's Compromise: The Dilemma of the American High School.* Boston: Houghton Mifflin, 1985.

Slavin, Robert E. *Using Student Team Learning.* Baltimore: Center for Research on Elementary and Middle Schools, Johns Hopkins University, 1986.

Smith, Page. *Killing the Spirit: Higher Education in America*. New York: Viking, 1990.

Steen, Lynn Arthur. "Forces for Change in the Mathematics Curriculum." Address to the School Mathematics Curriculum: Raising National Expectations, sponsored by Mathematical Sciences Education Board, University of California, Los Angeles, November 7, 1986.

———. "Teaching Mathematics for Tomorrow's World." *Educational Leadership* 47, 1 (September 1989), 18–23.

Stiggins, Richard. "Revitalizing Classroom Assessment: The Highest Instructional Priority." *Phi Delta Kappan* (January 1988), 363–368.

———. "Assessment Literacy." Paper prepared for the Northwest Regional Laboratory, Portland, Oregon, c. 1989.

———. Teacher Training in Assessment: Overcoming the Neglect. In Stephen Wise, ed., *Teacher Training in Assessment*. Buros Nebraska Symposium in Measurement and Testing, vol. 7. Forthcoming.

Stodolsky, Susan S. *The Subject Matters: Classroom Activity in Math and Social Studies*. Chicago: University of Chicago Press, 1988.

Strenio, Andrew J., Jr. *The Testing Trap: How It Can Make or Break Your Career and Your Children's Futures*. New York: Rawson, Wade Publishers, 1981.

Suen, Hoi K., and Bruce Davey. "Potential Theoretical and Practical Pitfalls and Cautions of the Performance Assessment Design." Paper presented at the Annual Meeting of the American Educational Research Association, Boston, 1990.

Trustees' Public Accountability Report. Princeton, N.J.: Educational Testing Service, 1990.

Tyson-Bernstein, Harriet. *A Conspiracy of Good Intentions: America's Textbook Fiasco*. Washington, D.C.: Council for Basic Education, 1988.

Tyson, Harriet, and Arthur Woodward. "Why Students Aren't Learning Very Much from Textbooks." *Educational Leadership* 47, 3 (November 1989), 14–17.

Vermont Department of Education. *Should These Be Vermont's Goals for Education?* Montpelier, Vt.: Department of Education, 1989.

Walker, Alice. *Meridian*. New York: Washington Square Press, 1976.

Washington Post. "Beyond the No. 2 Pencil." November 28, 1989.

Wiggins, Grant. "Creating A Thought Provoking Curriculum." *American Educator* (Winter 1987).

———. "Teaching to the (Authentic) Test." *Educational Leadership* 46, 7 (April 1989), 41–47.

———. "Rational Numbers: Scoring and Grading That Helps Rather Than Hurts Learning." *American Educator* 12, 4 (Winter 1988), 20–47.

Wiley, David E. "Test Validity and Invalidity Reconsidered." Unpublished paper.

Wolf, Dennis Palmer. "Opening Up Assessment." *Educational Leadership* (December 1987–January 1988) , 24–29.

———. "Portfolio Assessment: Sampling Student Work." *Educational Leadership* 46, 7 (April 1989), 35–39.

Index